MW00738117

Gender Issues in Development

Gender Issues in Development
Concerns for the 21st Century

Editors

Bhaswati Das
Vimal Khawas

RAWAT PUBLICATIONS

Jaipur ● New Delhi ● Bangalore ● Mumbai ● Hyderabad ● Guwahati

ISBN 81-316-0191-9

Published by
Prem Rawat for **Rawat Publications**
Satyam Apts, Sector 3, Jawahar Nagar, Jaipur 302 004 (India)
Phone: 0141 265 1748/7006 Fax: 0141 265 1748
E-mail: info@rawatbooks.com
Website: rawatbooks.com

New Delhi Office
4858/24, Ansari Road, Daryaganj, New Delhi 110 002
Phone: 011 2326 3290

Also at Bangalore, Mumbai, Hyderabad and Guwahati

Typeset by InosoftSystems, Noida
Printed at Chaman Enterprises, New Delhi

Contents

Acknowledgements

This book is a collective venture which was initiated by the inspiration of Prof. Muchkund Dubey, President, Council for Social Development (CSD) and Dr. N.J. Kurian, Director from the same institute who motivated us to organise a national level seminar on gender issues. Accordingly, the seminar was organised at India International Centre on 4-5 May 2006. The seminar mostly invited the social scientists to express their views on the gender and development. This book is an outcome of the deliberations made during the seminar. We take this opportunity to extend our heartiest thanks to both of them for their valuable time and support all through this work. We also would like to thank the support staff of CSD, who extended their help while conducting the seminar. Ms. Jaya Nair and Mrs. Chinmoyee Sanyal need special mention for their secretarial support while organising the event. We extend our thanks to Mr. R.S. Somi and other administrative staff of CSD for their cooperation and proactive participation which had relieved many of our stress and strains while organising the same.

Gender issues are wide and spread over the entire gamut of development. Until recently, development discourses did not put due weight to the issue. Over the decades it appeared to be the most intriguing for development plans. No one disagrees with the facts that the issues are diverse. However, within the limited scope of the conference we had to prioritised the areas of gender studies which are more critical and need special attention. However, in this venture we deliberately did not focus on women health issues which itself, with all its wide diversity, could form a discussion for two days.

We would use this as an opportunity to thank all the panelists, discussants and participants whose active participation enriched the seminar throughout. Special thanks are due to contributors for cooperating generously and patiently in the venture. Without their cooperation the journey we initiated with a conference and reached in this stage would not have been possible. I would like to highlight the acknowledgments mentioned by some of the contributors here. Dr. Pradeep Panda expressed his thanks to the Kerala Research Programme on Local Level

Development (KRPLLD) for providing financial support for a larger project from which data on domestic violence were drawn. Dr. Purnamita Dasgupta expressed her gratitude to South Asian Network for Development and Environment Economics (SANDEE) which had financed the study of CPR as Development Drivers in Himachal Pradesh. Her paper is based on the findings from that project. Dr. Abhijit Guha expressed in indebtedness to the village women whose participation in the workshop had enriched him. His paper is based on the interaction occurring during that workshop. He also had expressed his gratitude to Vina Majumder, Loknath Roy and Narayan Banerjee of the Centre for Women Development Study who dragged him out from the traditional anthropological pedagogy.

Last, but not the least, is the bearing of our family members, who have spared us from many of the essential family involvements and shouldered those responsibilities of their own. Without their passive but outstanding help it would not have been possible for us to reach at this stage.

Such a massive venture always involves many. If we have missed to acknowledge any ones' contribution, that is completely unwilling.

Bhaswati Das
Vimal Khawas

1

Gender Issues in Development
Concerns for the 21st Century

BHASWATI DAS AND VIMAL KHAWAS

From Women to Gender

The theoretical foundations of development discourse have experienced many changes over the decades. Theories with different perspectives emerged with changing situations of the world and changed the discourse sometimes in a completely opposite direction. The role of men and women in the development process has received much attention in the last few decades. Concerns with regard to women and their inclusion or exclusion in the development process have been increasingly examined. Although the principle of equality of men and women was recognised as early as 1945 in the UN Charter, and in the UN Declaration of Human Rights of 1948, several researchers have pointed out that development planners worked on the assumption that what would benefit one section of society (especially men) would trickle down to the other (women) and that they did not need to fully address women's position in the process of development.

The 20th century, probably, is one which has experienced the most trouble in defining the role of a person as male or female. Judith Butler has completely changed the direction of women's studies through her most influential book, *Gender Trouble* (1990). Early women's studies scholars tended to think of the differences between men and women as being innate and immutable. The new theory argues that a person's role was specified under a patriarchal framework where scope of gender (masculine or feminine) was limited within the understanding of biological understanding of sex (male and female). The theories of the 1990s emphasised that the concept of gender was fluid over time and over social situations. These modern theories leave enough space to create a persons own identity by favouring equal opportunities for both men and women.

Approaches in gender study, like the theories in gender study, have shown changes over time. Moser (1993), however, has tracked down the approaches in understanding women's position in development plans and processes in the Third World over the decades. Moser's analysis include five approaches in a sequence of welfare, equity, anti-poverty, efficiency, and empowerment. All the approaches identified by Moser have distinctive origins and purposes. But their implementation periods are mostly overlapping. As the purposes of the approaches are different, the planning for women in the society mixes up different approaches in different ways. This mixing of approaches helps the planners to identify the most suitable and also acceptable plan for different societies.

Incorporating Gender in Development

Considering the different roles and actions of men and women in the development process, different measures are taken to bring them on an equitable platform. Since the past decade onwards, there has been growing acceptance of the gender-focused approach to development. Gender equity was emphasised in the Programmes of Action of the International Conference on Population and Development in 1994 and the Fourth World Conference on Women in 1995. Two consecutive programmes have initiated the process of gender sensitive planning. India too, as part of these programmes of action, is making an effort to do gender justice through planning. It is worthwhile to mention here that while a person's sex does not change, the gender role is dynamic in nature and it includes all socially and culturally constructed relations between men and women. Gender roles vary from one culture to another and are supported by societal structures. Thus, an analysis of the position of Indian women will provide us the spectrum of women's development as well as the task ahead.

India's Female Population

According to the 2001 Census, India has 496 million women, which is almost equal to the combined total population of the countries of the US, the UK, and the Russian Federation. India singly accounts for 15 per cent of the world's women. Because of this huge share, any change and variation in women's status affects a substantial number of the woman population of the world. India, with its vast regional differences, has a variety of cultures which determine the differential status of women across the country. Nonetheless, social discrimination and economic deprivation on the basis of gender is common to all, irrespective of religion, caste, community or state.

Social Discrimination

The process of social discrimination starts in the family itself. The well-structured social institution of family sometimes fails to address the special needs of women. The culture of silence of Indian women has prohibited even the female members of society from extending their assistance to other women to cope with difficult situations. The Ministry of Women and Child Development (MWCD), Government of India, has identified different categories of women under difficult circumstances as follows:

> ...widows, destitute and deserted women, women ex-prisoners, victims of sexual abuse and crimes, including those trafficked and rescued from brothels, migrant or refugee women who have been rendered homeless due to natural calamities like flood, cyclone, earthquake, mentally challenged women, women victims of terrorist violence, etc.

The situation is worse when economic deprivation adds to the problem. The official statistics of India provide us the population below the poverty line by their place of residence. There are no official statistics available on the distribution of the poor by sex. This is with a view that if a family is poor, both the male and female members of the family will be poor. The proceedings of the first Asia Pacific Forum on Poverty, while discussing poverty among Indian women, says, "If we accept the definition of poverty as denial of choices and opportunities for a better life, then feminisation of poverty is less a question of whether more men than women are poor than of the severity of poverty and the greater hardship women face in lifting themselves and their children out of poverty" (Ganguly). However, the MWCD has enlisted the women in difficult circumstances with the specific purpose of rehabilitation; there are some other categories of women who are in the mainstream, but still in difficult circumstances. There are women who are neither deserted nor destitute, but the main or even only earning member in the family. Such women headed households are a phenomenon found irrespective of class. Female headship is likely to appear at a later stage of the life cycle, as compared with male headship. It may relatively be short-lived because of its late occurrence (Swain, 2004), but the severity of hardship could be more.

Even when women are not badly affected by some special situation, discrimination is visible. Education is seen as a basic investment for better earning in the future. It is also the key factor for better reception and delivery of social development. The need for universal education has long been realised. Since independence, the gender gap in education is continuously declining, but yet to be completely eliminated. The gap is more in technical, professional and higher education. This issue of the gender gap in higher and technical education among females, along with the policy analysis helping or hindering in bridging the gap, is required to be analysed.

It is important to mention that females are biologically more dominant and better care during the reproductive period can increase their life expectancy more than that of males. As per Census 2001, the total population of older persons in India is 7.66 crore. While in 1996, about 6.6 per cent of the total population was aged 60 years and above, the figure is projected to rise up to 8.94 per cent by 2016. Long life for the women in our society has certain important implications. Women with little empowerment, both economic and social, are mostly distressed in their old age. Moreover, longer lives than their male counterparts leads to a higher percentage of widowhood in a society practising almost universal marriage. At the age of 60–69 years, as high as 46 per cent of females are widowed, as compared to only 12 per cent of males (Census of India 1991).

Economics of Gender

For the purposes of this book, economics of gender will be discussed in two theoretical frames: firstly, the role of gender in natural resource management, and secondly, the feminisation of the labour market.

Women, in the Indian context, play the dual role of conservator and consumer of natural resources. However, their role as conservator is over emphasised because their role as consumer has hardly been commercialised. Moreover, in their traditional role of home managers (by collecting fuel, fodder, water and other non-timber forest products), they are the greatest victim of degradation of natural resources. With more commercialisation of natural resources when, as a conservator, she gets hardly any support from the existing system, the social harmony gets disturbed and the conservator's role gets marginalised. The lack of support from the system is embedded in the rule of possession, wherein the conservators do not have the right to the property they are conserving. But there are good practices also. What is required now is a situational review on whether women are more victims of degradation or winners as managers.

On the other hand, a study of the behaviour of the labour market through a gender lens is required in the context of most countries having accepted economic liberalisation and market oriented growth as a path for development. A lot of analysis has started coming up on the impact of liberalisation on the economy. Feminisation of the labour force is also forming an important part of this discourse. The concept of 'feminisation of the labour force' has opened up two drastically different dimensions. Firstly, the concept indicates an increasing participation of females in wage employment. Secondly, the term is used to describe the flexibilisation of labour for women and men, a fall-out of the changing nature of employment wherein irregular conditions, once thought to be the hallmark of women's secondary employment, has become widespread for both the sexes (Kanji and Menon-Sen, 2001).

The analysis of census data shows that there is near stagnation in male work participation. Considering the rural-urban differentials, it appears that there is slow decline in the share of male workers in the rural economy, and a slight increase in their share in the urban sector. Female participation, on the other hand, is increasing at a faster pace than male participation in both rural and urban areas. It is required to be seen whether women are really more efficient, cheaper or more flexible to succumb to the vulnerability of the job market.

Sensitisation and Empowerment

Gender budgeting is gaining increasing acceptance as a tool for engendering macroeconomic policy-making. The Fourth World Conference of Women held in Beijing in September 1995 and the Platform for Action that it adopted called for a gender perspective in all macroeconomic policies and their budgetary dimensions. In India, gender perspective on public expenditure has been gaining ground since the publication of the report of the Committee on the Status of Women in 1974. The Eighth Five-Year Plan (1992–97) highlighted for the first time the need to ensure a definite flow of funds from the general developmental sectors to women. The Ninth Five-Year Plan (1997–2002), while reaffirming the earlier commitment, adopted the Women Component Plan as one of its major strategies and directed both the Central and the state governments to ensure "not less than 30 per cent of the funds/benefits are earmarked in all the women's related sectors". It is also a time for us to see how far we have reached and how far we have to go.

To combat all the social and economic gender inequalities, empowerment is seen as very important. However, there is hardly any political will in the efforts towards political empowerment of women. To represent 496 million women, India has only 46 women in a house of 533 members in the 14th Parliament. Quoting Brinda Karat, who says "..it may be more appropriate, at least in so far as successful men in politics are concerned, to say that behind every successful man in politics there is a woman who was deprived of the chance". An indication of that inequality is visible from the fact that the number of female MPs has never crossed 10 per cent in the history of independent India. While this is the scenario at the centre, over a million women hold the reins of power at the village level. These women are the daughters of the 73rd and 74th Amendments of the Indian Constitution. Passed in 1993, these two amendments oblige all states to reserve one-third of seats in the three-tiered system of local government (village, block and district levels) – known as panchayati raj – for women. In a short time, women have shown their potential to wield power effectively at the village level and challenge feudal traditions. However, a law to boost their presence in parliament has been deadlocked for several years (Pande, 2000). The issue of empowerment touches upon the gender sensitivity of political parties, the problems of women participating in politics, and the political future of women in politics.

References

Bulter, Judith. 1990. *Gender Trouble: Feminism and the Subversion of Identity*, London: Routledge.

Census of India 1991. Table C-1, Part IV, Social and Cultural Tables.

Department of Women and Child 2004. Annual Report, Government of India.

Ganguly Thukral, Enakshi. *Poverty and Gender in India: Issues for Concern. http://www.adb.org/documents/books*

Kanji, Nazneen and Kalyani Menon-Sen. 2001. 'What Does the Feminisation of Labour Mean for Sustainable Livelihoods?' *Opinion*, London: International Institute for Environment and Development, August.

Karat, Brinda. 2005. 'Survival and Emancipation', *Three Essays Collective*. Haryana.

Moser, C. 1993. *Gender Planning and Development: Theory, Practice and Training*, London: Routledge.

ORGI. 2001. General Population Table, Government of India.

Pande, Mrinal. 2000. 'India's Nurseries of Politics: Political Rise of Women in India'. *UNESCO Courier*, June.

Swain, Pushpanjali. 2004. *Socio-demographic and Health Profile of Widows in India, www.nihfw.org/material/Research/R188.doc*

2

Agency, Structure and Women as Situated Subjects

Changing the Terms of Gendered Discourse and Exploring Ways to Crack the Gendered Codes

SARASWATI RAJU

I ssues related to gendered deprivation and discrimination are omni-present in the contemporary developmental and other discourses on women in India in much the same way empowerment is and yet much of these discourses limit themselves to systematically establish gender inequalities in terms of access to productive as well as reproductive resources. Some studies concentrate on interventions – formally institutionalised and operated through the state or members of civil society and NGOs as well as through informal mechanisms such as community networks and social capital. Very often if not always, these interventions rely on developing some sort of capabilities in women with a view to help build up their agency to contest, change and negotiate gendered asymmetries. Whether the changes that are induced through such social engineering are real changes or remain cosmetic or what changes are worth applauding and to be pursued and what are not because of double-edged implications can be a matter of debate (Nagar and Raju, 2003). Some sceptical scholars may suggest that the spaces occupied by women as spaces of occasional agencies are no more than cunning soci-etal sanctions providing vents to express pent-up anger and frustrations,[1] while others may talk about manipulative strategies that on the surface look like consent to existing constructs but are in fact strategic ways of resistance that may be termed as 'indirect agency' (Raheja and Gold, 1994; Niranjana, 1997; Raju, 2005).

Whichever way one looks at it, the concerns that most interventions despite their stated objectives/declaration to do so leave crucially fundamental issues of uneven and multilayered appropriation of power by men vis-à-vis women untouched continue to engage scholars. In fact, some interventions may end up reinforcing the already existing oppressive structures, even if the outcomes are entirely unintentional. One such example can be of an NGO that distributed free condoms to women agricultural labourers in Punjab villages, who ran the risk of sexual exploitation by landlords (personal communication). One can argue, and rightly so, that those who distribute condoms among these women, or for that matter, amongst sex workers, may not necessarily accept the moral, legal and ethical bases of exploitation by landlords and/or those involved in prostitution. Without intending to sit on judgement and with full realisation of the layered complexities of such situations, I maintain somewhere there is a compliance in these acts with the existing status quo or perhaps a tacit acknowledgement of the limits to which the ground realities can be altered given the means.

The fact remains that whenever any attempt is made to destabilise entrenched power structures, even the most potent and lauded projects get subverted and nipped or recast in an insipid new garb – the Sathins in Rajasthan are an exemplary case – too well-known to require a detailed account. Ironically, however troubling or hopeless the journey may be, there would be little disagreement that these struggles have to continue.

Can we then reconfigure the contours of such struggles in a more pragmatic incremental way as a starting principle to achieve a gender-just world? In responding to this issue, the paper takes as given as well as an uncontested proposition that in India, women do occupy subordinated spaces at every level even as the articulation of such subordination may differ.[2] Why this should continue to be so even after progressive and sustained constitutional and many a times politically correct processes in place, is an intriguing and complex question which the opening section of the paper attempts to address. In so doing, the author initiates a discussion on structure and agency in order to argue that, ironically, the very focus on women as agents of change disconnects the struggles from being located in larger sociocultural structures and discourses and is instrumental in creating the limits to gender justice. Scripting of women's agency, according to the author, is an extremely difficult and contested terrain even as it is widely debated. The concluding section is about the missing pieces in the puzzle as to why in India, gender justice goes 'two steps forward' and then 'a step backward' and poses a question if there is a way out of this conundrum.

Revisiting the Agency and Structure Debate

Agency is a widely discussed concept and yet I begin this discussion by revisiting it to set the stage for the subsequent discussion. The dictionary definition of agency is active force, action and power. An agent is one who performs an action or brings about a certain result; even if not explicitly defined, an agent moves things forward. Sen expands this and defines agency as the ability to set and pursue one's own goals and interests. To quote him (2006: 514):

> The expression 'agent' is sometimes employed in . . . economics and game theory . . . [as] a person who is acting on someone else's behalf . . . I am using the term 'agent' . . . in its older – and 'grander' – sense as someone who acts and brings about change, and whose achievement can be judged in terms of her own values and objectives, whether or not we assess them in terms of some external criteria as well. [Sen is] particularly concerned with the agency role of the individual as a member of the public and as a participant in economic, social and political actions . . .

If an individual aims at achieving certain values and objectives in the personal and public domains, there has to be freedom available to her/ him to adopt ways that s/he should prefer, to be able to act. The agency (to act) can be collectively invoked – very often effectively expressed in public arenas, or it can be enacted in personal spheres withholding the feminists' argument that the private and the public are not independently constituted, and therefore, gender inequalities in the personal spheres of domesticity cannot be delinked from inequalities in the public spheres. At this juncture, however, one needs to draw out the complexities involved in speaking about 'preferring' in exercising agency.

As Sen (2006) succinctly points out, individual 'preferences' can in fact be socially architectured in that the entrenched values may be internalised to such an extent that they appear as 'preferences' and 'choices' whereas in reality they are neither. Childcare, mothering-rearing and nurturing are some good examples – Badgett and Folbre, (1999: 316), quoted in Gasper and Staveren, 2006 call it 'socially imposed altruism' from which there cannot be much escape. Conventional preference-choice based evaluation, therefore, at best captures what can be termed as 'restricted agency' (Peter, 2006: 24). Conversely, some acts that superficially look like constraining 'choices' may in fact be exercising choices; my mother not wanting to learn ironing (a skill) because if she did, she would have to do all the ironing – that was her logic – can be a typical example to deconstruct the ideas surrounding 'choices' and 'preferences', which are often used rigidly and uncritically.

As Palriwala and Uberoi (2005) contend, the question of women's agency has been an important preoccupation in the literature on women's migration, whether for marriage or as workers. In the case of 'arranged marriages', marriage migration, for example, reflects not merely individuals, but family aspirations and mobility strategies whereby such marriages may be outcomes, compelled more by national and global economic disparities than by women's willing exercise of agency. In fact, the physical distance from critical support networks, particularly that of natal kin, in such marriages may turn the presumably liberating experiences into constraints and potentialities of women's agency.[3] Likewise, education and employment, conventionally thought of as inputs in agency enhancement, often reverberate with regressive logic, i.e., women should work because working women produce fewer children; women should be healthy because healthy women produce healthy children – instrumentality at its best (Raju, 2006)!

The point is that agency should be seen as neither a purely human accomplishment nor as being all about cognitive processes and intentionality. Rather, it should be conceived of as something that is the product of negotiations, of sorts, between all kinds of actors with seemingly autonomous (but actually mutually interdependent and determined) capacities (Knopp, 2004). Knopp's example of a person's open declaration of being a gay or a lesbian is:

> ... much more resonantly described (and fruitfully understood) as a highly contingent and contextualised *process* involving all manner of human and non-human forces than as an autonomous achievement of that individual coming to an epiphany and then 'choosing' to act (although that may be one component of the process). Indeed coming out, while frequently characterised in a kind of discursive shorthand as a key moment of decision, is much more commonly described by those experiencing it as an always unfolding and very compelling *process* ..., involving multiple parties, over which the individual possesses only partial control at best. The relevant 'actors' in this process are as likely to be other people and their actions, images, words, or even, scents or seemingly random objects, as the individual him or herself. (Knopp, 2004: 125)

What it means is that in order to evaluate agency and its efficacy, a broad-based informational basis as to motivations and constraints that may or may not allow individuals to act is a prerequisite. I would like to argue that such information that ostensibly relates to individuals' acts is located in a broader structural hold and ideology propounded institutionally as well as through informal norms and gendered codes.[4] These mechanisms are wide-ranging from caste and class locations to patriarchy and at times can even be enmeshed together (Chhachhi, 2005).

As I said earlier, the agential role of women in both social and lived experiences has to continue and be appraised and yet one needs to be careful as resistance – one of the constituent parts of agency – may not be romanticised however politically well-intentioned it may be (Thapan, 1997: 10), because agency without being grounded in social-structural realities remains at best fractured and superficially effective.

Social-structural realities work in a way that they do not allow the agency to actualise in certain spheres. For example, women may collectively be empowered by invoking their disapproval of public consumption of alcohol or step in to resolve issues related to pension distribution and so on, but the same women, despite their agency, may fail miserably to stop sex-selective abortions, inter-personal bargaining in intimate relations or abuse, thus enclaving certain matters in specialised discursive arenas outside the broad-based debates and contestation (Raju, 2006). As Anandhi (2002) reports from Tamil Nadu, a relatively better placed state in terms of gender-related indicators, even though questioned by some, there exists an interlocking of private and public patriarchy together with caste/class locations, which articulates itself in elected women members to grass-roots panchayat bodies into proxies representing either patriarchal or caste/class power interests – those who exhibit autonomous capacity to act independently are deliberately prevented from enacting on their own.[5] It is in this context that it is important to argue that the possibilities of social change are often contested by the dominant constructs.

At a workplace, my woman friend refused the suggestion that she should take charge of the tea club on the ground that for many years it has been looked after by women and it was high time that some man colleague came forward because at the workplace, they are all colleagues and not man and woman so that specific 'feminine' tasks are always assigned to women. Even before she could engage in any meaningful dialogue on her position with her colleagues, another slightly older woman said, 'I am old-fashioned and traditional and I really do not mind making tea!'

My friend, by invoking the collective identity as colleagues to argue out her case, was indeed making a point that men and women be treated as equal without stereotypical gendered constructs. Taking care of a tea club was incidental; it could have been presenting a bouquet to a visitor or singing a welcome song at an inaugural function. The older woman, however, framed her opposition as protecting tradition – a 'catch all' term and posited it against the individual's quest for 'gender equality', which in itself cannot be subjected to outright rejection for fear of being politically incorrect, but traditions enjoy a much larger and readily acceptable currency. The older woman's message thus was resonant with trivialising/rejecting a larger concern about typical gendered constructs by this younger friend of mine as being in confrontation with traditional values – a contest between tradition and gender-justice as a signature of modernity, 'marginalising everything that upsets founding values' (Prakash, 1992: 10), and therefore, unwelcome.

There is nothing new in the above incident and I am willing to buy the proposition that this older woman had no intention of strategising her opposition the way I am suggesting and that she was spontaneous in her response. This spontaneity is precisely what makes it more dangerous – acceptance and internalisation of values by women themselves as their 'defining characteristics' (Thapan, 1997: 11). Scholars have pointed out that in case of women, internalisation of oppression is stronger and deeply embedded in their consciousness, 'making allies out of the victims' (Sen et al., 2003: 320, also Kabeer, 1994) because of the cultural construction of femininity (Connell, 1995) and subjectivity (Ram, 1992), made worst by the interlocking nature of place, poverty and women's lack of access to productive resources. The big question that still remains is how to break free from this blinding trap.

Women have continuously been fixed as the site of repository of traditions and patriarchal values and any efforts to transcend the boundary is often questioned. In a volatile and confused state of threatened existence in the colonial India, home and domestic life were immediately seen as the inviolate site for the preservation of Indian values essentially because these domains were insulated from British interference and also provided a much easier domain to manipulate and dominate. As I discuss elsewhere (Raju, 1997), in an idealised demarcation of space, men negotiated the outside colonial world, whereas women were the custodians of the middle class moral values at home. Anchored thus, tradition at this juncture was often conceptualised as a highly precarious and contested realm to which indigenous resistance and identity could turn (Kumar, 1993: 7). Although much water has since flowed under the bridge and Indian women have made much headway in breaking several gendered codes, still, whenever the privileging (masculine) structures are threatened or even perceived as threatened, at such moments of indeterminacy, the discourses become ambivalent and yet often veer away implacably to take recourse to orthodoxy and traditional values. There are examples to substantiate this claim ad nauseam, but I would cite a more recent example of when the Miss World 1996 beauty contest in Bangalore was opposed both by right wing parties and progressive groups (amongst other issues) for being a masculine project in which women's sexuality and body exposure were commoditised, giving rise to a complex discourse on gender and sexuality in contemporary India (Oza, 2001). For our purpose, it is of interest to note that the primary site of the contestation remains women and their location. It is interesting to see how even women's groups circumvented the contested issues and I quote:

> . . . in the strategic rejection of the political right wing's version of culture, progressive groups relinquished the issue of culture so that the only visible opinion about culture was the conservative view of threatened Indian tradition and culture . . . Moreover, indigenous notions of sexuality that draw on a rich tradition of myth and legend remained silent in discourses of the [women's] opposition so that it became easier for the right wing to claim that any discourse on sexuality [was] outside Indian culture.[6] (Oza, 2001: 1080)

It is not very difficult to understand why progressive groups including those who work for women and gender equality go this far and no further when it comes to invoking complete agency. At the risk of repetition, it is because of the internalisation by women themselves as well as agency's limited capacity to question entrenched gendered coding.

Interestingly, much of the celebration about women's agency has come largely from Western scholarship. In my view, the discourses have to be more complex and nuanced. For one, as Rajan points out, 'reading' resistance in subaltern voices seems to be a postcolonial compulsion for some who, despite acknowledging that these voices can and are subsumed within 'the ideologies that shape [women's] worlds', still insist that they are different. Rajan goes on to elaborate that such scholars are "obliged to privilege something that has to be designated as 'women's experiences' – even the experience of ideology – as the invariant 'others' of male history, literary tradition, form and ideology, in order to make . . . women resistant by definition (1993: 3).[7] More often, 'the marginal and the dispossessed' are seen as 'cele[brating] their sheer defiance and their apparent autonomy' in 'ways that resistance also enters into the processes by which structures of domination persist or renew themselves' (O'Hanlon, 1992, quoted in Rajan, 1993: 4–5). Citing other examples, Rajan maintains that what is seen as some sort of assertive agency by women may in fact be 'precisely the reproduction, in an inverted form, of patriarchy's own forms of sexual essentialism, belittlement and contempt'(1993: 5). In this context, Tewari-Jassal's detailed exposition on rural women's work songs in the northern state of Rajasthan, which according to the author, transmit societal values such as 'licensing female subordination to patriarchal authority. . . as its ideological subtext' (2003: 203) from older to younger generations and in the process, spell out limits of transgressing these values, is extremely useful. Cutting across caste lines, the author argues that these songs, rather than empowering, suggest that women are complicit in their own oppression and as they speak within the operative social constraints and the subjugating discourses (Kumar, 1994: 15), they continue to align, even if partially, with the existing dominant structures.

Given this, I find Rao and Walton's (2004) notion of cultural capital extremely useful in unpacking further the agency-structure debate. They argue that people might have human and physical capabilities to exercise their agencies notwithstanding inherent biological differences, which may presumably provide women with 'the level playing field' and yet women may not be able to overcome ideological and structural barriers. This is because the majority of women have no or little access to social and symbolic resources, which are inherent in certain social relationships that can be drawn upon to maintain a position in the prevailing social order, so crucial in a status and hierarchy conscious society such as India. That is to say, the range of entitlements that women can draw upon may be circumscribed by rules, norms and practices such as legal or other restrictions on occupations in which women may work, prevailing ideas about appropriate gender divisions of labour, or husbands' prohibitions on wives working. Thus, the institutional rules, norms and practices governing families are of particular significance in reproducing gender differentials in entitlements and endowments despite parity in capabilities (Kabeer, 1994). Framed thus, institutional barriers articulated through patriarchal coding matter and they matter more to women because they are relatively less equipped to appropriate power relations that would have made cultural transgression across rigidly defined boundaries easier for them.

Does a refusal to accept the emancipatory role 'agency' is often assigned with amounts to saying that working towards agency is disposable? Not at all. Following Prakash's (1992) argument, although in quite a different context, and others as discussed above, my point is that agency alone cannot be a foundational theme in women's struggle for equality; that we recognise the structures of domination and women's placement in those structures because agency, even in its most potent/fully realisable avatar, exists in a form of relationality as even the most enlightened individuals cannot function in contextual isolation away from social constraints and the subjugating discourses within which they operate.

If so and if the idea of a relational realm is acceptable, it becomes quite clear that for the majority of women, patriarchal structures are here to stay – patriarchal structures may vary in their articulation and assume numerous forms. For example, there are enough cues to suggest that even as women's functional spaces are expanding and they are crossing over domestic spheres to market spaces as workers in almost every arena, the reverse – men crossing over to domestic spaces and breaking traditional gendered codes for domestic responsibilities, such as childcare and other household work, is either not happening or happening at a very slow rate. Increasingly, working housewives' tasks are being replaced by hired help, which often consists of women servants. The result is that the feminine/masculine division of labour does not really get reconfigured according to the changing times. The dual-triple burdens just get transferred from one set of women to another (Ehrenreich and Hochschild, 2003). Since provisioning of services continues undisturbed, the injustice of unequal burden-sharing in ongoing gendered division of labour is rarely subjected to social scrutiny. The patriarchal structures remain intact while somewhere in this drama, the concern for transformative changes in core asymmetries between women and men is sidetracked and unattended.

As argued by Gasper and Staveren (2006: 174), freedom – again an integral part of agency – has to go beyond just highlighting values 'related to the self, values that increase one's independence and autonomy, but also values related to relationships with others. . .' If we are looking at process changes rather than situational changes, and I think we do in arguing for women's agency, the approach to gendered agency had to be inclusive of stakeholders other than women – men partners, rather than being anchored on women, by women, and of women.

To expand Gasper and Staveren's proposition and to fit it in the present context, I would paraphrase it by saying that individualised/autonomous agency and 'the variety of values that may be promoted through such agency' cannot bring gender justice unless men are also liberated from the various constructs/traps that they are in. These are the social imposition of being the primary bread earners, being the custodians of societal values, of machismo, and so on. In this context, I am tempted to cite one example. In a training programme by an NGO which works in a rural Himalayan region, adolescent boys and girls were asked to describe what they see as advantageous if they were to belong to the opposite sex. Girls listed the freedom boys enjoy in terms of being able to go out at will, whereas boys saw this very mobility as a compulsion imposed upon them in that they had to loiter around so as to (a) have access to information about the job market, and (b) because young men cannot stay at home doing nothing.

Many more examples of socially sanctioned/imposed codes can be unearthed for men as well. The point is loosening of these codes through conscious efforts and providing for unconventional spaces that men can occupy is the other side of the same coin for women's freedom.

Concluding Remarks

An inclusive of men's framework for gender equality would eventually legitimise it in the minds of people at large and not amongst a select few feminist scholars/activists. A broad-based legitimising will have to eventually address unequal power relations and asymmetrical gendered order. In order

> to reclaim the transformative aspects of the concept of . . . [agency] we need to move [beyond the issues of] 'access to', 'participation in', and 'self-help' to ideas of contestation, and struggle, in which alliances can be formed with different groups, *including men* in specific times and places, for purposes of transforming institutions of the state, the economy, the community and the family (emphasis added). (Bisnath and Elson, 2002)

However, it is an extremely complicated and rather prolonged process and is not an easy task and does run the risk of appropriating women's spaces by vocal, authoritative men and yet many NGO experiences in India have shown that with proper care and sensitivities and checks in place, men have become supportive partners in women's struggles (Raju and Leonard, 2000).

That such an approach is required has now been institutionally acknowledged. In fact, some projects and the Tenth Five-Year Plan categorically seek the active participation and involvement of men (Planning Commission, 2004). However, despite international and national strictures regarding male partnership as a strategy, men are rarely part of intervened constituencies – it remains tokenism at best. Unless proactively created, much wider constituencies beyond the obvious are created, partial agential successes will continue, and in some cases, may even lead to the backlash that we encounter from time to time. This proposition asks for a much embedded and complex framework for gender development than is currently available.

Notes

1. *Barsane ki Holi* in the Mathura region in Uttar Pradesh is a good example when women beat their male partners with sticks.
2. I do not, therefore, intend to make an inventory of various aspects of deprivation and subordination that women experience in every walk of their lives (I have discussed various issues related to gender-related deprivation elsewhere. See Raju, 2006).

3. In one of our recent works on declining sex-ratios in Himachal Pradesh, it came out quite clearly that the increasing mobility of married/unmarried daughters to distant places has an adverse effect on parents' perception of daughters' availability when they needed them, further reducing their 'utility' value in popular imagination!

4. A news item published in *The Times of India* dated September 24, 2006, is a pointer. In the city of Kolkata, which is better placed than Delhi in the treatment of its women, even women-managed Puja committees resisted employing trained women priests during the *pujas*. If not as the leading priest, women could have definitely lent a helping hand, but even that was not accepted.

5. In a Haryana village, a Dalit woman *sarpanch* (panchayat head) used her second-in-command, a high-caste woman member, to advance her agenda because she knew that even though she was the *sarpanch*, her lower caste status placed her in a significantly disadvantaged position, adversely affecting her bargaining power.

6. Activists may enter the debate from an entirely different angle arguing that they understand the caveats, nuances and finer points in questioning the framing of women as the primary site of their resistance, but they do not have the luxury of incorporating such restricting assumptions into their actions and their fight is against commodification of all kinds. Such a focus may overtake the issues of diversity of the indigenous notions of sexuality, not only for setting up on an active agenda and to get going with it, but also because for each example of signs of alternative sexuality, right-wing activists can come up with loads of arguments to show what real indigenous stands for and how the texts and symbols represent deeper and higher level justification of what they are claiming as the essence of the (Indian) civilisation. I thank my colleague, Deepak Mishra, at the Centre for the Study of Regional Development, for pointing out this important aspect to me. The fact, however, remains that the movement in Bangalore revolved primarily around 'protecting the *izzat* (honour) of (Indian) women', rather than positing it as a struggle against capitalism, perhaps because it is easier to invoke popular sentiments and garner wider support when movements are pitched against tradition with women in the eye of the needle.

7. Rajan's observation is confined to the 'problem of subaltern, specifically gendered, *resistance* (emphasis in the original), in relation to [women's] writing' (1993: 2), but I find her arguments equally useful in understanding other means of expressions that have been seen as 'resistance'.

References

Anandhi, S. 2002. 'Interlocking Patriarchies and Women in Governance: A Case Study of Panchayati Raj Institutions in Tamil Nadu' in K. Kapadia (ed.), *The Violence of Development: The Politics of Identity, Gender and Social Inequalities in India*, New Delhi: Kali for Women, pp. 425–458.

Bisnath, S. and D. Elson. 2002. 'Women's Empowerment Revisited', in UNIFEM, Progress of the World's Women: A New Biennial Report, www. undp.org/unifem/progressive/empower.html, February 4, 2006.

Chhachhi, A. 2005. 'The State, Communalism, Fundamentalism and Women in India' in M. Khullar (ed.), *Writings the Women's Movement: A Reader*, New Delhi: Zubaan, pp. 218–242.

Connell, R.W. 1995. *Masculinities*, Oxford: Polity Press.

Ehrenreich, B. and A.R. Hochschild. 2003. *Global Women: Nannies, Maids and Sex Workers in the New Economy*, London: Granta Books.

Gasper, D. and I.V. Staveren. 2006. 'Development as Freedom' – And As What Else?' in B. Agarwal, J. Humphries and I. Robeyns (eds.), *Capabilities, Freedom and Equality: Amartya Sen's Work from a Gender Perspective*, New Delhi: Oxford University Press, pp. 152–179.

Kabeer, N. 1994. *Reversed Realities: Gender Hierarchies in Developmental Thought*, New Delhi: Kali for Women.

Knopp, L. 2004. 'Ontologies of Place, Placelessness, and Movement: Queer Quests for Identity and Their Impacts on Contemporary Geographic Thought' in *Gender, Place and Culture*, 11(1): 121–134.

Kumar, R. 1993. *The History of Doing: An Illustrated Account of Movements for Women's Rights and Feminism in India, 1800–1990*, New Delhi: Kali for Women.

Nagar, R. and S. Raju. 2003. 'Women, NGOs and the Contradictions of Empowerment and Disempowerment: A Conversation', in *Antipode*, 35(1): 1–12.

Niranjana, S. 1997. 'Femininity, Space and the Female Body: An Anthropological Perspective', in M. Thapan (ed.), *Embodiment: Essays on Gender and Identity*, New Delhi: Oxford University Press, pp. 107–124.

Oza, R. 2001. 'Showcasing India: Gender, Geography and Globalization' in *Signs*, 26(4): 1067–1095.

Palriwala, R. and P. Uberoi. 2005. 'Marriage and Migration in Asia: Gender Issues' in *Indian Journal of Gender Studies*, 12(2–3): 1–25.

Planning Commission. 2004. Tenth Five Year Plan (2002–07), Chapter 2.11, Downloaded Google.com, September 1, 2004.

Peter, F. 2006. 'Gender and the Foundations of Social Choice: The Role of Situated Agency' in B. Agarwal, J. Humphries and I. Robeyns (eds.),

Capabilities, Freedom, and Equality: Amartya Sen's Work from a Gender Perspective, New Delhi: Oxford University Press, pp. 17–38.

Prakash, G. 1992. 'Postcolonial Criticism and Historiography' in *Social Text*, 31–32, pp. 8–19.

Raheja, G.G., and A.G. Gold. 1994. *Listen to the Heron's Words: Reimagining Gender and Kinship in North India*, Berkeley: University of California Press.

Rajan, Sunder R. 1993. *Real and Imagined Women: Gender, Culture and Postcolonialism*, London and New York: Routledge.

Raju, S. 1997. 'The Issues at Stake: An Overview of Gender Concerns in Post-independence India' in *Environment and Planning A* Vol. 29, pp. 2191–2206.

———— 2005. 'Limited Options: Rethinking Women's Empowerment 'Projects' in 'Development Discourses: A Case from Rural India' in *Gender Technology and Development*, 9: 253–271.

———— 2006. 'Locating Women in India's Development' in A. Kundu (ed.), *Social Development Report*, New Delhi: Oxford University Press, pp. 78–95.

Raju, S. and Ann Leonard. 2000. *Men as Supportive Partners in Reproductive Health: Moving from Rhetoric to Reality*, New Delhi/New York: Population Council.

Ram, K. 1992. *Mukkuvar Women, Gender Hegemony, Capitalist Transformation in a South Indian Fishing Community*, New Delhi: Kali for Women.

Rao, V. and M. Walton. (eds.), 2004. *Culture and Public Action*, Stanford: Stanford University Press.

Sen, A. 2006. 'Development as Freedom' in B. Agarwal, J. Humphries, and I. Robeyns (eds.), *Capabilities, Freedom, and Equality: Amartya Sen's Work from a Gender Perspective*, New Delhi: Oxford University Press, pp. 501–531.

Sen, A., B. Agarwal, J. Humphries and I. Robeyns. 2003. 'Continuing the Conversation' in *Feminist Economics*, 9(2–3): 319–332.

Thapan, M. 1997. 'Introduction: Gender and Embodiment in Everyday Life' in M. Thapan (ed.), *Embodiment: Essays on Gender and Identity*, New Delhi: Oxford University Press, pp. 1–34.

Tewari, Jassal. 2003. 'Bhojpuri Songs, Women's Work and Social Control in Northern India' in *The Journal of Peasant Studies*, 30(2): 159–206.

3

Bridging the Gender Gaps
An Analysis of the Educational Situation with Special Emphasis on Higher, Technical and Professional Education

ANITA NUNA

In India, since the 19th century, social reformers have given high priority to women's education. Though their approach to women's education was very much limited to preparing women for their role in the family, yet women's education, for whatever reason, has always been high on the national agenda. But their efforts at educating women could not get translated into action to a large extent due to serious social-cultural barriers till the early 20th century. In 1945, the All India Women's Conference for the first time pleaded for expansion of education for women with a view to enable them to be independent. At the time of independence, gender equality was adopted as one of the major goals in the Constitution of India.

At the time of independence (1947), India had large regional imbalances in terms of educational spread and also in terms of girls' participation at all levels and types of education. The enrolment of women students, both in the school sector and higher education sector, was abysmally low. At the national level, their participation was 12.8 per cent in recognised high schools; 9.6 per cent in higher education; and just 5.2 per cent in professional courses of the total enrolled children (Progress of Education in India, 1937–47).

After independence, the Government of India looked at women's education as a challenge in national development. To this end, a number of commissions and committees such as the University Education Commission (1948–49); Durga Bai Deshmukh Committee on Women' Education (1958–59); Committee to Look into the Causes for Lack of Support Particularly in Rural Area, for Girls' Education and to Enlist Public Cooperation (1963); Education Commission (1964–66); Committee on the Status of Women in India (1971); Committee on Differentiation of Curricula for Boys and Girls (1964); and Committee for Review of National Policy on Education, 1986 (1990), etc., were set up to look into the status and causes of low participation of girls and women in education at different levels, including higher, technical and professional education and also to suggest ways and means to enhance their participation and retention. These committees broadly concluded that the gender gaps in education were mainly due to a mix of sociocultural and economic constraints and that the same could be reduced by making special provisions for women's education. Subsequently, the concern for girls' education has been placed on the forefront in all the Five-Year Plan programmes. A number of programmes concerning 'Education for All' have been launched during the last five decades with special emphasis on promoting girls' education in general, and that of those belonging to socially disadvantaged groups in particular.

Efforts made in the past seem to have paid good dividends, though much remains to be achieved. During the six decades or so since independence, there have been improvements in the status of girls education. The statistics reveal that the proportion of girl students to the total enrolled students have increased at all levels. In higher education, their percentages have gone up from 10 per cent in 1950–51 to nearly 40.4 per cent in 2004–05 (UGC, 2004–05). Likewise, their proportion in technical and other professional courses has also increased over time. However, this change is primarily seen among the higher and middle classes, with higher levels of education among people in urban areas; in rural and remote areas and among certain social groups and communities, girls and women are still facing problems in deriving the benefits of existing educational structures. There are wide inter-state disparities in gender gaps at all levels of education and these gaps seem to be wider at the district and sub-district levels. Girls are unable to complete even their basic education in many remote areas because they do not enjoy easy access to schools. Access to higher education is still a dream for many girls. Further, the analysis indicates wide disparities in the education of rural males and rural females; urban females and rural females, and between females belonging to scheduled and non-scheduled groups and between certain minority communities. The reasons for these inequalities are varied and vary even from one location to another.

This paper is an attempt to bring out some of the issues and challenges that need to be addressed to bridge gender gaps in education in general and in higher, technical and professional education in particular. This paper is broadly divided into three sections. The first one focuses on the national perspective on girls' education and initiatives to bridge gender gaps in education. The second section analyses the progress and shortfalls in terms of educational expansion and status of girls' education both in the school sector and higher education, including technical and professional education. The last concluding section highlights challenges and priorities that need to be addressed in the coming years so that the existing weaknesses in efforts for bridging gender gaps in education, especially in higher, technical and professional courses, can be addressed. The last section is based on an analysis of both secondary and primary data/information collected through household surveys and field observations. A total of 250 households were surveyed to ascertain the perceptions of parents of school-going girls and the girls themselves studying in classes VI, IX and X in different locations of states namely, Andhra Pradesh, Jharkhand, Chhattisgarh, Haryana, Punjab and Madhya Pradesh on some of the following questions: Why is there gender disparity in higher education? Why do urban-rural disparities exist in girls' education? How do the major stakeholders, the girls/parents/community in rural areas view women's participation in higher/technical/professional courses? What is the attitude of the rural community towards government efforts in promoting girls' education?

National Perspective on Girls' Education

Major Recommendations of Different Committees and Commissions set up by the GoI in the Post-independence Period for Girls' Education

(i) The University Education Commission, as early as in 1948, gave a prominent place to women's education. The commission included a separate chapter on women's education and recommended that there should be no curtailment in educational opportunities for women, but rather a great increase.

(ii) The Durga Bai Deshmukh Committee on Women' Education in 1958–59, recommended scholarships for girls based on merit for continuation of secondary and higher education. The committee also recommended establishment of more secondary schools for girls and further development of existing ones, especially in rural areas, with provisions for staff quarters, hostels and even free or subsidised transport, where necessary.

(iii) The Committee to Look into the Causes for Lack of Support Particularly in Rural Areas, for Girls' Education and to Enlist Public Cooperation (1963) stressed on introducing the Compulsory Education Act in states where it did not exist and free education for all girls upto the secondary stage.

(iv) The Education Commission (1964–66) believed that at the secondary stage, separate schools, hostels, scholarships and special efforts to encourage girls to study mathematics and science were to be encouraged. At the higher secondary level (Classes XI and XII), alongside the polytechnics, possibilities to exploit a range of interesting courses in commercial, clerical, scientific and industrial trades and in areas of special interest to girls were emphasised.

To promote higher education, a programme of scholarships and provision of suitable but economical hostel accommodation for women students with all the necessary amenities on a large scale were emphasised to encourage girls from rural areas to seek higher education. At the undergraduate stage, the commission envisaged separate colleges for women as per local demand and incentives for academically inclined girls with ambitions of pursuing a career in research and teaching at the college or university level, or in professions such as medicine or technology. The need to provide facilities for advanced training in business administration and management to women candidates was also stressed.

To promote girls' participation in technical and engineering education, particular attention ought to be given to developing courses of special interest to girls in all polytechnics at both certificate and diploma levels. The commission also visualised the need to open more polytechnics for girls in order to attract them into these courses.

(v) The Committee on the Status of Women: Towards Equality (1971) stressed on the establishment of ashram *shalas* or residential schools, to serve clusters of villages scattered in difficult terrain and to post at least 50 per cent women teachers in schools.

At the secondary stage, free education for all girls upto the end of the secondary stage; quality education and provision of facilities for important subjects like science, mathematics and commerce; and introduction of job oriented work experience, keeping in view the needs, resources and employment potential of the region were proposed.

To promote higher education, the committee focused on the development of more employment opportunities, particularly part-time in nature and the development of employment information and guidance services for women entering higher education.

(vi) The National Perspective Plan for Women (1988–2000) stressed on flexible school timings and availability of schools within walking distance. It was analysed that the recommended distance of 3 kilometers for a middle school was a handicap for many girls; hence, it was considered necessary to provide hostel facilities. Opening of more colleges and polytechnics for girls, especially in rural areas; special scholarships for rural girls opting for science courses at the secondary and higher education levels; and incentives like scholarships, freeships and bursaries to meet their requirements for food and lodging, etc., to enable girls belonging to weaker sections from rural areas to pursue higher education were considered necessary. An initial reservation of 30 per cent seats for rural girls in higher education courses was also put forward as a proposal.

(vii) The Committee for Review of National Policy on Education, 1986, in 1990 recommended crèches and hostel facilities to help women continue higher education; relaxation of age limits and the possibility of continuing education and re-entry into the mainstream after a break. Further, the committee said there should be at least one women's polytechnic in each district.

The above analysis clearly indicates that all the committees and commissions have recommended every effort to bridge gender gaps at all levels and in every type of education. To promote higher education, separate institutions for girls as per demand; residential schools; hostels; relaxation of age limits; development of employment information and guidance services for women entering higher education regarding job opportunities; incentives for pursuing careers in research and teaching at the college or university level, or in professions such as medicine or technology were considered to be focus areas. To bridge gender gaps in professional colleges, polytechnics were proposed for each district.

Girls' Education and Policy Perspectives

There has been a marked shift in policy perspectives towards girls' education since independence. While the National Policy on Education, 1968, emphasised equalisation of educational opportunities, the

National Policy on Education (NPE), 1986, revised in 1992, emphasised education for women's equality and ending social evils and practices derogatory to women. The NPE, 1986/1992 places the role of education as an agent of basic change in the status of women. The NPE and its Programme of Action (PoA), 1992, laid major emphasis on increasing women's participation in vocational, technical and professional education at different levels. The policy of non-discrimination is recommended to eliminate sex stereotyping in vocational and professional courses and to promote women's participation in non-traditional occupations, as well as in existing and emergent technologies. The National Policy for the Empowerment of Women, 2001, also focuses on equal access to women to quality education at all levels; career and vocational guidance; and special measures for the development of vocational/technical skills. Reducing the gender gaps in secondary and higher education found special mention in the National Policy for the Empowerment of Women, 2001.

Girls' Education and Five-Year Plans

The First Five-Year Plan (1951–56) included a chapter on education in which women's education was given a prominent place. Targets were laid down for women's education at the secondary stage. Emphasis was placed on opening institutions for girls and the appointment of women teachers to promote girls' education. During the Fourth Plan period, among the special programmes undertaken to encourage girls' education, stress was laid on providing sanitary facilities in schools for girls. In the Sixth Plan period, special emphasis was placed on meeting the special needs of women, who might have faced an interruption in their higher studies. The Seventh Plan envisaged free education for girls upto the secondary stage and stressed on the promotion of vocational and technical education for girls by setting up more women's polytechnics and by opening access to all technical institutions to women. The Eighth Plan stressed on the creation of conditions that would enable women to participate in the educational process in a more meaningful way. The Nineth Plan recognised education of girls as a non-negotiable area. The National Agenda for Governance stated, "We will institute plans for providing free education for girls up to college levels, i.e., undergraduate level including professional courses would be made free." This includes tuition fees, basic textbooks, maintenance expenditure in hostels and library books. The scheme was to be devised and implemented in a time-bound manner. Additional hostel facilities for girls, particularly in tribal and remote areas, to improve attendance rates were also proposed. The Women's Component Plan (WCP) was adopted as a special strategy in the Nineth Plan period directing the Central and state governments to ensure that not less than 30 per cent of the funds/benefits were ear-marked in all the women related sectors.

The Tenth Five-Year Plan (2002–07) viewed girls' education as a major area of concern. The plan fixed targets to bridge gender gaps in enrolment, retention and learning achievements. Special efforts were proposed to provide easy and equal access to free education for girls and women at all levels and in the field of technical and vocational education and training in upcoming and job-oriented trades and reduce dropout rates by expanding support services through mid-day meals, hostels and incentives like free supply of uniforms, textbooks, transport charges and appointing more women teachers at the primary level (at least 90 per cent). The scheme of providing boarding and hostel facilities for girls, initiated in 1993, has been revised with the intent of increasing girls' enrolment at the secondary level. Steps to remove gender bias and ste-reotypes in the curricula, textbooks and learning material were envisaged as major areas of concern. Under the recast programme of the Balika Samridhi Yojna (BSY), the Tenth Plan focuses on educating and empow-ering the girl child living below the poverty line with adequate financial support till she completes her higher secondary education or gets equipped with the necessary skills to earn her livelihood. To encourage more and more girls to enter into the mainstream of higher education, the Tenth Plan endeavours to put into action the governmental commitment of providing free education for girls upto the college level, including in professional courses.

Vocationalisation of secondary education and vocational training for women was another priority area which got greater attention in the Tenth Plan. The plan commits to initiate efforts to extend the existing network of regional vocational training centres to all states and women's indus-trial institutes and women's wings with general industrial training insti-tutes with residential facilities in all districts and sub-districts.

In the field of science and technology, special measures have been suggested to train women in areas such as communication and informa-tion technology. Incentives of various kinds have also been suggested to encourage girls and women to opt for the emerging trades/areas of tech-nical education with high employment potential, such as electronics, computer applications, bio-engineering, biotechnology, food processing, fabric designing, beauty culture, communications, media, etc.

National Initiatives to Bridge Gender Gaps in School Education since 1950

In pursuance of the abovementioned commitments, a number of programmes concerning 'Education for All' have been launched during the last five decades in which special emphasis has been placed on promoting girls' education in general and the education of girls belonging to socially disadvantaged groups and educationally backward minorities in particular. The District Primary Education Programme (DPEP) launched in 1993–94, which was shaped on the experiences of state-specific projects launched in the early 1980s, such as the Bihar Education Project, Lok Jumbish in Rajasthan and Uttar Pradesh Basic Education Projects, gave adequate importance to girls' education and gender concerns in its design. The programme was implemented primarily in low female literacy districts and the focus was to increase the participation of girls and lower significantly gender gaps in the enrolment and retention rates. The Mahila Samakhya (MS) programme has also contributed a lot to promoting girls' education. The Sarva Shiksha Abhiyan (SSA) too recognises girls' education as a major challenge. The goals of this mission mode campaign are: providing access to all 6–14 year old children through various strategies, including the Education Guarantee Scheme, Alternative Schooling and Back to School Camps and bridging gender and social gaps at the primary stage by 2007 and at the elementary level by 2010. Within the ambit of the SSA, Kasturba Gandhi Balika Vidyalaya (KGBV), a special programme for girl children from the Scheduled Castes (SCs), Scheduled Tribes (STs), other backward communities (OBCs) and minorities, has been started in the Tenth Five-Year Plan to support the opening of residential girls' schools in educationally backward blocks. It aims to ensure access and quality education to girls through residential schools and boarding facilities at the elementary level.

Special Provisions to Bridge Gender Gaps in Secondary Education

Though secondary education is primarily the responsibility of states, the Centre also intervenes through centrally sponsored schemes. Some of the centrally sponsored schemes launched for increasing girls' access to secondary education are:

1. Strengthening of boarding and hostel facilities for girls: This scheme was launched in 1993–94 with a view to support voluntary efforts

in facilitating the access of girls residing in districts predominantly inhabited by socially disadvantaged groups (SCs and STs) and educationally backward minorities, to secondary education.

2. Setting up of schools in educationally backward blocks through the provisions of a one-time Central grant to state governments, NGOs and registered societies. To address the issue of access with equity in providing education to girls at the secondary stage, provisions of providing grants for setting up new secondary schools and up-grading of existing primary schools to secondary/higher secondary levels have been made during the Tenth Plan period.

3. Area Intensive Programme: The scheme of the Area Intensive Programme was launched in 1993 to promote the participation of Muslim children in general and Muslim girls in particular through the opening of multistream residential schools in Muslim dominated pockets.

4. Jawahar Navodaya Vidayalaya (JNV): The JNV scheme was launched in 1985–86 with the objective of setting up one school in each district for providing good quality modern education to talented children in rural areas. There quarters of the seats are reserved for rural areas with proportional representation for SCs, STs and one-third seats for girls.

Initiatives to Bridge Gender Gaps in Higher Education

The following schemes have been launched by the University Grants Commission (UGC) to promote women's participation in higher education:

- A special scheme of hostels for women was introduced in 1995–96 to enable girls and women to pursue higher studies in universities and colleges.
- Part-time research associateship for women: This scheme was started to provide opportunities for unemployed women who have PhD degrees to their credit and have an aptitude for research, but are unable to pursue research work on a regular basis due to personal reasons. The UGC has made provisions to provide such benefits to 100 girls every year.
- Day care centres have been set up within universities on a payment basis for children from three months to six years of age to help women pursue their academic careers.
- Women studies centres have been set up to undertake research, develop curricula and organise training and extension work in the

Table 1: Percentage Increase in Number of Schools in India between the 5th and 6th, and 6th and 7th All India School Education Survey Periods

Surveys	No. of Primary Schools		No. of Upper Primary Schools		No. of Secondary Schools		No. of Higher Secondary Schools	
	Rural	*Urban*	*Rural*	*Urban*	*Rural*	*Urban*	*Rural*	*Urban*
Fifth Survey, 1986	475,823	52,907	113,087	25,929	38,862	13,698	7,136	8,329
Sixth Survey, 1993	507,581 (6.68%)	62,874 (18.84%)	129,246 (14.29%)	33,559 (29.43%)	47,870 (23.18%)	17,694 (29.17%)	11,600 (62.56%)	12,062 (44.82%)
Seventh Survey, 2002	572,814 (12.85%)	78,250 (24.52%)	193,947 (50.06%)	51,375 (53.09%)	63,576 (32.81%)	27,165 (53.53%)	22,847 (97.14%)	21,022 (74.79%)

Source: All India School Education Surveys, NCERT, New Delhi.
Note: Figures in parentheses indicate percentage increase during successive survey periods.

areas of gender equity, economic self-reliance of women and girls' education. The scheme was started in 1986 with the objective of promoting studies on women's issues. The UGC has already set up women studies centres in 34 universities.

- To bridge educational gaps in higher education between non-scheduled children and children belonging to socially disadvantaged groups including girl students (SCs and STs), the Union government has launched various schemes such as scholarships; remedial coaching assistance at the undergraduate and postgraduate levels; coaching for the National Eligibility Test (NET); coaching for entry in services etc. The UGC has also planned a new scheme of research associateship and scholarships to undertake postgraduate studies in professional courses.

Progress and Shortfalls in School Education

During the last five decades, there has been considerable growth in the number of schools across the country (Table 1). But the percentage increase in number of schools is more in urban areas as compared to rural areas in relation to the rural area population.

Though there has been a substantial increase in the category of higher secondary schools in rural areas across the country, shortage of higher secondary schools still persists in many states. It has emerged from the analysis that there are states in which the number of higher secondary schools in rural areas was less than 10 per 100 upper primary schools as per the 7th All India School Education Survey, 2002 (Annexures I and II). If we go by statistics, we find that the coverage of rural population by higher secondary classes within was only 8.30 per cent and 68.51 per cent upto 8 kilometres (7th All India School Education Survey, 2002). This means 91.70 per cent of the rural population in the country is yet to be served by higher secondary classes within and 31.49 per cent upto 8 kilometres (the national norm for access to higher secondary classes). Inter-state variations were much wider. There were many states in which the rural population served by higher secondary classes within was much below the national average (8.30%). These states were Jharkhand (0.51%); Bihar (0.67%); Assam (1.15%); Jammu & Kashmir (2.61%); Orissa (2.60%); West Bengal (2.96%) and Uttar Pradesh (5.72%). The survey data also reveal that 70 per cent of the rural population was yet to be served by higher secondary classes upto a distance of 8 kilometres in Bihar and Jharkhand. Non-availability of easy access to higher secondary education acts as a major impediment for girls' entry into higher education.

Table 2: Percentage of Children Enrolled in Different Levels of Schooling (All Communities)

Year	Primary (Classes I-V)		Upper Primary (Classes VI-VIII)		High/Hr. Sec./ Pre-Degree	
	Boys	Girls	Boys	Girls	Boys	Girls
1946–47	73.3	26.7	82.0	18.0	87.2	12.8*
1950–51	71.9	28.1	83.9	16.1	86.7	13.3
1960–61	67.4	32.6	76.1	23.9	79.4	20.6
1970–71	62.6	37.4	70.7	29.3	75.0	25.0
1980–81	61.4	38.6	67.1	32.9	69.1	30.9
1990–91	58.5	41.5	63.2	36.8	67.0	33.0
As on September 30, 2003	53.3	46.7	55.9	44.1	58.9	41.1

Source: Selected Educational Statistics, 2003–04, MHRD, GoI, New Delhi.
*quoted in Durga Bai Deshmukh Committee Report, 1958–59.

The education of girls in India since independence started on a very low key note. The gaps between the enrolment of boys and girls at all levels of education were very high at the time of independence. But these have reduced at a faster rate at the national aggregative level during the last two decades (Table 2).

The state-level analysis in Table 3 indicates that though the gender gaps in primary education are reducing, they are continuing at the secondary and higher secondary stages in many states. The states where gender gaps have been registered as comparatively very high are Bihar, Chhatisgarh, Jharkhand, Madhya Pradesh, Rajasthan, Orissa and Uttar Pradesh. The participation of girls in these states at the higher secondary stages was recorded much below the national average. For instance in Bihar, girls formed 35 per cent of the total enrolled children at the upper primary stage; 29.2 per cent at high; and 24.7 per cent at the higher secondary stages as on September 30, 2003. Similarly, in Rajasthan, girls formed 36 per cent of the total enrolled children at the upper primary stage; 28.6 per cent at the high; and 28.8 per cent at the higher secondary stages (Table 3). These gaps were increasing at the higher levels.

Rural-urban disparities in enrolment at the secondary and higher secondary levels continued after five decades of planned development. The states where the rural-urban differentials in secondary and higher secondary enrolments were very sharp are Bihar, Chhatisgarh, Jharkhand, Madhya Pradesh, Rajasthan and Uttar Pradesh (Table 4).

At the national aggregative level, the gender gaps in education among children belonging to socially disadvantaged groups (SC/ST) and Mus-

Table 3: Statewise Percentage of Girls Enrolled to Total Enrolled Children at Different School Stages in India as on September 30, 2003 (All Communities)

S.No.	States/UTs	Primary	Upper Primary	Secondary	Higher Secondary	Higher Education
1.	Andhra Pradesh	49.29	46.80	44.79	40.15	37.03
2.	Arunachal Pradesh	46.00	45.65	42.28	38.99	36.47
3.	Assam	48.99	46.76	44.04	37.46	33.60
4.	Bihar	42.16	35.25	29.23	24.68	24.35
5.	Chhattisgarh	48.02	43.24	38.10	37.84	36.87
6.	Goa	47.55	47.21	48.65	49.10	56.83
7.	Gujarat	45.04	38.25	40.67	41.51	44.21
8.	Haryana	46.75	44.53	41.59	41.10	41.09
9.	Himachal Pradesh	48.00	47.90	47.84	45.14	43.59
10.	Jammu & Kashmir	45.23	43.18	42.34	39.89	46.59
11.	Jharkhand	43.82	41.10	37.18	39.18	32.23
12.	Karnataka	48.34	47.15	46.51	46.15	41.16
13.	Kerala	48.90	47.73	49.80	50.24	60.57
14.	Madhya Pradesh	45.59	40.30	35.05	36.73	37.00
15.	Maharashtra	47.84	46.84	45.45	42.70	41.21
16.	Manipur	48.27	47.17	48.71	44.54	44.83
17.	Meghalaya	50.01	50.13	50.29	48.11	46.34
18.	Mizoram	47.92	48.90	51.08	49.50	45.42
19.	Nagaland	47.84	49.21	48.01	45.05	39.98
20.	Orissa	47.29	44.94	43.38	36.58	35.76
21.	Punjab	46.91	46.92	46.99	44.84	51.41
22.	Rajasthan	45.09	36.14	28.55	28.82	33.82

Contd.

Contd.

23.	Sikkim	49.77	53.43	50.41	48.87	38.76
24.	Tamil Nadu	48.26	47.67	47.73	50.00	45.51
25.	Tripura	47.79	47.13	46.78	42.35	40.96
26.	Uttar Pradesh	46.16	41.24	34.70	40.53	36.66
27.	Uttaranchal	48.33	47.83	41.79	38.55	42.20
28.	West Bengal	48.86	47.49	42.39	39.04	36.93
29.	Andaman and Nicobar Islands	48.05	46.82	49.21	50.37	53.27
30.	Chandigarh	45.34	46.51	46.48	48.73	52.01
31.	Dadra and Nagar Haveli	45.83	38.50	40.04	41.06	–
32.	Daman & Diu	47.12	46.23	46.24	40.87	46.77
33.	Delhi	46.44	47.29	46.04	47.83	48.60
34.	Lakshadweep	46.75	45.03	47.26	47.10	34.65
35.	Pondicherry	48.19	48.03	49.43	51.89	50.89
	India	46.70	44.01	41.18	40.99	39.68

Source: Selected Educational Statistics, 2003–04, MHRD, GoI, New Delhi, 2006.

Table 4: Areawise Percentage of Girls Enrolled to Total Enrolled Children in Different School Stages

S.No.	States/UTs	Primary		Upper Primary		Secondary		Higher Secondary	
		Rural	Urban	Rural	Urban	Rural	Urban	Rural	Urban
1.	Andhra Pradesh	49.83	50.08	48.21	47.98	43.01	49.40	35.79	41.87
2.	Arunachal Pradesh	44.76	48.03	45.25	47.02	43.79	46.49	43.94	44.10
3.	Assam	48.41	48.48	48.06	52.79	49.60	54.74	38.84	39.21
4.	Bihar	42.88	49.29	38.43	47.21	29.98	41.73	30.49	28.32
5.	Chhattisgarh	48.29	49.71	42.74	46.04	39.52	45.41	33.41	45.31
6.	Goa	48.64	47.63	48.87	47.40	47.16	48.07	45.36	48.79
7.	Gujarat	47.36	47.42	45.17	44.85	37.49	39.36	37.61	43.65
8.	Haryana	47.05	48.22	44.54	40.86	42.29	41.90	39.79	43.92
9.	Himachal Pradesh	48.81	47.90	47.20	44.06	46.87	48.43	45.96	44.14
10.	Jammu & Kashmir	47.46	47.86	43.74	44.25	40.30	48.61	36.14	41.64
11.	Jharkhand	44.22	49.72	41.01	49.75	33.78	47.35	27.98	35.71
12.	Karnataka	50.17	49.35	47.40	49.09	44.40	48.19	41.04	43.50
13.	Kerala	49.20	50.73	47.93	46.65	50.44	53.03	48.03	50.30
14.	Madhya Pradesh	47.75	47.92	39.67	44.24	34.50	42.84	29.22	40.75
15.	Maharashtra	48.16	47.16	48.10	48.30	44.76	47.29	42.51	45.10
16.	Manipur	49.01	53.20	47.59	46.97	47.82	49.48	47.79	44.10
17.	Meghalaya	50.16	51.67	52.02	51.59	50.66	50.33	49.93	54.06
18.	Mizoram	47.30	49.18	47.72	48.76	49.22	49.46	45.16	50.38
19.	Nagaland	48.89	50.41	47.22	47.09	48.26	46.37	45.49	46.95
20.	Orissa	47.44	48.91	45.76	46.54	43.24	46.84	37.85	43.76
21.	Punjab	47.70	48.97	47.08	44.79	47.18	47.49	44.61	47.41
22.	Rajasthan	46.24	49.20	40.80	42.20	32.27	38.14	23.09	39.78
23.	Sikkim	49.84	–	52.00	49.35	49.91	43.22	49.41	67.02

Contd.

Contd.

24.	Tamil Nadu	48.38	48.74	48.99	49.00	49.61	51.90	42.09	48.44
25.	Tripura	47.47	49.30	47.59	47.82	47.63	53.09	44.84	47.38
26.	Uttar Pradesh	46.64	44.62	40.53	43.02	33.48	42.99	35.04	43.49
27.	Uttaranchal	49.49	45.76	47.57	43.37	44.46	38.55	40.35	48.51
28.	West Bengal	49.34	49.82	56.79	58.02	50.75	57.15	34.99	41.65
29.	Andaman and Nicobar Islands	48.03	46.58	48.31	44.76	46.53	47.05	48.08	48.94
30.	Chandigarh	43.84	47.47	42.04	38.28	47.40	42.73	56.69	48.91
31.	Dadra and Nagar Haveli	48.59	39.31	42.53	46.43	33.95	43.62	39.11	42.75
32.	Daman & Diu	47.84	48.91	49.73	49.00	45.74	44.84	40.46	40.37
33.	Delhi	50.12	48.99	37.64	40.65	40.85	42.18	48.79	47.70
34.	Lakshadweep	45.91	46.23	50.03	45.01	42.64	46.63	46.60	43.76
35.	Pondicherry	49.47	49.80	45.51	55.37	50.92	50.77	43.52	46.55
	India	47.29	47.87	44.36	46.32	43.23	47.34	38.26	44.50

Source: Seventh All India School Education Survey, 2002, NCERT, New Delhi.

lims have been reducing at a faster rate at the primary and upper primary levels. But these gaps are still high at the secondary and higher secondary levels.

The gender gaps in dropout rates have come down substantially during the last five decades. But high dropout rates are still seen in Classes I-VIII and in Classes I-X in the case of both boys and girls as given in Table 5. High dropout rates appear to be the major cause of low participation of girls in higher education.

Table 5: Dropout Rates (All Communities)

Year	(Classes I-V)		(Classes I-VIII)		Classes I-X	
	Boys	Girls	Boys	Girls	Boys	Girls
1960–61	61.7	70.9	75.0	85.0	NA	
1990–91	40.1	46.0	59.1	65.1	67.5	76.9
As on Sept. 30, 2003	33.74	28.57	51.85	52.92	60.98	64.92

Source: Selected Educational Statistics, 2003–04, MHRD, GoI, New Delhi.

Higher, Technical and Professional Education

Higher education in colonial India was mainly concentrated in and around Indian port cities. The Calcutta, Bombay and Madras port towns were the apex centres of higher learning. The rural areas, inhabited by the vast majority of the Indian people, were almost completely devoid of educational facilities. The level of female education was particularly low. However, a sharp increase is noticed in the growth of higher educational institutions in the country after independence, both in the government and non-government sectors. It is evident from the latest available data that there were 325 universities (including 18 Central, 211 state, and 96 deemed universities); five institutions established under state legislation; 13 institutes of national importance; and 17,625 colleges, including 1,849 womens colleges in 2004–05 in the country as a whole (UGC, 2004–05). In the professional education sector, there were 1,068 engineering; technical and architecture colleges; 783 medical colleges including homeopathy; Ayurvedic and Unani; 900 teacher training colleges; 4,877 technical; industrial and arts and crafts schools; and 1,105 polytechnic institutes as on September 30, 2003 (MHRD, 2003–04). Besides, there were six Indian Institutes of Technology (IITs) located in different parts of the country.

In the school education sector, there was a national level institute known as National Council of Educational Research and Training (NCERT) to look at different aspects of school education. The NCERT had a network of six institutes located in six regions of the country. These regional institutes train science graduates for school education as teachers. Despite a wide network of educational institutions in different areas, it has been observed that the rural remote areas were still lagging behind in the required educational facilities. An analysis of statewise data of educational institutions reveals that educational institutions of higher learning were very few in many states in relation to their population size (Annexures III and IV).

At the time of independence (1947), girls' participation in higher education was abysmally low. The statistics reveal that girls formed 9.6 per cent in higher education and just 5.2 per cent in professional courses of the total enrolled children in 1946–47. The last five decades have witnessed a sharp increase in girls' participation in higher, technical and professional courses. According to UGC 2004–05 figures, a total of 104.81 lakh students were enrolled in higher education institutions during 2004–05, of whom 42.34 lakh were women, constituting about 40.40 per cent of the total enrolment. This indicates that the number of women enrolled per hundred men has increased tremendously during the last five decades. It has gone up from 14 in 1950–51 to 68 in 2004–05. Though enrolments at the national level seem to be quite impressive, inter-state gender disparities in higher education are still very high. The statistics reveal that there were states in which girls' participation in higher education was much below the national average (40.40 per cent). For instance, women's participation in higher education (colleges and universities) was as low as 24.5 per cent in Bihar, 30.5 per cent in Jharkhand; 36 per cent in Orissa; and 37.2 per cent in Madhya Pradesh (Table 6).

Analysis indicates that there were wide gender gaps in facultywise enrolments. The participation of girls in all the faculties was recorded low as compared to boys with the exception of education (Table 7). The gender gaps were registered as very sharp in mainly engineering/technology; agriculture; veterinary science and law, despite strong emphasis being placed in the National Policy on Education, 1986 revised in 1992 (NPE), on increasing girls' participation in technical and professional courses. The participation of girls in education seems to be high mainly because of their preference for teaching as a profession over other professions. Moreover, teacher training schools and colleges are now available in rural areas after the declaration of the NPE, in which the opening

**Table 6: Percentage of Girls Enrolled to Total Enrolled Children
in Colleges and Universities, 2004–05**

S.No.	States/UTs	Total Enrolments	Girls' Enrolments	% of Girls' Enrolment to Total
1.	Andhra Pradesh	866,489	348,097	40.17
2.	Arunachal Pradesh	5,806	1,748	30.10
3.	Assam	214,342	88,732	41.40
4.	Bihar	551,888	134,986	24.46
5.	Chhattisgarh	163,607	60,601	37.04
6.	Delhi	197,652	96,497	48.82
7.	Goa	21,172	12,503	59.05
8.	Gujarat	631,865	280,632	44.41
9.	Haryana	264,331	109,106	41.28
10.	Himachal Pradesh	99,067	43,379	43.79
11.	Jammu & Kashmir	72,875	34,107	46.80
12.	Jharkhand	209,176	63,887	30.54
13.	Karnataka	673,069	278,278	41.34
14.	Kerala	313,155	190,559	60.85
15.	Madhya Pradesh	566,188	210,445	37.17
16.	Maharashtra	1,431,971	592,798	41.40
17.	Manipur	38,679	17,421	45.04
18.	Meghalaya	30,716	14,778	48.11
19.	Mizoram	12,180	5,554	45.60
20.	Nagaland	13,356	5,324	39.86
21.	Orissa	367,187	131,926	35.93
22.	Punjab	279,707	144,446	51.64
23.	Rajasthan	388,479	131,992	33.98
24.	Sikkim	4,695	1,954	41.62
25.	Tamil Nadu	800,005	365,762	45.72
26.	Tripura	21,268	8,749	41.14
27.	Uttar Pradesh	1,361,749	501,540	36.83
28.	Uttaranchal	131,742	55,848	42.39
29.	West Bengal	685,964	270,160	39.38
30.	Andaman and Nicobar Islands	2,127	1,202	56.51
31.	Chandigarh	39,477	20,628	52.25
32.	Lakshadweep	240	84	34.81
33.	Daman & Diu	619	291	47.01
34.	Dadra and Nagar Haveli	0	0	–
35.	Pondicherry	20,199	10,326	51.12
	India	10,481,042	4,234,340	40.40

Source: Annual Report 2004–05, University Grants Commission, New Delhi.

of the a District Institute of Educational Training (DIET) in each district has made it mandatory to train teachers for elementary schools. A certain proportion of seats in such institutes has also been reserved for women candidates. The policy of districtwise recruitment of school teachers as adopted by many states and posting women teachers near their home towns, if possible, also encourages women to opt for teaching as a profession.

If we see girls' participation in different courses at the higher education level, it can be said on the basis of the analysis in Table 8 that girls who get enrolled in higher education generally opt for humanities subjects. Their participation in other faculties was registered as very low. The field observations highlight the fact that the non availability of quality mathematics and science courses in secondary schools, especially in rural areas, is a major reason for the low participation of girls in technical and professional courses. Lack of women science teachers in rural areas was also reported as one of the major reasons for low participation of girls in technical courses.

According to figures from the Ministry of Human Resource Development (MHRD), girls' participation in technical courses was comparatively very low. At the national level, girls' participation in technical/industrial and arts and crafts schools was as low as 6.6 per cent and in

Table 7: Facultywise Percentage of Girls Enrolled to Total Enrolled
Students in Higher Education, 2004–05

S. No.	Faculty	Total Enrolments	Girls' Enrolments	% of Girls' Enrolment to Total
1.	Arts	4,729,048	2,162,482	45.73
2.	Science	2,142,325	850,255	39.69
3.	Commerce/ Management	1,885,539	696,548	36.94
4.	Education	154,071	78,758	51.12
5.	Engineering/ Technology	654,635	175,725	26.84
6.	Medicine	330,153	153,706	46.56
7.	Agriculture	61,838	10,585	17.12
8.	Veterinary Science	15,721	3,387	21.54
9.	Law	319,671	68,596	21.46
10.	Others	88,041	34,298	38.96
	Total	10,481,042	4,234,340	40.40

Source: Annual Report 2004–05, University Grants Commission, New Delhi.

Table 8: Facultywise Percentage of Girls Enrolled to Total Enrolled
Girls in Higher Education

S. No.	Faculty	Facultywise Girl's Enrolment	Facultywise % age of Girls' Enrolment to Total Enrolled Girl Students in Higher Education
1.	Arts	2,162,482	51.07
2.	Science	850,255	20.08
3.	Commerce/Management	696,548	16.45
4.	Education	78,758	1.86
5.	Engineering/Technology	175,725	4.15
6.	Medicine	153,706	3.63
7.	Agriculture	10,585	0.25
8.	Veterinary Science	3,387	0.08
9.	Law	68,596	1.62
10.	Others	34,298	0.81
	Total	4,234,340	100.00

Source: Annual Report 2004–05, University Grants Commission, New Delhi.

polytechnics, just 22.5 per cent, despite national recommendations to open polytechnics in each district (1990). A statewise analysis indicates wide inter-state gender disparities in polytechnic and Industrial Training Institute (ITI) courses. For instance, in technical/industrial and arts and crafts schools, their percentages ranged from 3 per cent in Andhra Pradesh, Kerala and Gujarat to 39 per cent in Manipur; 36 per cent in Punjab; and 27 per cent in Chandigarh. Similarly, in polytechnics, their percentages ranged between 5 per cent in Dadra and Nagar Haveli and 6 per cent in Uttar Pradesh to 49 per cent in Mizoram (Table 9).

The gender gaps in technical degree courses were also very high. At the national level, girls formed 23.8 per cent of the total enrolled students in BE/BSc (Engg)/BArch courses. Inter-state differentials were registered as being more wide. As per the 2003–04 figures of the MHRD, there were more than 20 states in the country in which girls' participation in technical degree courses was below the national average (23.8 per cent). However, the gender gaps in medicine and teacher training colleges were comparatively low. Girls formed 42 per cent in MBBS and 49.8 per cent in BEd/BT courses of the total enrolled children (Table 9).

Due to the strong efforts made by the government and by non-government organisations in the post-independence period for the educational development of socially disadvantaged groups, remarkable progress was noticed in the participation of girls in higher education at the national

Table 9: Percentage of Girls Enrolled to Total Enrolled Children in Professional Institutions as on September 30, 2003

S.No.	States/UTs	Polytechnic Institutes	Tech./Industrial, Art & Craft Schools	Teacher Training Schools	BEd/ BT	BE/BSc (Engg.)/B Arch	MBBS
1.	Andhra Pradesh	33.01	3.31	44.15	43.14	30.62	48.27
2.	Arunachal Pradesh	33.33	0.00	0.00	25.00	12.73	47.22
3.	Assam	11.22	16.71	50.35	40.09	9.18	30.94
4.	Bihar	12.61	4.37	42.50	36.75	4.37	11.56
5.	Chhattisgarh	27.45	3.96	48.23	37.48	37.46	37.38
6.	Goa	17.31	0.00	92.59	83.08	32.20	68.58
7.	Gujarat	17.58	2.63	52.32	36.24	17.91	46.34
8.	Haryana	17.72	16.88	36.26	41.96	18.76	27.38
9.	Himachal Pradesh	21.80	13.76	43.01	41.82	16.22	45.26
10.	Jammu & Kashmir	28.19	17.19	29.23	58.17	13.38	45.48
11.	Jharkhand	9.83	6.37	59.32	33.26	6.67	66.59
12.	Karnataka	29.72	5.18	50.71	54.47	25.52	34.62
13.	Kerala	30.44	2.63	82.78	80.78	40.16	57.45
14.	Madhya Pradesh	26.90	7.00	32.33	43.66	36.90	36.88
15.	Maharashtra	30.00	9.06	48.57	50.40	21.07	48.68
16.	Manipur	23.18	38.52	73.33	58.62	14.87	41.66
17.	Meghalaya	20.93	5.62	47.79	70.10	0.00	0.00
18.	Mizoram	48.85	16.33	41.86	50.00	0.00	0.00
19.	Nagaland	18.45	23.76	77.78	52.44	0.00	0.00
20.	Orissa	35.06	6.83	48.65	50.48	12.79	40.99
21.	Punjab	28.90	35.92	61.53	73.70	20.55	63.34
22.	Rajasthan	23.67	6.36	54.65	50.18	17.14	19.77

Contd.

Contd.

23.	Sikkim	12.22	0.00	65.38	50.27	22.23	51.51
24.	Tamil Nadu	12.52	2.73	56.28	64.33	13.23	55.97
25.	Tripura	30.06	21.00	55.44	38.99	19.59	27.65
26.	Uttar Pradesh	5.71	8.52	49.45	41.82	14.72	43.90
27.	Uttaranchal	47.31	9.81	40.55	45.32	49.10	37.47
28.	West Bengal	18.85	5.64	30.80	52.34	18.29	25.39
29.	Andaman and Nicobar Islands	37.50	0.00	76.92	73.11	0.00	0.00
30.	Chandigarh	35.15	27.17	51.43	91.30	26.78	72.85
31.	Dadra and Nagar Haveli	4.93	7.02	–	–	0.00	0.00
32.	Daman & Diu	12.30	0.00	100.00	63.33	0.00	0.00
33.	Delhi	36.67	24.70	45.19	68.54	46.11	51.66
	Lakshadweep	–	16.67	–	–	0.00	0.00
34.	Pondicherry	36.45	16.67	62.22	69.72	25.32	41.73
35.	India	22.45	6.59	50.48	49.88	23.82	42.03

Source: Selected Educational Statistics, 2003–04, MHRD, GoI, New Delhi, 2006.

Table 10: Percentage of SC and ST Girls Enrolled to Total Enrolled Children in Higher and Professional Institutions

S.No.	States/UTs	Higher Education		Polytechnic Institutes		Tech./Industrial, Arts & Crafts Schools		Teacher Training Schools	
		SC	ST	SC	ST	SC	ST	SC	ST
1.	Andhra Pradesh	32.22	28.84	32.99	32.99	3.31	3.31	36.62	32.62
2.	Arunachal Pradesh	–	38.95	–	34.43	0.00	0.00	–	–
3.	Assam	34.02	34.30	16.43	13.02	27.33	40.12	50.00	50.00
4.	Bihar	10.65	23.52	10.29	18.82	4.38	4.32	48.21	50.00
5.	Chhattisgarh	31.21	33.38	33.33	46.67	3.96	4.00	38.51	77.02
6.	Goa	47.84	32.70	21.05	20.83	0.00	0.00	66.67	–
7.	Gujarat	30.20	39.54	18.50	16.81	2.64	2.63	47.80	46.27
8.	Haryana	38.28	–	14.16	–	16.88	–	18.18	–
9.	Himachal Pradesh	36.30	41.81	19.94	16.90	13.80	13.67	42.86	52.00
10.	Jammu & Kashmir	58.88	58.85	30.00	17.86	–	–	33.33	23.08
11.	Jharkhand	34.55	49.24	16.00	8.33	6.42	6.29	63.64	63.16
12.	Karnataka	37.72	35.48	24.16	16.73	5.18	5.18	50.69	50.64
13.	Kerala	61.89	60.44	35.06	244.19	2.64	2.64	78.02	73.08
14.	Madhya Pradesh	24.40	21.53	31.34	22.30	7.02	7.03	29.15	35.46
15.	Maharashtra	37.19	30.21	16.14	23.60	9.06	9.05	40.94	31.78
16.	Manipur	50.09	47.05	35.90	19.61	41.67	39.25	–	0.00
17.	Meghalaya	42.89	46.84	33.33	26.32	11.11	5.60	22.22	49.21
18.	Mizoram	0.00	46.06	–	48.85	–	14.76	–	41.54
19.	Nagaland	82.67	40.18	–	18.45	–	23.65	–	75.68
20.	Orissa	27.17	27.68	29.88	29.93	6.84	6.83	46.48	42.58
21.	Punjab	46.98	–	22.10	–	27.65	–	58.75	–
22.	Rajasthan	32.81	32.33	14.57	7.14	6.33	6.41	53.87	54.68

Contd.

Contd.

23.	Sikkim	47.60	44.47	11.11	19.35	0.00	0.00	50.00	45.45
24.	Tamil Nadu	42.33	33.21	6.25	16.30	2.59	2.70	50.46	45.05
25.	Tripura	39.67	37.65	31.17	23.13	21.67	21.43	52.27	51.49
26.	Uttar Pradesh	24.08	20.77	5.81	17.24	8.51	8.51	25.45	28.57
27.	Uttaranchal	27.76	17.45	37.78	45.95	32.30	38.03	29.70	50.00
28.	West Bengal	32.81	32.49	3.00	12.96	5.64	5.60	22.11	24.35
29.	Andaman and Nicobar Islands	–	47.95	–	71.43	–	0.00	–	100.00
30.	Chandigarh	48.07	49.82	30.61	50.00	27.03	–	50.00	40.00
31.	Dadra and Nagar Haveli	–	–	35.29	32.43	0.00	6.78	–	–
32.	Daman& Diu	57.69	24.73	21.43	0.00	0.00	0.00	100.00	100.00
33.	Delhi	40.94	40.96	15.54	17.86	24.71	24.65	45.28	34.78
34.	Lakshadweep	–	35.98	–	–	–	16.85	–	–
35.	Pondicherry	45.04	46.34	37.23	–	17.13	–	46.15	–
	India	32.31	34.22	21.09	22.81	6.97	6.24	44.66	43.29

Source: Selected Educational Statistics, 2003–04, MHRD, GoI, New Delhi, 2006.

aggregative level. The latest available data (Selected Educational Statistics, 2003) indicates that percentages of SC and ST girls to total SC and ST children enrolled in higher education were 32.3 per cent and 34.2 per cent respectively. Similarly, their participation in teacher training schools was also very high. But the gender gaps among both SCs and STs were registered as very high in technical courses (Table 10).

Rural-urban gender gaps in higher, technical and professional courses could not be assessed due to non-availability of data. However, field experiences highlight that participation of rural girls is comparatively low in higher education, including professional and technical courses, among all communities, due to poor availability and accessibility of higher education institutions in rural areas.

The status of higher education of Muslim minorities cannot be assessed analytically due to non-availability of data. Inferences can be drawn only on the basis of research studies. Based on field-based studies on education of Muslim minorities, it can be said that the status of higher education of Muslim girls is very low in the country. The findings of a survey, based on the Census 2001 educational data on the education levels of Indians reveals that the average level of education in the country is in any case poor. There is a frighteningly large gap between the education levels of Muslims and non-Muslims. This gap widens dramatically as you go further up the educational ladder, especially at the level of Class XII and college. Only one in 101 Muslim women is a graduate compared with one in 37 non-Muslim women (Goswami and Malik, 2006).

Gender stereotypes also prevail in the choice of subjects. At the higher secondary stage, girls in rural areas are generally forced to opt for arts streams because of non-availability of women science teachers. At the graduation level, they opt for common subjects in which job opportunities are very few. Although a number of courses are available in polytechnics and in ITIs, yet urban girls also opt for office management and secretarial courses, fashion design/textile design and other similar subjects.

Concluding Observations

The overall assessment is that India has made tremendous progress in reducing the gender gaps in education among all communities and different social groups after independence. There is no doubt that by and large, the gender gaps at the national aggregative level have reached a satisfactory level in terms of enrolments. The analysis of enrolment statistics indicates that girls formed 40.4 per cent of the total enrolled students in higher education (UGC, 2004–05). Similarly, participation of SC and ST girls has also gone up. According to MHRD figures for 2003–04, SC girls formed 32.3 per cent and ST girls, 34.2 per cent of the total enrolled students in higher education. This indicates that the gender gaps in enrolments have reduced sharply during the last six decades. However, the statistics reveal that there are wide inter-and intra-state differentials in gender gaps at the higher levels of education despite five decades of planned development and the adoption of decentralised planning and management systems of education. Gender gaps are still evident in technical courses, too.

Broadly speaking, though girls' education has been considered crucial for national development, the empirical reality is not very convincing. There are many states in which participation of girls in higher education is very low. According to the UGC annual report for 2004–05, there were states in which girls' participation in higher education (colleges and universities) was much below the national average (40.4 per cent). These states were Bihar (24.5 per cent), Jharkhand (30.5 per cent), Rajasthan (34 per cent), Orissa (36 per cent) and Madhya Pradesh (37.2 per cent). This means that despite the strong policy perspective on girls' education and the adoption of multi-pronged strategies to promote girls' education, many girls are still out of the ambit of the education system. High dropout rates by the end of the secondary stage of education is indicative of the malady. The data shows that 65 per cent girls drop out of school by the end of class X (MHRD, 2003). This clearly indicates that non-completion of the plus 2 stage of school education leads to low participation of girls in higher education. The reasons for this are varied. Besides the sociocultural constraints in certain social groups and communities, non-availability of higher secondary schooling facilities leads to girl dropping out of school before completing 12 years of schooling.

Analysis of data on the availability and accessibility to the+2 stage of schooling facilities shows that urban areas are apparently better served than rural areas. Though considerable progress has been made in the expansion of schooling facilities in both rural and urban areas, from the point of view of increasing girls' participation in higher, technical and professional courses, there are several major weaknesses in the system that need attention. It has emerged from the analysis that there are states in which the number of higher secondary schools in rural areas was less than 10 per100 upper primary schools as per the 7th All India School Education Survey, 2002. These states are mainly Bihar (2), Jharkhand (1) and Orissa (3). Similarly, the rural population served by higher secondary classes within these states was also comparatively well below the national average (8.30 per cent); 0.67 per cent in Bihar, 0.51 per cent in

Jharkhand and 2.6 per cent in Orissa. Non-availability of easy access to higher secondary classes acts as a major factor in low participation of girls in higher education as completion of the+2 stage is a precondition for entry into higher education. Many scholars who have worked on these issues have reached the conclusion that utilisation of school facilities is subject to distance, whereby the nearer a person lives to this facility, the more likely it is that he or she will use it, assuming of course that there are no socio-economic barriers to access (Ramachandran, 1988; Raza and Nuna, 1990; Nayar, 2000; Karlekar, 2000; Nuna, 2003). A study by Lingam (1993), quoted in Karlekar (2000), highlighted that in Maharashtra, girls in rural areas which did not have high schools were not sent to school alone. The national norms of upto 5 kilometers for secondary classes and 8 kilometers for higher secondary classes do affect the participation of girls in higher education. Parents find it very hard to support girls' education at any level if education facilities are not available within a village boundary. Hence, states with poor accessibility to secondary education still witness low participation of girls in higher education.

The problem gets compounded with lack of physical infrastructure in schools and continuous shortages of women teachers in rural areas. Although many initiatives have been undertaken by state governments to construct toilets in schools on a priority basis under the Education For All programmes, analysis of the 7th All India School Education Survey (2002) data indicates that there were wide inter-state differentials in the availability of infrastructure facilities such as urinals in schools with girls' enrolment (Table 11).

Table 11: Percentages of Schools with Girls' Enrolments having Urinals

States	School Category	
	Primary	*Upper Primary*
Kerala	89.0	97.6
Orissa	26.0	57.8
Bihar	4.2	22.7
Jharkhand	5.4	28.2
Chhatisgarh	31.1	59.5
U.P.	39.7	60.3
M.P.	42.5	63.7
India	33.2	59.1

Source: Seventh All India School Education Survey, NCERT, New Delhi, 2002.

Though lack of urinals affects the participation of both boys and girls, it affects girls more especially at the post primary stages. Parents find it difficult to send daughters, especially after the onset of puberty, to schools that lack proper toilet facilities. The old tradition of leaving school at puberty is still a reality. In a study of Gujarat by Bhatty et al. cited in the Human Development Report, 2000, pointed out that the proportion of girls attending school increased until the age of 10–11 years, after which it declined. Caldwell et al. cited in the Human Development Report, 2000, found that by age 15 in Karnataka, only 11 per cent of girls were still enrolled in schools. Further, they found that one fifth of all girls were removed from school at puberty, usually to be married as soon as possible.

Shortage of women teachers in rural area schools is also identified as a major hurdle in bridging the gender gaps in education, especially in states with low female literacy rates. The 7th All India School Education Survey, 2002, data indicates that percentages of women teachers to total teachers are very low in rural areas at all levels of school education. At the national level, women teachers formed 31 per cent at the primary; 30 per cent at the upper primary; 26 per cent at the secondary; and 27 per cent at the higher secondary school categories. Their percentages were much below the national average in states such as Bihar, Chhatisgarh, Jharkhand, Madhya Pradesh, Uttar Pradesh and Rajasthan at all stages, despite the declaration of national policies to appoint 50 per cent women teachers in elementary schools on a priority basis. The Tenth Five-Year Plan commits as much as 90 per cent women teachers in elementary schools.

Cultural factors also play an important role in determining the level of education girls attain in rural areas. Karlekar (2000) was of the opinion that whether a girl should be educated or not is part of the familial world views. Nuna (2003) pointed out that among certain tribal groups in Chhatisgarh, parents feel that education will empower women and they will demand their rights. It was also noticed that in the rural backward communities of Giridih district of Jharkhand, girls were sold to older men at a very young age. Sudarshan (2000) was of the opinion that the intangibles influencing girls' education are inherent in the gender roles ascribed by society, which encourage participation in domestic duties as a priority.

Nuna (2003) found that centrally sponsored schemes that are launched to bridge gender gaps in higher education did not achieve their objectives due to the lack of proper implementation, monitoring and evaluation of such schemes. For instance, one of the major objectives of the Area Intensive Programme (a centrally sponsored scheme), which was launched in 1993 to promote participation of Muslim girls in technical, professional and vocational courses remained unfulfilled as no multistream residential higher secondary schools have been opened for girls in any state, except to Kerala. Many states have not even prepared grant proposals for such schools.

Besides inter-state and rural-urban gender disparities, gender gaps are also visible in the courses taken, particularly in the technical and professional courses. Facultywise enrolment figures of the UGC for 2004–05 indicate wide gender gaps. The participation of girls in all the faculties was recorded lower than that of boys, except in education (51.1 per cent of the total enrolled students). It is also evident from the data that girls who enroll for higher education largely take humanities subjects. The percentage of girls in the arts faculty was 51.07 per cent as compared to 20 per cent in science; 16 per cent in commerce; 4.15 in engineering/technology; and 3.6 per cent in medicine. Their share in agriculture, veterinary science and law was less than 2 per cent (UGC, 2004–05).

Gender gaps in technical, industrial and arts and crafts schools were also very high. Girls' participation in technical, industrial and arts and crafts schools was only 6.6 per cent and in polytechnics only 22.5 per cent. The analysis indicates that lack of institutions affect girls' participation in such courses. It has emerged from the analysis that there were many states in which the number of colleges, including technical, industrial and arts and crafts schools and polytechnics, was very few in relation to their population size, despite various recommendations of national committees to open at least one women's polytechnic in each district. The predominance of girls in the arts faculty has implications on access to jobs and power positions.

India inherited serious social and gender imbalances and our Constitution tries to find solutions to these problems. The proclaimed goals of correcting inherited imbalances through the intervention of gender sensitive planning and gender budgeting is a very positive step towards bridging gender gaps in development, especially in education. However, the planning process needs stronger commitment to fulfil the needs of the deprived areas and deprived sections of our society.

References

Annual Report of the University Grants Commission, 2003–04. New Delhi.

Caldwell, J.C., P.H. Reddy and P. Caldwell. 1985. 'Educational Transition in Rural South India', in *Population and Development Review*, 1.1(1).

Goswami, Omkar and Kabir Malik. 2006. 'A Shocking Divide', *India Today*, August 14.

Government of India. 'Report of the Durgabai Deshmukh Committee (1958–59)', New Delhi: Ministry of Education.

———. 'Report of the Education Commission (1964–66): Education and National Development', New Delhi: Ministry of Education.

———. 1971. 'Towards Equality: Report of the Committee on the Status of Women in India', New Delhi: Ministry of Education and Social Welfare.

———. 'National Perspective Plan for Women (1988–2000)', New Delhi: Department of Women and Child Development, MHRD.

———. 1990. 'Towards an Enlightened and Humane Society NPE, 1986', New Delhi: A Review Committee for Review of National Policy on Education, MHRD.

———. 2005. 'Report of the CABE Committee on Girls' Education and the Common School System', New Delhi: MHRD, June, 2005.

———. 1937–47. 'Progress of Education in India: Decennial Review, Vol. II' (For official use only), New Delhi: Central Bureau of Education, Ministry of Education.

———. 'Five Year Plan Documents', New Delhi: Planning Commission.

———. 'National Policies on Education', New Delhi: MHRD.

———. 'Selected Educational Statistics', New Delhi: MHRD.

Hasan, Z. and M. Ritu. 2004. *Unequal Citizens: A Study of Muslim Women in India*, Oxford University Press.

Karlekar, Malavika. 2000. 'Girls' Access to Schooling: An Assessment' in Rekha Wazir (ed.), *The Gender Gap in Basic Education: NGO as Change Agents*, New Delhi: Sage Publications.

Mahbub ul Haq. 2000. 'Human Development in South Asia: The Gender Question', The Mahbub ul Haq Human Development Centre, Oxford University Press.

Naik, J.P. 1975. *Equality Quality and Quantity: The Elusive Triangle in Indian Education*, New Delhi: Allied Publishers.

Nayar, U. 2000. *Education of Girls in India: Progress and Prospects*, New Delhi: NCERT.

NCERT. 'All India School Education Surveys'.

Nuna, A. 2003. Cultural Impediments in Learning Opportunities for Girls: A Case Study of District Giridih in Jharkhand and Dantewada in Chhatisgarh, DWS, New Delhi: NCERT, Unpublished Report.

———. 2003. 'Education of Muslim Girls: A Study of the Area Intensive Programme', DWS, New Delhi: NCERT, Unpublished Report.

Ramachandran, V. 1998. 'The Indian Experience' in V. Ramachandran (ed.), *Bridging the Gap between Intention and Action: Girl's and Women's Education in South Asia*, New Delhi: Asian-South Pacific Bureau of Adult Education, UNESCO-PROAP.

Raza, Ahmed and A. Nuna. 1990. *School Education in India: The Regional Dimension*, New Delhi: NIEPA.

Rekha, Wazir (ed.). 2000. *The Gender Gap in Basic Education: NGOs as Change Agents*, New Delhi: Sage Publications, pp. 1–260.

Sudarshan, Ratna M. 2000. 'Educational Status of Girls and Women: The Emerging Scenario' in Rekha Wazir (ed.), *The Gender Gap in Basic Education: NGO as Change Agent*, New Delhi: Sage Publications.

Sultan, N. 1995. 'Education of Women after Freedom' in Usha Sharma and B.M. Sharma (eds.), *Women's Education in Modern India*, New Delhi: Commonwealth Publishers.

Annexure 1: Schools Belonging to Different Categories in the 6th (1993) and 7th Survey (2002)

S.No.	States/UTs	Primary Schools				Upper Primary Schools			
		Rural		Urban		Rural		Urban	
		1993	2002	1993	2002	1993	2002	1993	2002
1.	Andhra Pradesh	44,412	53,916	4,729	7,251	4,724	11,905	1,657	3,191
2.	Arunachal Pradesh	1,109	1,263	37	74	261	308	16	51
3.	Assam	27,584	28,630	1,306	1,415	6,485	7,242	458	484
4.	Bihar	34,697	38,428	1,990	2,083	8,369	8,493	1,306	1,193
5.	Chhattisgarh	19,843	22,477	1,155	1,474	3,338	5,358	405	886
6.	Goa	821	745	207	292	92	55	26	20
7.	Gujarat	12,081	5,862	1,501	1,383	14,475	24,511	4,140	6,174
8.	Haryana	4,680	8,510	526	1,109	1,250	1,831	229	396
9.	Himachal Pradesh	7,470	10,614	251	254	1,056	1,837	52	64
10.	Jammu & Kashmir	8,091	9,745	652	743	2,110	3,233	432	761
11.	Jharkhand	15,193	16,164	943	895	3,308	3,528	723	742
12.	Karnataka	20,198	23,450	1,758	2,804	13,566	17,893	4,717	5,732
13.	Kerala	4,727	5,251	1,192	1,446	2,856	2,332	848	653
14.	Madhya Pradesh	44,153	47,383	7,074	6,850	8,331	20,208	4,027	7,338
15.	Maharashtra	34,732	34,560	5,217	6,290	16,093	20,104	4,123	5,705
16.	Manipur	2,590	2,175	441	377	556	600	146	194
17.	Meghalaya	3,919	5,439	180	368	743	926	77	150
18.	Mizoram	663	938	280	314	420	534	188	313
19.	Nagaland	1,181	1,288	44	64	319	400	66	69
20.	Orissa	34,221	34,541	2,085	2,136	9,536	10,724	723	942
21.	Punjab	11,605	12,042	1,134	1,298	1,225	2,262	145	283

Contd.

Contd.

22.	Rajasthan	29,168	29,438	4,181	3,515	7,599	17,646	2,577	5,591
23.	Sikkim	524	497	0	–	118	133	0	2
24.	Tamil Nadu	26,620	26,341	3,465	7,053	4,349	4,567	1,360	2,005
25.	Tripura	1,942	1,996	87	58	400	406	34	29
26.	Uttar Pradesh	64,989	96,331	11,568	17,215	13,340	22,016	3,712	6,855
27.	Uttaranchal	9,094	12,466	888	1,436	1,799	2,952	263	519
28.	West Bengal	40,435	41,845	8,122	8,006	2,313	1,663	550	326
29.	Andaman and Nicobar Islands	181	197	7	10	38	50	6	6
30.	Chandigarh	14	8	28	18	4	4	25	3
31.	Dadra and Nagar Haveli	123	123	2	3	38	76	4	10
32.	Daman & Diu	25	33	5	17	16	16	9	8
33.	Delhi	304	222	1,664	1,889	61	47	445	614
34.	Lakshadweep	7	3	5	1	6	13	5	7
35.	Pondicherry	185	170	150	149	52	74	65	59
	India	507,581	573,091	62,874	78,290	129,246	193,947	33,559	51,375

Source: Seventh All India School Education Survey, 2002, NCERT, New Delhi.

Annexure 2: Schools Belonging to Different Categories in the 6th (1993) and 7th Survey (2002)

S.No.	States/ UTs	Secondary Schools				Higher Secondary Schools			
		Rural		Urban		Rural		Urban	
		1993	2002	1993	2002	1993	2002	1993	2002
1.	Andhra Pradesh	4,762	8,272	2,197	4,071	523	1,368	769	1,362
2.	Arunachal Pradesh	72	109	7	23	47	47	14	25
3.	Assam	2,503	3,247	409	467	436	563	161	202
4.	Bihar	2,495	2,524	530	533	200	159	162	163
5.	Chhattisgarh	441	967	131	246	424	942	308	618
6.	Goa	203	191	128	153	29	28	29	48
7.	Gujarat	2,937	3,256	831	1,362	769	1,118	1,066	1,345
8.	Haryana	1,667	2,548	508	888	252	898	284	743
9.	Himachal Pradesh	916	1,167	109	153	167	643	74	164
10.	Jammu & Kashmir	820	1,054	221	449	114	207	126	179
11.	Jharkhand	705	800	309	365	43	39	95	158
12.	Karnataka	3,219	4,631	1,761	3,090	696	884	580	905
13.	Kerala	1,621	1,049	565	365	205	1,045	90	555
14.	Madhya Pradesh	1,232	2,504	867	1,590	914	1,680	1,267	2,247
15.	Maharashtra	6,498	8,825	3,339	4,337	1,308	2,073	1,064	1,415
16.	Manipur	316	376	155	164	14	62	22	50
17.	Meghalaya	289	356	120	158	4	37	5	46
18	Mizoram	138	208	115	132	0	6	0	39
19.	Nagaland	124	162	60	94	0	9	4	18
20.	Orissa	4,677	5,681	633	717	302	345	81	71
21.	Punjab	1,717	1,758	437	472	366	1,178	378	571

Contd.

Contd.

22.	Rajasthan	2,643	3,862	687	1,781	461	1,654	743	1,276
23.	Sikkim	65	81	1	7	21	39	2	4
24.	Tamil Nadu	2,344	2,404	1,041	1,921	1,008	1,351	1,242	2,727
25.	Tripura	305	362	32	41	96	161	56	79
26.	Uttar Pradesh	1,329	2,823	635	1,657	1,931	3,881	1,649	3,111
27.	Uttaranchal	520	645	49	114	519	761	212	307
28.	West Bengal	3,182	3,542	1,405	1,248	609	1,531	656	1,364
29.	Andaman and Nicobar Islands	25	37	6	8	31	32	10	16
30.	Chandigarh	10	13	58	57	2	4	41	52
31.	Dadra and Nagar Haveli	7	11	1	4	5	5	2	4
32.	Daman & Diu	15	11	13	9	0	3	3	3
33.	Delhi	38	43	273	409	90	74	835	1,097
34.	Lakshadweep	5	6	3	1	1	2	3	3
35.	Pondicherry	30	51	58	79	13	18	29	55
	India	47,870	63,576	17,694	27,165	11,600	22,847	12,062	21,022

Source: Seventh All India School Education Survey, 2005, NCERT, New Delhi.

**Annexure 3: Statewise Higher Education Institutions in
India as on September 30, 2003**

Sl. No.	States/UTs	Pre-Degree Junior Colleges/Higher Secondary Schools	Technical Industrial/ Arts & Crafts Schools	Polytechnic Institutes
1.	Andhra Pradesh	3,267	556	104
2.	Arunachal Pradesh	74	2	1
3.	Assam	731	27	8
4.	Bihar	685	47	13
5.	Chhattisgarh	1,439	134	1
6.	Goa	80	15	5
7.	Gujarat	2,427	254	52
8.	Haryana	1,776	105	31
9.	Himachal Pradesh	820	63	6
10.	Jammu & Kashmir	380	38	12
11.	Jharkhand	122	33	10
12.	Karnataka	2,237	588	186
13.	Kerala	1,286	549	56
14.	Madhya Pradesh	4,211	166	44
15.	Maharashtra	4,212	613	164
16.	Manipur	112	7	1
17.	Meghalaya	80	7	1
18.	Mizoram	71	1	2
19.	Nagaland	52	3	2
20.	Orissa	744	177	27
21.	Punjab	1,695	158	19
22.	Rajasthan	3,159	123	17
23.	Sikkim	41	1	2
24.	Tamil Nadu	4,136	681	165
25.	Tripura	242	4	1
26.	Uttar Pradesh	7,369	307	81
27.	Uttaranchal	1,071	72	18
28.	West Bengal	2,868	64	40
29.	Andaman and Nicobar Islands	49	1	2
30.	Chandigarh	52	2	2
31.	Dadra and Nagar Haveli	9	1	1
32.	Daman & Diu	6	2	1
33.	Delhi	1,212	61	25
34.	Lakshadweep	4	1	0
35.	Pondicherry	77	14	5
	India	46,796	4,877	1105

Source: Selected Educational Statistics, 2003-04, MHRD, GoI, New Delhi, 2006.

Annexure 4: Statewise Higher Education Institutions in India as on September 30, 2003

S.No.	States/UTs	Univ.	Arts, Science & Commerce Colleges	Engg, Tech., & Arch. Colleges	Others including Law, Management, MCA/IT, Agriculture, etc.	Medical Colleges (Allo/Ayur/ Unani/Nurs./ Pharm etc.	Teacher Training Schools	Teacher Training Colleges
1.	Andhra Pradesh	18	1,330	238	93	53	25	87
2.	Arunachal Pradesh	1	10	1	0	1	0	2
3.	Assam	5	317	3	21	7	1	40
4.	Bihar	11	743	7	63	23	58	15
5.	Chhattisgarh	9	213	2	32	2	13	1
6.	Goa	1	24	4	5	7	1	2
7.	Gujarat	10	422	32	111	41	168	51
8.	Haryana	4	163	41	35	8	37	24
9.	Himachal Pradesh	4	69	2	24	7	7	7
10.	Jammu & Kashmir	5	73	4	34	6	14	8
11.	Jharkhand	4	146	5	14	8	22	9
12.	Karnataka	13	930	120	214	172	134	70
13.	Kerala	7	186	66	82	40	102	21
14.	Madhya Pradesh	14	513	56	209	28	27	21
15.	Maharashtra	19	1,208	177	128	116	286	251
16.	Manipur	2	58	1	1	1	1	3
17.	Meghalaya	1	48	0	0	0	7	2
18.	Mizoram	1	26	0	2	0	2	2
19.	Nagaland	1	36	0	18	0	1	2
20.	Orissa	8	567	19	153	16	67	16

Contd.

Contd.

21.	Punjab	5	209	16	53	42	26	23
22.	Rajasthan	9	456	39	96	24	46	51
23.	Sikkim	1	2	1	1	1	1	1
24.	Tamil Nadu	16	441	96	184	97	82	22
25.	Tripura	1	14	1	5	1	2	1
26.	Uttar Pradesh	22	733	69	273	34	70	121
27.	Uttaranchal	4	47	2	28	1	9	1
28.	West Bengal	14	354	43	46	19	58	26
29.	Andaman and Nicobar Islands	0	2	0	1	0	1	1
30.	Chandigarh	1	12	2	3	4	1	3
31.	Dadra and Nagar Haveli	0	0	0	0	0	0	0
32.	Daman & Diu	0	1	0	0	0	1	1
33.	Delhi	5	63	16	56	18	23	10
34.	Lakshadweep	0	0	0	0	0	0	0
35.	Pondicherry	1	11	5	6	6	10	5
	India	217	9,427	1,068	1,991	783	1,303	900

Source: Selected Educational Statistics, 2003-04, MHRD, GoI, New Delhi, 2006.

4

Feminisation of Segregation
Insights from at Disaggregate Analysis of NSSO Data

NEETHA N.

Feminisation of labour is one of the central concepts around which much of the gender-oriented discourses on the impact of globalisation has been evolved. The term was identified with a sharp increase in the share of women's employment, either due to a relatively faster expansion of certain sectors which are dominated by female workers (like electronics and garments) or by the replacement of male workers by female workers in select or all sectors. The process, which has received attention in academic debate and discussion since the 1980s, was viewed as a solution to gender-based discrimination in the labour market, especially in terms of women's participation in paid employment. The rising proportion of women in manufacturing industries, which are export oriented, provided much empirical support to this argument. The growing evidence of the reversal of such trends,[1] and the exploitative and precarious nature of employment where women are concentrated, have given rise to complex directions and, thus, debates around the issue. There is also evidence of defeminisation of labour during the period where less mobile women are found to be replaced by more mobile male workers with shifting production centres.

In India, too, the debate on feminisation has found central place in all the discussion around globalisation and its impact on the labour market. Globalisation is often argued to have increased economic opportunities for a large group of workers, especially women, by linking urban centres to the global economy. Central to this hypothesis has been the focus on flexible production organisations, which is often argued to bring in more and more flexible workforces, especially those including women. Thus, in the aura that has been created around liberalisation, there is a wider understanding that new opportunities of employment are opening up for women. While some focus on the high-end sectors of IT services, others stress on export manufacturing, both considered to be favouring the hiring of women and both linked to the processes associated with globalisation. Studies further suggest that the process has been accompanied by increasing trends of casualisation, contract labour and home-based work, further worsening the conditions of work. The question before us is how far the processes related to globalisation have contributed to women's employment either in terms of availability of opportunities or towards improving conditions of work.

The data collected by the NSSO in its employment and unemployment surveys give a large wealth of information on labour, which is available for both sexes. Although employment data sets are generally quite inadequate for comprehending the nature of social and economic forces at work in the sphere of labour and employment relations, and even more so as they operate in relation to women, there is an increasing recognition that they are important for identifying major shifts and changes taking place between specific points in time. For such purposes, some distinctive features that emerge from the data are quite revealing. Using the various rounds of NSSO data, the paper attempts to analyse the dynamics of women's employment during the 1990s, which witnessed several structural changes in the economy. Thus, the discussion that follows presents some of the changes in recent years in women's employment and examines the overall direction of such changes with a view to position women workers in the context of the overall economic changes and the resultant changes in the size and structure of the Indian labour force.

Trends in Women's Participation Rates and Sectoral Distribution

Work participation of women is an issue that got much attention in the debates around globalisation and women internationally and in India. The term has been much debated and contested, drawing insights from different sectors and regions. At the macro level, the declining employment opportunities seem to have affected both men and women. Within this context of declining overall employment, changes in women's participation across sectors/sub-sectors could provide important insights into the processes that are under way. Increased share of women in sectors in which the conditions of work are better would mean an entirely different process when compared to a situation where women are pushed to sectors that are known for poor conditions of work. The process becomes all the more different when one takes into account the conditions under which women take up work. For many women, labour market participation is an outcome of poverty and livelihood, which have strong implications on their sectoral concentration, nature of work, and bargaining position.

The aggregate data during the period shows a somewhat stagnant picture, or a reversal trend. Over the years, as revealed by the data (Table 1),·trends in work participation rates show a stagnant picture with some decline during the period from 1993–94 to 2004. Work participation of women remained low, though what is normally expected is an increase in the rate, especially in urban areas where the impacts of globalisation would be more pronounced. Participation rates of women remained as low as 12 per cent in urban areas and have stagnated during the period. In rural areas, though the rates have been comparatively better at around 23 per cent, it shows a declining trend during the period, where principal status employment is concerned, leading to a decline in the aggregate women's participation rate in terms of principal status.

When both principal and subsidiary status employment is taken, overall the rates show a stagnant picture across the period for both and rural

Table 1: Workforce Participation Rate in NSSO Rounds

Rounds	UPS*			UPSS**		
	M	F	T	M	F	T
Rural						
43rd	51.7	24.5	38.5	53.9	32.3	43.4
50th	53.8	23.4	39.0	55.3	32.8	44.4
55th	52.2	23.1	38.0	53.1	29.9	41.7
60th	52.7	22.8	38.1	54.2	31.5	43.1
Urban						
43rd	49.6	11.8	31.5	50.6	15.2	33.7
50th	51.3	12.1	32.7	52.1	15.5	34.7
55th	51.3	11.7	32.4	51.8	13.9	33.7
60th	53.1	12.1	33.5	54.0	15.0	35.4
Total						
43rd	51.2	21.7	36.9	53.1	28.5	41.2
50th	53.2	20.6	37.5	54.5	28.6	42.0
55th	52.0	20.3	36.5	52.7	25.9	39.7
60th	52.8	20.1	36.9	54.2	27.4	41.1

Source: NSSO Employment and Unemployment Data, Various Rounds.
*UPS: Usually employed (Primary Status)
**UPSS: Usually employed (Primary + Subsidary Status)

Table 2: Women's Share in Employment across Various Rounds

Year	UPS			UPSS		
	Rural	Urban	Total	Rural	Urban	Total
1993-94	29.06	17.60	26.57	35.87	21.18	32.85
1999-00	29.85	17.24	27.00	35.02	19.69	31.72
2004	29.31	17.19	26.51	35.70	20.20	32.30

Source: NSSO Employment and Unemployment Data, Various Rounds.

areas. However, between 1999–00 and 2004 the rates show a small increase, though the increase still could not make up for the loss during the period 1993–94 and 1999–00.

The share of women in total employment has also shown a stagnating trend across the period both in rural and urban areas, standing at around 29 per cent and 17 per cent respectively, (Table 2) with some small decline over the period. Women's share in total employment in the UPSS category also shows a declining trend, though the share is much larger at around 32 per cent, with rural areas having 35 per cent of women in the

Table 3: Percentage Distribution of Total Female Employment
by Broad Economic Sectors

Sector	Total		
	1993–94	1999–2000	2004
Primary	78.41	76.55	75.38
Secondary	11.09	11.42	11.94
Tertiary	10.50	12.03	12.68
Total	100	100	100

Sector	Rural		
	1993–94	1999–2000	2004
Primary	86.51	85.6	84.67
Secondary	7.89	8.7	9.02
Tertiary	5.59	5.7	6.31
Total	100.00	100	100

Sector	Urban		
	1993–94	1999–2000	2004
Primary	25.27	18.02	16.73
Secondary	32.07	29.03	30.36
Tertiary	42.66	52.95	52.91
Total	100.00	100.00	100

Source: NSSO Employment and Unemployment Data, Various Rounds.

total workforce. Thus, the data indicate that in the period of liberalisation and export oriented growth, unlike many other countries, the trends in women's employment in India show a regressive picture in terms of participation of women in paid employment.

In a sectorwise analysis, the picture becomes all the more complicated. The distribution of female workers across broad economic sectors for the last three rounds of the NSSO is given in Table 3. The data shows that agriculture still constitutes the largest chunk for all women workers. The share shows a small decline over the period, mostly in urban areas, with a sharp fall during the period from 1993–94 and 1999–2000.

In urban areas, the tertiary sector accounted for the largest chunk of women workers – more than half of women workers. This share rose sharply during the period from 1993–94 to 1999–2000, and then stagnated in the second period. The share of the secondary sector shows a small increase in rural areas, but not in urban areas. To further examine the industrywise changes within these broad categories, the distribution of women at the disaggregate industrial category is examined in the subsequent section.

Changing Employment Scenario at a Disaggregate Level

A longstanding feature of women's employment in the country has been the persistent and substantially high concentration of women in agriculture. This is reflective of the fact that for most women, urbanisation and the pattern of industrial development did not mean expanding opportunities for employment. It is for this reason that even within urban India, agriculture, which is elsewhere peripheral to the urban context and urban employment, continue to account for a far larger share of the female workforce than one would expect.

As has been seen earlier, the share of agriculture has more or less stagnated with some negligible decline over the period. Within the category of agriculture, again, there is near stagnation, though there are some negligible increases in the categories of forestry and fishing. Though the share of mining and quarrying has shown some increase, overall, there has been a decline in the share of the primary sector.

The industrial sector, including repair services, does not show much change though on the whole, the sector shows a marginal decline in terms of its share; the number of women in this category has increased. Among the industrial categories the trend in food products and tobacco, two core sectors of women's employment, show negative rate of growth. In these sectors, there has also been an absolute decline in the number of women

Table 4: Industrial Distribution of Female Workforce: All India

Industrial Category	1999–2000		2004	
	No. of Workers	% age	No. of Workers	% age
Agriculture, Forestry and Fishing	93,792	76.23	102,563	75.02
Agriculture, Hunting and Related Service Activities	93,226	75.77	101,729	74.41
Forestry, Logging and Related Service Activities	443	0.36	588	0.43
Fishing, Operation of Fish Hatcheries and Fish Farms; Service Activities Incidental to Fishing	123	0.10	232	0.17
Mining and Quarrying	381	0.31	465	0.34
Manufacturing and Repair Services of which:	12,058	9.80	13,248	9.69
Manufacture of Food Products and Beverages	1,427	1.16	1,353	0.99
Manufacture of Tobacco Products	3,470	2.82	3,117	2.28
Manufacture of Textiles	2,645	2.15	2,461	1.80
Manufacture of Wearing Apparel; Dressing and Dyeing of Fur	714	0.58	2,338	1.71
Manufacture of Wood and of Products of Wood and Cork, except Furniture; Manufacture of Articles of Straw and Plating Materials	1,120	0.91	1,080	0.79
Manufacture of Chemicals and Chemical Products	627	0.51	561	0.41
Manufacture of Other Non-Metallic Mineral Products	898	0.73	998	0.73
Manufacture of Furniture; Manufacture of N.E.C.	504	0.41	684	0.50
Electricity, Gas and Water	37	0.03	55	0.04
Construction	1,969	1.60	2,598	1.90
Trade, Hotels and Restaurants	4,897	3.98	5,154	3.77

Contd.

Contd.

Retail Trade	3,962	3.22	4,019	2.94
Hotels and Restaurants	787	0.64	916	0.67
Transport, Storage and Communication	406	0.33	424	0.31
Finance, Insurance, Real Estate and Business Services	418	0.34	670	0.49
Community, Social and Personal Services of which:	9,068	7.37	10,978	8.03
Public Administration and Defence	1,070	0.87	1,025	0.75
Education	3,039	2.47	4,142	3.03
Health and Social Work	935	0.76	1,244	0.91
Private Households with Employed Persons	1,070	0.87	3,062	2.24
Other Community and Personal Services	2,854	2.32	1,518	1.11
Total	123,038	100	136,714	100

Source: NSSO Employment and Unemployment Data, Various Rounds.
N.E.C.: Not elsewhere classified.

workers. Here it needs to be noted that during the period between 1993–94 and 1999–2000, the only sector which has shown some increase is beverages and tobacco.[2] While manufacture of textiles shows a decline in share, manufacture of wearing apparel and dressing and dyeing of fur show a major increase in terms of share as well as number of women employed. The increase in the sector invites special attention not only because it is the only industry which has shown a positive growth rate within manufacturing in contrast to that of 1993–94 and 1999–2000, but also because of its importance in the context of export led growth and use of flexible labour.

The construction industry, again accounting for a considerable proportion of women workers, has almost stagnated over the period, while in absolute terms, there has been much increase. The most important trend that needs to be highlighted, which is quite the reverse of the trend observed during the previous periods, is the decline in the share of women engaged in trade, hotels and restaurants, though in terms of absolute numbers, there is a small increase. Within this category, retail trade, which accounts for the majority of the workers, shows a decline in its share, while the number of women workers has stagnated. This needs to seen in contrast to the trend during 1993–94 and 1999–2000, when the number of women engaged in retail trade increased substantially. In the category of community, social and personal services, except for other community and personal services and public administration, all the categories have registered growth. The sectors which have registered maximum growth rates are education and private households with employed persons, which are basically the group of domestic workers. Education seems to be growing as an important area of occupation of women workers, which clearly shows further signs of segmentation of the market in terms of gender and this is emerging as an accepted area of women's employment. The more than doubled increase in the share as well as number of women engaged in private households with employed persons[3] reflects the pattern of change taking place in the country, where women who are pushed away from agriculture, manufacturing and trade are being segregated and concentrated into low paid domestic work.

Pattern of Employment Change in Urban Areas

In the 1990s, there has been a precipitous fall in women's employment in urban agriculture, reflected both in the reduced number of women in agriculture and also in its share. During the period 1999–2000 and 2004, though the number of women engaged in agriculture stagnated, in terms of share there has been a decline.

The data on women across various manufacturing industries shows a decline in the share of women workers in tobacco, textiles and chemical products. Manufacture of food products and beverages shows a small increase in terms of share, while the increase in absolute numbers has been quite substantial. The increase in the number as well as share of manufacture of wearing apparel and dressing and dyeing of fur has been phenomenal with the share increasing from 2.4 per cent to 6.2 per cent. The construction industry shows a decline in its share, while in terms of numbers, it has shown a marginal increase.

The share of trade in employment, which rose sharply during the period 1993–94 and 1999–2000, and could absorb some of the displaced workers from agriculture and manufacturing during the period, seems to have lost its importance in the later period. Within this category, it could be seen that it is the category of retail trade that has declined dramatically during the period, reducing from 13.7 per cent to 9.5 per cent.

In the urban areas, private households with employed persons as a separate category accounted for a substantial share of women workers and is next to agriculture and education for the first time. The increasing demand for domestic service in urban areas coupled by the large-scale rural-urban migration, which has been induced by rural impoverishment during the period of globalisation, explains the sizeable proportion of women in domestic service. Thus, the data clearly shows a pattern of expansion of manual and low paid jobs where more women can find greater place.

Education and health account for a substantial share of women workers, with a small increase during the period. The substantial share of women in this category is reflective of another category of jobs where women are finding place, which are mostly white collared. However, it needs to be noted that most of the expansion in these segments has been in the private sector, as a resultant of the privatisation process, whereby a large unorganised sector in such services has also grown. In education, for example, the proliferation of teaching shops with commercial objectives has not offered any great quality of employment. In fact, it is quite known that in several such institutions, teachers are paid wages lower than the statutory minimum wages for unskilled labour and below the actual wages received by factory workers or domestic servants. The same is true in the case of health services.[4]

Table 5: Industrial Distribution of Female Workforce: All India: Urban

Industrial Category	1999–2000		2004	
	No. of Workers	%age	No. of Workers	%age
Agriculture, Forestry and Fishing	2,904	17.62	3,494	16.1
Agriculture, Hunting and Related Service Activities	2,871	17.42	3,494	16.1
Forestry, Logging and Related Service Activities	16	0.10	0	0.00
Fishing, Operation of Fish Hatcheries and Fish Farms; Service Activities Incidental to Fishing	16	0.10	0	0.00
Mining and Quarrying	66	0.40	130	0.6
Manufacturing and Repair Services of which:	3,959	24.02	5,491	25.3
Manufacture of Food Products and Beverages	363	2.20	608	2.8
Manufacture of Tobacco Products	808	4.90	738	3.4
Manufacture of Textiles	941	5.71	1,063	4.9
Manufacture of Wearing Apparel; Dressing and Dyeing of Fur	396	2.40	1,346	6.2
Manufacture of Wood and of Products of Wood and Cork, except Furniture; Manufacture of Articles of Straw and Plating Materials	165	1.00	152	0.7
Manufacture of Chemicals and Chemical Products	313	1.90	239	1.1
Manufacture of Other Non-Metallic Mineral Products	148	0.90	195	0.9
Manufacture of Furniture; Manufacture of N.E.C.	297	1.80	521	2.4
Electricity, Gas and Water	33	0.20	65	0.3
Construction	791	4.80	955	4.4
Trade, Hotels and Restaurants	2,772	16.82	2,821	13

Contd.

Contd.

Retail Trade	2,260	13.71	2,062	9.5
Hotels and Restaurants	363	2.20	521	2.4
Transport, Storage and Communication	297	1.80	347	1.6
Finance, Insurance, Real Estate and Business Services	412	2.50	781	3.6
Community, Social and Personal Services of which:	5,229	31.73	7,509	34.6
Public Administration and Defence	643	3.90	781	3.6
Education	1,864	11.31	2,604	12
Health and Social Work	610	3.70	890	4.1
Private Households with Employed Persons	859	5.21	2,452	11.3
Other Community and Personal Services	1,254	7.61	803	3.7
Total	16,481	100	21,702	100

Source: NSSO Employment and Unemployment Data, Various Rounds.
N.E.C.: Not elsewhere classified.

Pattern of Employment Change in Rural Areas

In rural areas, agriculture and manufacturing show marginal declines, while construction, trade, hotels and restaurants, and community, social and personal services show very marginal increases when the two time periods are compared. Unlike the trend observed in urban, areas where there has been a substantial decline in the share of women in trade, hotels and restaurants, rural areas show an almost a stagnant picture, with just a small increase. Community, social and personal services also show a marginal increase. Overall, this reveals that there have not been substantial changes across the major industrial categories of women workers in the rural areas.

Within manufacturing, the major declines have been in tobacco and beverages, food products and textiles. Manufacture of wearing apparel and dressing and dyeing of fur shows increase in both share and number of women, though it still does not constitute for a reasonable proportion of women workers. Within trade, retail trade shows a marginal increase unlike in urban areas. Though education, health and private households with employed persons show an increase, the increase is negligible, except in education. These patterns, though not sharp, do indicate the nature of change that is happening in women's employment, a trend towards further segregation and informalisation of women workers. The extent of these trends of segregation could be further examined by an analysis of data under various National Classifications of Occupations (NCO), which is attempted in the following section.

Sex-Based Occupational Segmentation and Segregation

Socio-economic determinants do not permit women to participate in the market on an equal footing with men workers. Employment is fraught with constraints for women workers, particularly since cultural and social norms position women in a secondary or marginal status. In our country, where patriarchal institutions are a ubiquitous feature, there is a close relationship between patriarchal norms and labour market trends. Occupational segregation is a central instrument for perpetuating patriarchy since it reinforces gender division of labour, encourages payment of low wages to women, and maintains women's economic dependence. Concurrently, the gender division of labour reinforces occupational segregation by weakening the status of women in the labour market. In this context, the distribution of workers across various NCO categories could reveal important insights into occupational segregation of work across

Table 6: Industrial Distribution of Female Workforce: All India: Rural

Industrial Category	1999–2000		2004	
	No. of Workers	% age	No. of Workers	%age
Agriculture, Forestry and Fishing	90,893	85.3	99,544	84.37
Agriculture, Hunting and Related Service Activities	90,360	84.8	98,718	83.67
Forestry, Logging and Related Service Activities	426	0.4	590	0.50
Fishing, Operation of Fish Hatcheries and Fish Farms; Service Activities Incidental to Fishing	107	0.1	236	0.20
Mining and Quarrying	320	0.3	354	0.30
Manufacturing and Repair Services of which:	8,098	7.6	8,507	7.21
Manufacture of Food Products and Beverages	1,066	1	826	0.70
Manufacture of Tobacco Products	2,664	2.5	2,478	2.10
Manufacture of Textiles	1,705	1.6	1,534	1.30
Manufacture of Wearing Apparel; Dressing and Dyeing of Fur	320	0.3	1,180	1.00
Manufacture of Wood and of Products of Wood and Cork, except Furniture; Manufacture of Articles of Straw and Plating Materials	959	0.9	944	0.80
Manufacture of Chemicals and Chemical Products	320	0.3	354	0.30
Manufacture of Other Non-Metallic Mineral Products	746	0.7	826	0.70
Manufacture of Furniture; Manufacture of N.E.C.	213	0.2	236	0.20
Electricity, Gas and Water	0	0	0	0.00
Construction	1,172	1.1	1,770	1.50
Trade, Hotels and Restaurants	2,131	2	2,714	2.30

Contd.

Contd.

Retail Trade	1,705	1.6	2,242	1.90
Hotels and Restaurants	426	0.4	472	0.40
Transport, Storage and Communication	107	0.1	118	0.10
Finance, Insurance, Real Estate and Business Services	0	0	0	0.00
Community, Social and Personal Services of which:	3,836	3.6	4,495	3.81
Public Administration and Defence	426	0.4	354	0.30
Education	1,172	1.1	1,888	1.60
Health and Social Work	320	0.3	472	0.40
Private Households with Employed Persons	213	0.2	944	0.80
Other Community and Personal Services	1,598	1.5	826	0.70
Total	106,557	100	117,985	100

Source: NSSO Employment and Unemployment Data, Various Rounds.
N.E.C.: Not elsewhere classified.

male and female workers. Since the data across NCO categories for the latest round of NSSO data have just been made available, the analysis below is limited to the previous two rounds, the 55th and 50th rounds.

Distribution of Women across NCO Categories

The occupational segregation pattern shows some interesting changes. The data show high concentration of women workers in the category of farmers, fishermen, hunters, loggers and related workers, though there has been a decline in the proportion over the years. Production and related workers represents the next major category, which show an increase from 11.54 per cent to 12.06 per cent. Professional, technical and related workers, administrative, executive and managerial workers, clerical and related workers all show some increase in share over the period. In these categories, it is important to note the increase in the shares of professional, technical and related workers and administrative, executive and managerial workers, which are generally considered to be skilled, quality jobs. This points to some degree of reduction in sex-based occupational segmentation.

The distribution of women across various NCO categories at further disaggregate levels was analysed to find their industrial concentration for both rural and urban areas. The prominent industries and their share of employment in total women's employment are calculated for 1999–2000. In rural areas, the sectoral distribution of women across occupations, where the share is more than 0.5 per cent, is given in Table 8. Agriculture occupies the majority of women in rural areas, accounting for more than 82 per cent women, of which 41.51 per cent belong to the category of agricultural workers alone. From the data, it can be seen that other prominent occupations of women are teaching, trade, textiles and tobacco, of which tobacco preparers and tobacco product makers account for the largest share of women's non-farm employment, with a share of 2.27 per cent.

The 17 industries where women's employment is above 0.5 per cent accounted for 95.71 per cent of the workers, of which 10 prominent categories accounted for more than 91 per cent of the workers. The fact that about 82 per cent belonged to agriculture highlights the high degree of women in agriculture in rural areas in the event of no alternative source of employment and livelihood. In the urban areas also, concentration of women in a few occupations is quite substantial, though the extent of occupational concentration seems to be somewhat less compared to rural areas, with the prominent 10 industries accounting

Table 7: Male and Female Workers' Percentwise Share across Various NCO Categories

NCO Categories	1993–94		1999–2000	
	Male	Female	Male	Female
Professional, Technical and Related Workers	3.91	3.51	3.66	3.65
Administrative, Executive and Managerial Workers	2.31	1.14	3.50	1.54
Clerical and Related Workers	3.84	1.39	3.88	1.44
Sales Workers	8.40	3.03	8.42	2.88
Service Workers	3.38	4.11	3.81	4.86
Farmers, Fishermen, Hunters, Loggers and Related Workers	57.67	75.28	53.37	72.56
Production and Related Workers, Transport Equipment Operators and Labour	20.49	11.54	22.58	12.06
Workers Not Classified by Occupations	0.00	0.00	0.78	1.01
Total	100.00	100.00	100.00	100.00

Source: NSSO Employment and Unemployment Data, Various Rounds.

Table 8: Female Workers' Share across Various NCO Categories, 1999–2000: Rural

NCO Categories	Percentage of Women's Workforce in the Specified Occupational Category
Working Proprietors, Directors and Managers Mining, Construction, Manufacturing and Related Concerns	0.57
Maids and Other Housekeeping Service Workers N.E.C.	0.65
Food and Beverage Processors	0.69
Tailors, Dress Makers, Sewers, Upholsterers and Related Workers	0.77
Bricklayers and Other Construction Workers	0.82
Production and Related Workers, N.E.C.	0.88
Launderers, Drycleaners and Pressers	0.93
Spinners, Weavers, Knitters, Dyers and Related Workers	1.15
Teachers	1.27
Merchants and Shopkeepers, Wholesale and Retail Trade	1.29
Plantation Labourers and Related Workers	1.50
Labourers, N.E.C.	2.23
Tobacco Preparers and Tobacco Product Makers	2.27
Farmers Other than Cultivators	4.39
Cultivators	34.79
Agricultural Labourers	41.51

Source: NSSO Employment and Unemployment Data, Various Rounds.
N.E.C.: Not elsewhere classified.

for around 62 per cent of the workers. The distribution of women across various occupations where the share is at least 1 per cent is given in Table 9.

The occupational distribution of women clearly highlights the concentration of women in low skilled and thus underpaid activities, which are largely concentrated in the informal sector. Teachers and maids and other service workers account for the largest share of women's employment. Maids and service workers are accepted categories of women's employment, and women's large share in these categories is an expected outcome. However, teaching, which turns out to be the prominent occupation of women in urban areas, reveals the increasing trend of feminisation that is happening as far the education sector is concerned. The social acceptability of the occupation as a female friendly one may have been the reason for the increased presence of women in this occupation.

To examine further the trend in occupational segmentation or the feminisation process, the male-female shares across various categories are examined for the two NSSO rounds, 1993–94 and 1999–2000. The data shows that women's share has been higher in categories such as farmers and related workers, workers not classified by occupations, and service workers, which clearly reveal the extent of sex-based concentration that exists in the labour market. The substantial share of workers in the category of not classified by occupations suggests that a good proportion of workers are not classified properly in terms of occupation. The sectors which have registered increase in the share of women are women oriented occupations such as clerical and related workers, service workers and agriculture and related workers. The only sign of a change is the growing share of women in professional, technical and related workers. However, the optimism about a waning sex-based concentration gets complex when the share of administrative, executive and managerial workers is examined – this segment shows a decline in share over the years.

To understand the rural-urban picture, it both rural and urban areas have been examined separately. The data, however, does not provide any conclusive result. In rural areas, the occupations where the share of women workers is high are farmers, fishermen, hunters, loggers and related workers and service workers. In fact, for both these categories, there has been an increase during the period. The only category which has shown substantial change in terms of sex segmentation, is again professional, technical and related workers, where women workers' share increased from 19.5 per cent to 23.12 per cent. However, the drastic

Table 9: Female Workers' Share across Various NCO Categories, 1999–2000: Urban

NCO Categories	Percentage of Women's Workforce in the Specified Occupational Category
Hotel and Restaurantkeepers	0.99
Food and Beverage Processors	1.06
Working Proprietors, Directors and Managers, Other Services	1.07
Clerical and Other Supervisors	1.13
Cooks, Waiters, Bartenders and Related Workers (Domestic and Institutional)	1.15
Farmers Other than Cultivators	1.45
Working Proprietors, Directors and Managers, Wholesale and Retail Trade	1.66
Launderers, Drycleaners and Pressers	1.76
Production and Related Workers, N.E.C.	1.97
Working Proprietors, Directors and Managers, Mining, Construction, Manufacturing and Related Concerns	2.02
Nursing and other Medical and Health Technicians	2.56
Building Caretakers, Sweepers, Cleaners and Related Workers	2.66
Salesmen, Shop Assistants and Related Workers	2.72
Bricklayers and Other Construction Workers	3.19
Clerical and Related Workers, N.E.C.	4.14
Spinners, Weavers, Knitters, Dyers and Related Workers	4.16
Cultivators	4.27

Contd.

Contd.

Tobacco Preparers and Tobacco Product Makers	4.64
Tailors, Dress Makers, Sewers, Upholsterers and Related Workers	4.83
Merchants and Shopkeepers, Wholesale and Retail Trade	5.29
Labourers, N.E.C.	5.31
Agricultural Labourers	8.27
Maids and Other Housekeeping Service Workers N.E.C.	10.47
Teachers	10.98
Total	87.73

Source: NSSO Employment and Unemployment Data, Various Rounds.
N.E.C.: Not elsewhere classified.

Table 10: Male-Female Workers' Share across Various NCOs-Total (% age)

NCO Categories	1993-94		1999-2000	
	Male	*Female*	*Male*	*Female*
Professional, Technical and Related Workers	75.50	24.50	72.98	27.02
Administrative, Executive and Managerial Workers	84.81	15.19	85.96	14.04
Clerical and Related Workers	88.42	11.58	87.94	12.06
Sales Workers	88.45	11.55	88.74	11.26
Service Workers	69.47	30.53	67.91	32.09
Farmers, Fishermen, Hunters, Loggers and Related Workers	67.93	32.07	66.50	33.50
Production and Related Workers, Transport Equipment Operators and Labour	83.08	16.92	83.48	16.52
Workers Not Classified by Occupation			67.68	32.32
Total	73.44	26.56	72.96	27.04

Source: NSSO Employment and Unemployment Data, Various Rounds.

decline in the share of administrative, executive and managerial workers from 24.69 per cent to 18.93 per cent seems to suggest an increasing gender division. Administrative, executive and managerial workers normally represent categories of workers who are in decision-making roles. This with the decline in the shares of clerical and related workers and production and related workers and an increase in the share of service workers and agriculture and related workers indicate a trend towards an increasing concentration of women in low skilled and poorly paid employment in rural areas, which characterises the occupations in these categories.

In the urban areas also, women's largest shares are in agriculture and related workers and service workers. However, quite contrary to the trend in rural areas for all sectors, the share of administrative executive and managerial workers shows an increase. Except for production and related workers, the share of women shows an increase in all sectors, which is reflective of an increased entry of women in general to all occupations in urban areas.

The analysis above is highly aggregative and cannot reveal the pattern within one category. To explore this aspect, occupational classification at the two-digit level was examined both for rural and urban areas. The occupations at the two-digit level, where the shares of women workers are at least 18 per cent, are given in the following table for 1999–2000.

The occupational concentration for both sexes in rural areas is clearly visible from the table. In occupations such as teachers, nursing and other medical and health technicians, tobacco preparers and tobacco product makers, maids and other housekeeping service workers. NEC (not elsewhere classified) women had a larger share than male workers. Women workers accounted for about 88 per cent of the workers among maids and other housekeeping services, followed by tobacco (75.42 per cent), which suggests the existence of a high degree of sex-based segregation at work. As seen earlier, tobacco preparers and tobacco product makers also account for the largest share of women's employment in rural areas.

In urban areas, too, the sex-based segregation across occupations seems to be pronounced, with women constituting about 86 per cent of maids and housekeeping workers and about 77 per cent of tobacco workers. Sex-based segregation is also found to be sharp in categories such as launderers, dry-cleaners and pressers, nurses and other medical and health technicians, with women accounting for a considerably large proportion of workers in these sectors.

Even in occupations where women are concentrated, it has been argued that there exists a hierarchy of jobs, where women occupy the lower

Table 11: Male-Female Workers' Share across Various NCOs: Rural (% age)

NCO Categories	1993-94		1999-2000	
	Male	*Female*	*Male*	*Female*
Professional, Technical and Related Workers	80.46	19.54	76.88	23.12
Administrative, Executive and Managerial Workers	75.31	24.69	81.07	18.93
Clerical and Related Workers	91.66	8.34	92.09	7.91
Sales Workers	85.56	14.44	86.40	13.60
Service Workers	69.92	30.08	68.10	31.90
Farmers, Fishermen, Hunters, Loggers and Related Workers	67.93	32.07	66.56	33.44
Production and Related Workers, Transport Equipment Operators and Labour	80.38	19.62	80.73	19.27
Workers Not Classified by Occupation			65.01	34.99
Total	70.96	29.04	70.18	29.82

Source: NSSO Employment and Unemployment Data, Various Rounds.

Table 12: Male-Female Workers' Share across Various NCOs: Urban (% age)

NCO Categories	1993–94		1999–2000	
	Male	Female	Male	Female
Professional, Technical and Related Workers	70.75	29.25	69.84	30.16
Administrative, Executive and Managerial Workers	90.35	9.65	88.77	11.23
Clerical and Related Workers	86.73	13.27	85.62	14.38
Sales Workers	91.05	8.95	90.69	9.31
Service Workers	69.12	30.88	67.75	32.25
Farmers, Fishermen, Hunters, Loggers and Related Workers	67.86	32.14	63.59	36.41
Production and Related Workers, Transport Equipment Operators and Labour	86.22	13.78	86.93	13.07
Workers Not Classified by Occupation			80.28	19.72
Total	82.41	17.59	82.86	17.14

Source: NSSO Employment and Unemployment Data, Various Rounds.

Table 13: Male-Female Workers' Share across Various NCOs, 1999–2000: Rural (% age)

Occupational Categories	Share of Women in the Occupational Category	Share of Men in the Occupational Category
Glass Formers, Potters and Related Workers	18.21	81.79
Hotel and Restaurantkeepers	19.74	80.26
Telephone and Telegraph Operators	19.87	80.13
Computing Machine Operators	21.25	78.75
Cultivators	22.72	77.28
Social Scientists and Related Workers	23.77	76.23
Tailors, Dress Makers, Sewers, Upholsterers and Related Workers	26.55	73.45
Spinners, Weavers, Knitters, Dyers and Related Workers	26.88	73.12
Stenographers, Typists and Card and Tape Punching Operators	27.21	72.79
Building Caretakers, Sweepers, Cleaners and Related Workers	30.39	69.61
Farmers Other than Cultivators	32.56	67.44
Plantation Labourers and Related Workers	33.03	66.97
Production and Related Workers, N.E.C.	33.23	66.77
Housekeepers, Matrons and Stewards (Domestic and Institutional)	34.78	65.22
Elected and Legislative Officials	35.98	64.02
Launderers, Drycleaners and Pressers	36.54	63.46
Paper and Paper Board Product Makers	40.98	59.02
Agricultural Labourers	46.16	53.84
Teachers	51.09	48.91
Nursing and Other Medical and Health Technicians	56.81	43.19
Tobacco Preparers and Tobacco Product Makers	75.42	24.58
Maids and Other Housekeeping Service Workers NEC	87.76	12.24

Source: NSSO Employment and Unemployment Data, Various Rounds.

Table 14: Male-Female Workers' Share across Various NCOs, 1999–2000: Urban (% age)

Occupational Categories	Share of Women in the Occupational Category	Share of Men in the Occupational Category
Physical Scientists	30.06	69.94
Hotel and Restaurantkeepers	30.94	69.06
Forestry Workers	30.98	69.02
Glass Formers, Potters and Related Workers	32.50	67.50
Spinners, Weavers, Knitters, Dyers and Related Workers	33.78	66.22
Food and Beverage Processors	34.16	65.84
Cooks, Waiters, Bartenders and Related Workers (Domestic and Institutional)	35.50	64.50
Plantation Labourers and Related Workers	37.56	62.44
Agricultural Labourers	38.75	61.25
Building Caretakers, Sweepers, Cleaners and Related Workers	40.36	59.64
Stenographers, Typists and Card and Tape Punching Operators	41.00	59.00
Production and Related Workers, N.E.C.	43.13	56.87
Nursing and Other Medical and Health Technicians	43.30	56.70
Farmers Other than Cultivators	45.80	54.20
Life Science Technicians	46.76	53.24
Launderers, Dry-cleaners and Pressers	51.97	48.03
Tobacco Preparers and Tobacco Product Makers	77.42	22.58
Maids and Other Housekeeping Service Workers NEC	86.01	13.99

Source: NSSO Employment and Unemployment Data, Various Rounds.

rungs. Women's segregation into 'female' occupations implies that there is a higher likelihood of these occupations being poorly paid, and gender-based wage differentials do reflect these biases. Labour market trends, clearly, reflect social attitudes that consider women's work to be inferior to that of men. It is also an extension of the human capital discrimination faced by women.

Emerging Scenario

The analysis of the NSSO data thus gives a complex picture, which makes it difficult to arrive at any specific conclusion. Does this mean that female workers are marginalised in the labour market.? Or does it imply that the conditions in the labour market have improved so much so that female workers are withdrawing from the labour market? As has been seen, there are no visible signs of feminisation at the macro level; rather, the trends available seem to suggest increasing marginalisation and seg-mentation of women. The decline in participation rates in the principal status category, alongside betterment in the participation rates by all statuses, suggests the possibility of many women being unable to find employment throughout the year. Thus, this points to the lack of ad-equate employment opportunities for the female labour force.

The sectoral distribution shows a stagnant and highly segregated pic-ture, with women concentrated in the primary sector as against the trends in other liberalised economies. Within the manufacturing and services sector, segregation seems to be powerful, with women getting further concentrated in stereotypical occupations. Agriculture still accounts for the largest share of female workers. The macro data shows that in India, the expansion of the manufacturing sector, which has been the major source of female employment in other developing countries, has been very limited. Within the manufacturing sector, export oriented units are the major absorbent of female workers and this has been brought out by many micro level studies. The substantial increase in women in the manufacturing of garments, which have a substantial export market, point in this direction. Such units are known for their exploitative and insecure nature and hence do not contribute to much betterment for the women workers.

The services sector contributes a substantial proportion of women workers, and the degree of concentration that is visible in the sector, especially in personal services in the urban areas and in education, points to the broad contours of change other in the sector. It also needs to be noted that unlike other countries, in India, the growth of the services sector has not been substantial enough to absorb a large proportion of the female population. The increased concentration of women in categories such as education and health further reveals the conservative approach towards women's employment. These not only restrict the entry of women in the labour market, but also decide the pattern of the employment. The sudden increase and fall in trade (both in terms of employment and share) points to the fact that the changes that happen in the short run may not be sustainable, as these are largely the results of impulsive responses. In the category of trade as has been seen, retail trade dominates and the period of its sudden upsurge matched a decline in the primary and secondary sectors. That reduced employment opportunities for women workers in agriculture; manufacturing and construction have all played a role in pushing or crowding large numbers of women into petty retail trade. Thus, what seems to have happened is that people who are out of the workforce through shifts in traditional occupations have tried alternative sources of livelihood and, because of different reasons, petty retail trade is often seen as an important source of employment for poor women, who are uneducated and lack specific skills. The perceived relative skills required for entering retail trade, especially small vending, are not too many as compared to other categories of work. The self-employed nature of the occupation makes the entry of poor and vulnerable groups easier, which is furthered by the requirement of very low capital investment. Further, with reduced family incomes and rapid impoverishment, it is quite likely that more and more women who are entering the workforce will take up different tasks at different points in time, which could fluctuate in quantum, depending on the opportunities available, such as petty trade, adding to fluctuations in such categories of work.

With the slow growth of the manufacturing sector, poor educational background and prevailing social attitudes to women's work, the picture does not seem to change in the near future. Women thus are likely to remain increasingly concentrated in agriculture and other low-paid, less-skilled occupations in the manufacturing and services sector. Further, within the broad category of manufacturing and services, new areas of women's work are emerging. Domestic work, export oriented manufacturing work, and part-time work constitute a significant proportion of work in urban and rural areas. Thus, in the job pyramid, women will tend to be concentrated in jobs that require limited skills and education, and that pay low wages, with less scope for skill development and career growth, unless structural changes in the economy are preceded by social transformations which could alter women's position in society.

Notes

1. See J. Ghosh, *Export Oriented Employment for Women and Social Policy*, UNRISD, 2002
2. During this period, there has also been an absolute decline in male employment in tobacco and beverages, which highlights an overall decline in employment in the sector. To some extent this could be attributed to the declining demand for tobacco products, especially bidis, the production of which is highly labour intensive. The overall decline in number of smokers and a shift in the profile of tobacco consumers alongside bans on smoking in public places seem to have contributed to this decline.
3. As per NIC, private households with employed persons include the activities of private households employing all kinds of domestic personnel such as maids, cooks, gardeners, gatekeepers, secretaries, governesses, baby sitters, etc.
4. See Rama Baru.

References

Banerjee, Nirmala. 1997. 'How Real is the Bogey of Feminisation?' in *The Indian Journal of Labour Economics*, Vol. 40, No. 3, July-September.

Deshpande, Sudha. 2003. 'Changing Employment Structure in Large States of India: What do the NSSO Data Show?' *Indian Journal of Labour Economics*, Vol. 46, No. 4.

Ghosh, Jayati. 2002. *Export Oriented Employment for Women and Social Policy*, UNRISD.

National Sample Survey Organisation. 1996. *Sarvekshana*, New Delhi: Department of Statistics, Government of India, Vol. 20, No. 1, July-September.

———. 2000. *Report on Employment and Unemployment in India 1999–2000, Key Results,* NSS 55th Round July 1999-June 2000, December.

———. 2001. Draft Report No 458, *Employment and Unemployment in India 1999–2000*, Parts I and II, NSS 55th Round July 1999-June 2000, April, 2001.

Neetha, N. 2001. 'Feminisation and Marginalisation: Revelations of NSS 55th Round' in *Labour and Development*, Vol. 7, No. 2.

Neetha, N. and Indrani Mazumdar. 2005. 'New Developments in Labour Hiring and Women's Employment in Urban India', Paper presented at the seminar on *Globalisation and Women's Movement in India*, January 20–22, New Delhi: Centre for Women Development Studies.

Sundaram, K. 2001. 'Employment-Unemployment Situation in the Nineties: Some Results from NSS 55th Round Survey' in *Economic and Political Weekly,* March 17.

———. 2001. 'Employment and Poverty in 1990s: Further Results from NSS 55th Round Employment – Unemployment Survey, 1999–2000' in *Economic and Political Weekly*, August 11.

5

Determinants of Sexual Violence within Marriage in Kerala

PRADEEP PANDA

Violence against women, including physical, sexual and psychologi cal violence, is increasingly viewed as a serious violation of human rights. The varied forms of such violence are currently recognised as public health and social issues in developing countries, including India (WHO, 2002; Jewkes, 2002). Sexual violence is also emerging as a major health and human rights issue over the past decade. Sexual violence is defined as 'any sexual act, attempt to obtain a sexual act, unwanted sexual comments or advances, or acts of traffic, or otherwise directed against a person's sexuality using coercion, by any person regardless of their relationship to the victim' (WHO, 2002). One of the most recent works addresses the magnitude, determinants and consequences of sex without consent among young people in developing countries (Jejeebhoy, Shah and Thapa, 2005).

Although prevalence of sexual violence against women varies considerably across countries, it is believed to be a common problem worldwide. Globally, the estimate shows that one in three adult women has experienced sexual violence, mostly perpetrated by women's intimate partners (Beckerman, 2002).

Sexual violence against women is a risk factor for many physical and psychological health problems. In recent years, research shows that sexual violence leads to poor physical outcomes, including increased rates of sexually transmitted infections, pelvic pains and urinary tract infections (Campbell and Alfred, 1989; Eby and Campbell, 1995) as well as poor mental health outcomes, including depression and poor body image (Campbell and Soeken, 1999; Dutton et al., 2005). In spite of such physical and psychological risks, little research has been done on the prevention of sexual violence.

Sexual Violence in India

A growing number of studies have examined the underlying causes and correlates of domestic violence against women in India. Also, there are some qualitative studies that have examined sexual violence within marriage in India. However, quantitative studies on the prevalence and determinants of sexual violence within marriage are scanty. This paper is an attempt to quantify sexual violence within marriage and identify its correlates in the state of Kerala in India.

In spite of a steep rise in the reported rape cases and other forms of sexual assault, there is lack of much-needed research on sexual violence in India. Of course, there are many reasons for this inadequate attention to sexual violence research, such as sensitivity and the stigma surrounding sexual violence, the culture of silence and taboos on the topics of sex and women's sexuality, restricted legal and professional definitions of sexual violence, patriarchal ideologies and denial of sexual violence by institutions such as the police, judiciary, health systems and social systems.

Sexual violence is found to have many negative impacts on women's health and well-being. In a population-based representative sample of 2,496 women in Goa, India, sexual violence by the husband was found to be a risk factor for chronic fatigue in women (Patel et al., 2005). In a qualitative pilot study of HIV-positive women in Kolkata, sexual violence was found to be an indirect social factor for the source of infection (Majumdar, 2004). Other qualitative studies in India revealed women's submission to sex for fear of abandonment and many psychological and emotional consequences (Santhya and Jejeebhoy, 2005; George and Jaswal, 1995; Khan et al., 1996). In spite of such negative impacts of sexual violence on women, victims receive little help or redress.

Although the prevalence rates vary across studies, there are indications that sexual violence against women within marriage is fairly prevalent. In general, sexual violence within marriage is determined on the basis of the response to a question whether the husband had physically forced his wife to have sexual relations during the year preceding the survey. Following such definition, the incidence of sexual violence was found to be 30.1 per cent in Uttar Pradesh, as reported by husbands (Koenig et al., 2006). The incidence of sexual violence as reported by wives was found to be 15 per cent in a multisite household survey of nearly 10,000 women in India. It may be noted that the level of sexual violence was similar across the three strata, i.e., rural, urban slum and urban non-slum (INCLEN, 2000). Although it is difficult to compare these estimates due to differences in samples, methodologies, definition used and gender differences in responses, these studies point to a serious problem faced by women within marriage.

A host of social, economic, cultural and community factors are responsible for the occurrence of sexual violence. There is a common perception in India that it remains the husband's prerogative to physically compel his wife to engage in sexual relations when desired (Maitra and Schensul, 2004; Sodhi and Verma, 2003; Khan et al., 1996). In popular Hindi films in India, an exploratory content analysis found that while severe sexual violence was portrayed as criminal and serious, moderate sexual violence was treated as fun and romantic (Ramasubramanian and Oliver, 2003). Feminist scholars are concerned that sexual violence is shown as a normal part of relationships with men and, most often, it is glorified within Indian cinema (Gandhi and Shah, 1992; Derne, 1995, 1999). The limited evidence available from India suggests a host of underlying risk factors for sexual violence: women marrying in adolescence, lack of familiarity with husbands prior to marriage, women's lack of preparedness for sex, women's limited knowledge of sexual and rights information, gender power inequalities and lack of social support due to rigid community norms (George, 2002; Santhya and Jejeebhoy, 2005; Joshi et al., 2001; Khan et al., 1996; Sodhi and Verma, 2003)

A study in Uttar Pradesh did not find strong associations between higher levels of education among both husbands and wives and greater household wealth with a lower risk of sexual violence. On the contrary, the study found that women married to more educated husbands (seven or more years of schooling) experienced significantly higher risks of coercive sexual intercourse. Husbands who had witnessed their fathers beating their mothers as children, and childless husbands are more likely to sexually coerce their wives. Furthermore, a contextual or community-level factor that was found to have a positive effect on sexual violence within marriage was violent crime rates (Koenig, 2006).

On the basis of a representative sample of married women, an attempt has been made in this paper to examine the prevalence and correlates of sexual violence within marriage in Kerala state in India.

The Context of Kerala

Kerala is considered one of India's most progressive states due to its exceptionally high female literacy and life expectancy as well as related health indicators, which are comparable to those of many developed countries (Dreze and Sen, 1989; Government of Kerala, 2006). But there is another side to this picture reflected in rising consumerism, escalating dowry demands, high unemployment, and persisting pockets of poverty. Modern Kerala thus represents a paradox with dynamic social movements, Dalit emancipation, high emigration (indicating exposure to other cultures), and political decentralisation (in recent times) on the one hand, and high suicide rates, unemployment, male dominance and gender-based violence on the other. To understand the phenomenon of gender-based violence, dowry and related issues, there have been several recent studies (INCLEN, 2000; Panda, 2003; Panda and Agarwal, 2005; Eapen and Kodoth, 2003; Kodoth, 2005).

The issue of sexual violence within the general community and in institutions has been widely prevalent and documented in Kerala (Devika and Kodoth, 2001). However, there is limited quantitative empirical evidence of the prevalence and determinants of sexual violence within marriage in Kerala. This paper attempts to fill this gap, and looks at identifying the risk and protective factors for sexual violence against women in Kerala. The results may help in developing appropriate interventions to prevent sexual violence.

Methodology

The data for this study comes from a household survey conducted in 2001 in three rural and three urban settings in Thiruvananthapuram district of Kerala state. A total of 10 wards (six rural and four urban) were selected from these six settings. From each ward, 50 households were selected at random. Thus, a total of 500 households (300 rural and 200 urban) were selected. The study participants were ever-married women aged 15–49 years. The survey included 502 women (302 rural and 200 urban). The participation rate was 92 per cent, similar across both rural and urban areas.

Informed consent was taken from the women respondents prior to interview. Interviews were undertaken in places that ensured maximum privacy. Confidentiality of information was strictly maintained. A team of six local female investigators conducted the interviews. The investigators were given extensive training for a comprehensive understanding of each survey instrument item. The data collection instruments were field tested. All questionnaires were reviewed for completeness and correctness of recording after interview.

Information was collected on demographic variables such as age, duration of marriage and number of children as well as socio-economic variables such as consumption expenditure (food and non-food), possession of consumer durables, ownership of assets (i.e., title to land and house) by the women, education and employment. Information was also collected on social support received from the natal family and neighbours, childhood experience or witnessing of violence, and alcohol consumption and substance abuse by husband. The index woman was a respondent for the abovementioned information, excluding information on consumption expenditure. For consumption expenditure, a trained male investigator collected information from the head of the household at each site.

The operational definitions of prevalence rates (lifetime and current) and of physical and psychological violence in this study are similar to those used by the International Clinical Epidemiology Network (INCLEN) study (INCLEN, 2000). Domestic violence was defined as any reported violence, either physical or psychological, perpetrated by a husband against his wife. Accordingly, physical and psychological violence were measured with specific discrete behaviours (See Panda, 2003, 2004; Panda and Agarwal, 2005, for details).

This paper focuses on sexual violence within marriage, and the underlying risk and protective factors. Sexual violence is defined as whether husbands had physically forced their wives to have sexual intercourse without their consent or willingness. As such, it was determined from the response to a single question asking the woman respondent whether her husband had physically forced her to have sexual intercourse during the year preceding the survey. This definition is also similar to forced sex or coerced sex in the literature. The analysis in this paper is restricted to 443 women as the focus of this paper is on current sexual violence. The remaining 59 women were excluded from the analysis because they were widowed, divorced, separated, or women whose husbands had been absent for more than one year prior to the survey due to out-migration.

Results

Sample Profile

Table 1 presents the profile of the sample. The average age of the women respondents is 32.4 years and the average duration of marriage is 11.9 years. The average spousal age difference is higher in urban areas as compared to rural areas (7.4 and 6.2 years, respectively). More than 70 per cent of the couples have one or two children. More than 95 per cent of the men and women are literates in both rural and urban areas. There is not much sex differential in the levels of education. Less than 10 per cent of rural women and men have more than 12 years of education as compared to 40 per cent of men and women in urban areas, showing rural-urban differentials in the levels of education.

More than two-thirds of the women in rural and urban areas do not engage in outside employment compared to 6 per cent of the men. Women in rural areas are more likely to be engaged in seasonal and irregular employment (16.9 per cent), whereas women in urban areas are more likely to be employed in regular employment (24.6 per cent). As one would expect, men are more likely to be employed in both rural and urban areas. A substantially higher proportion of men are likely to be engaged in regular employment, in both rural and urban areas.

The households are spread across all income groups. However, while a larger proportion in rural areas belongs to the middle income group, the concentration in urban areas is for the high income group. In the sample, more than one-third of the women own immovable property: 5.4 per cent own only land, 15.6 per cent own only a house and 14.7 per cent own both land and a house. Ownership of land and a house is much higher in urban areas as compared to rural areas (32.7 and 3.3 per cent, respectively). In the sample, 56 per cent of women reported some form of social support, either from the natal family (33 per cent) or from both the natal family and neighbours (23 per cent).

Table 1: Sample Profile (Percentage)

Characteristics	Total (N=443)	Rural (N=272)	Urban (N=171)
Age of the Respondent (Years)			
15–24	14.0	16.9	9.4
25–34	51.9	48.2	57.9
35+	34.1	34.9	32.7
Duration of Marriage (Years)			
<7	30.0	29.4	31.0
7–14	37.9	38.6	36.8
15+	32.1	32.0	32.2
Number of Children			
0	9.5	9.2	9.9
1–2	74.0	76.8	69.6
3+	16.5	14.0	20.5

Contd.

Contd.

Spousal Age Difference (Years)			
<5	28.0	32.4	21.1
5–8	44.9	46.3	42.7
9+	27.1	21.3	36.3
Per Capita Expenditure (Rs/Yr)			
<6,000	22.3	29.4	11.1
6,000–11,999	51.7	63.2	33.3
12,000+	26.0	7.4	55.6
Education of Respondent (Years)			
<6	13.6	17.3	7.6
6–12	64.1	72.4	50.9
13+	22.3	10.3	41.5
Employment of Respondent			
Unemployed	70.0	69.1	71.3
Regular	18.1	14.0	24.6
Seasonal/Irregular	11.9	16.9	4.1
Education of Husband (Years)			
<6	16.5	22.4	7.1
6–12	62.3	69.5	50.9
13+	22.3	8.1	42.1
Employment of Husband			
Unemployed	5.6	4.4	7.6
Regular	83.1	78.7	90.1
Seasonal/Irregular	11.3	16.9	2.3
Ownership of Property			
None	64.3	72.4	51.5
Land	5.4	7.0	2.9
House	15.6	17.3	12.9
Land and House	14.7	3.3	32.7
Social Support			
None	44.0	42.3	46.8
Natal Family	33.4	38.6	25.1
Natal Family and Neighbour	22.6	19.1	28.1
Woman Witnessing Marital Violence in Childhood			
Did not Witness	68.6	58.1	85.4
Witnessed	31.4	41.9	14.6
Husband's Alcohol Consumption			
Teetotaler	51.2	50.0	53.2
Drinker	48.8	50.0	46.8
Husband Witnessing Marital Violence in Childhood			
Did not Witness	73.4	64.7	87.1
Witnessed	26.6	35.3	12.9

Nearly 31 per cent of women reported witnessing their father beating their mother during their childhood. The witnessing of this parental behaviour was substantially higher in rural areas. Half of the women reported that their husbands drank occasionally or regularly over the past one year. Nearly 27 per cent of women reported that their husbands had witnessed their father beat their mother during childhood, the percentage being higher in the rural areas.

Women's Experience of Sexual Violence

The prevalence rate of sexual violence against women within marriage was 15 per cent. In other words, nearly 15 per cent of the total sample of women reported one or more incidents of forced sex during the 12 months preceding the survey. This rate is similar across rural and urban areas (Table 2). This shows how sexual violence is made legitimate by ideas of male sexual entitlement in both rural and urban areas.

Correlates of Sexual Violence

In order to find the correlates of sexual violence, we followed an ecological perspective (Heise, 1998). Accordingly, we explored the bivariate relationships between sexual violence among women and some of the individual, household and community factors. These factors include:

(a) Demographic characteristics: Age of the woman; duration of marriage; age difference between husband and wife; number of children; residence;
(b) Socio-economic status: Education and employment status of the woman and her husband; per capita expenditures per annum;
(c) Social support from the natal family and neighbours;
(d) Ownership of property by the woman respondent: Title to land or house, or both;
(e) Woman's witnessing father beating mother in childhood; and
(f) Specific characteristics of husband: Husband's alcohol consumption; husband's witnessing father beating mother in childhood.

Table 2 presents the bivariate relationship between women's experience of sexual violence and selected characteristics as mentioned above. There is no significant association between demographic variables and women's experience of sexual violence. This suggests an early onset of sexual violence in the marital relationship, which continues as age progresses.

On the other hand, there is a striking differential between socio-economic variables and women's experience of sexual violence. For instance, per capita expenditure has a sharp negative association with sexual violence. While 44 per cent of the women from poor households experience sexual violence, only 6 per cent of the women from non-poor households experience sexual violence. Similarly, educational status of men and women is also negatively associated with sexual violence.

While employment status of women is not associated with sexual violence, there is a striking diffential between husband's employment status and women's experience of sexual violence. For instance, the prevalence of sexual violence is as high as 48 per cent if the husband is unemployed, and only 11 per cent if the husband has a regular job.

Ownership of property by the woman has a strong negative effect on sexual violence. Among those who do not own property, 21 per cent experienced sexual violence. In contrast, those who own only land or only house or both land and house reported substantially less sexual violence (0.0, 2.9 and 6.2 per cent, respectively). Due to a small sample for women's ownership of only land, we cannot make a meaningful relationship between this with women's experience of sexual violence.

Women's experience of sexual violence is likely to be higher when a woman has no social support from the neighbours or natal family.

Table 2: Sexual Violence against Women by Select Characteristics (Percentage)

Sexual Violence (at least one incident of forced sex during the previous 12 months)	14.7
Age of the Respondent (Years)	
15–24	16.1
25–34	14.3
35+	14.6
Duration of Marriage (Years)	
<7	17.3
7–14	12.5
15+	14.8
Number of Children	
0	14.3
1–2	13.4
3+	20.5
Spousal Age Difference (Years)	
<5	16.1
5–8	15.1
9+	12.5

Contd.

Contd.

Residence	
Rural	14.0
Urban	15.8
Per Capita Expenditure (Rs/Yr)	
<6,000	44.4
6,000–11,999	6.1
12,000+	6.1
Education of Respondent (Years)	
<6	36.7
6–12	11.6
13+	10.1
Employment of Respondent	
Unemployed	14.5
Regular	13.8
Seasonal/Irregular	17.0
Education of Husband (Years)	
<6	28.8
6–12	13.4
13+	7.4
Employment of Husband	
Unemployed	48.0
Regular	11.7
Seasonal/Irregular	20.0
Ownership of Property	
None	20.7
Land	0.0
House	2.9
Land and House	6.2
Social Support	
None	22.6
Natal Family	5.4
Natal Family and Neighbour	13.0
Woman Witnessing Marital Violence in Childhood	
Did not Witness	6.3
Witnessed	33.1
Husband's Alcohol Consumption	
Teetotaller	7.0
Drinker	22.7
Husband Witnessing Marital Violence in Childhood	
Did not Witness	5.5
Witnessed	39.8

In families in which the husband or wife has witnessed their father beat their mother as a child, sexual violence is likely to be much higher. Similarly, sexual violence is likely to be much higher when the husband is an alcoholic.

Multivariate Analysis

Due to possible confounding among the independent factors in the bivariate analysis, a logistic regression model was used for women's experience of sexual violence (1 if experienced sexual violence; 0 otherwise) to assess the effect of each independent factor in the presence of other variables in the model. The logistic regression results in terms of beta coefficients are presented in Table 3.

A significant finding is that women's ownership of property has a strong and negative relationship with sexual violence. Even after controlling for a host of other well-known correlates, women's property ownership emerges as a strong predictor of the risk of sexual violence. Women's property ownership enhances their bargaining power within marriage. It also enhances their dignity and self-worth. It provides an exit option for women to be free from sexual violence. In earlier research in Kerala, we had established that women's ownership of property had a strong and negative relationship with women's experience of physical and psychological violence, both long term and current (Panda and Agarwal, 2005). In addition, employing both quantitative and qualitative data, the various pathways by which property ownership impacts domestic violence have also been established (Panda, 2006). The present study provides evidence for the importance of women's property ownership in reducing yet another important form of domestic violence against women, i.e., sexual violence within marriage. In future research, this relationship should be empirically validated in other states and settings in India, along with examining the pathways.

The multivariate analysis also shows a significant and negative association between household economic status (measured as per capita expenditure) and sexual violence. Husband's employment status is also strongly related with sexual violence – the risk of sexual violence is heightened if the husband is unemployed as compared to his having regular or even irregular/seasonal employment. Unlike husband's employment status, women's employment status is not significantly associated with sexual violence. While husband's education level is not associated with sexual violence, women' with 6–12 years of education experience less sexual violence as compared to women with less than six years of education.

Women's social support from the natal family or neighbours does not seem to make a difference to the risk of sexual violence. Similarly, husband's alcohol consumption is not significantly related with sexual violence. While women's witnessing their father beat their mother as a child is not related with sexual violence, their husband's childhood experience of witnessing such violence is a strong predictor of the risk of sexual violence. This positive association between the husband's childhood experience of violence and women's experience of sexual violence is consistent with research in India or other settings (Koenig et al., 2006). This suggests that violent behaviour may be learned from childhood experience. This intergenerational transmission of violence has a serious negative effect on the well-being of the family.

To sum up the multivariate results, four factors act as protection against sexual violence – household economic status, women's education, women's ownership of property and husband's employment status. In addition, the husband's witnessing his father beat his mother as a child acts as a risk factor for sexual violence.

Table 3: Logistic Analysis: Women's Experience of Sexual Violence

Variable	Sexual Violence (Beta Coefficient)
Per capita expenditure (Rs/Yr)	
<6,000 (rc)	
6,000–11,999	−2.73***
12,000+	−2.28***
Education of Respondent (Years)	
<6 (rc)	
6–12	−0.99**
13+	0.48
Employment of Respondent	
Unemployed (rc)	
Regular	−0.66
Seasonal/Irregular	−0.42
Education of Husband (Years)	
<6 (rc)	
6–12	0.30
13+	1.26
Employment of Husband	
Unemployed (rc)	
Regular	−1.32*
Seasonal/Irregular	−1.61*
Ownership of Property	
Did not Own (rc)	

Contd.

Contd.	
Owned (Land or House or Land and House)	−1.84***
Social Support	
None (rc)	
Natal Family	−0.72
Natal Family and Neighbour	−0.50
Woman Witnessing Marital Violence in Childhood	
Did not Witness (rc)	
Witnessed	0.15
Husband's Alcohol Consumption Teetotaller (rc)	
Drinker	−0.31
Husband Witnessing Marital Violence in Childhood	
Did not Witness (rc)	
Witnessed	2.93***
Number of Cases	443
-2 Log Likelihood	200.84
Model Chi-Square	168.62

Notes: *Significant at the 10% level
**Significant at the 5% level
***Significant at the 1% level
rc: reference category

Discussion and Conclusions

Sexual violence against women in India is a significant public health and human rights issue, but remains inadequately studied. It is still considered a domestic/private matter not relevant to state policy. While NGOs and feminist scholars have been continuously striving for the prevention of sexual violence within and outside marriage, the achievement so far are not very satisfactory. Specifically, the issue of fighting rape and other forms of sexual assault through the women's movement was not sustained. Establishment of crisis centres is one major accomplishment of the women's movement. There is a need for effective implementation of existing law, to change the law, and to ensure accountability of the police and judiciary in terms of responsiveness to the needs of victims of sexual violence.

In India, marital rape is not recognised as an offence under the law. Also, the legal definition of rape is limited to penetration of the vagina by the penis. Due to this narrow definition of only penile penetration, many sexual assaults against women, including sex without consent, remain unadressed and fall outside legal remedy (Singh, 2004). There are also inadequacies in the existing medico-legal services for the survivors/victims of sexual violence (Bakshi, 1994). The inadequacy and gender bias of the criminal justice system in India are widely acknowledged (Agnes, 1992, 1995). The judiciary as well as police and those who have to deal with such cases of sexual violence, have to be sensitised regarding gender issues. There is an urgent need for more research to formulate strategies to prevent sexual assault and rape.

The present study is an attempt to build the evidence on the correlates of sexual violence within marriage. In terms of policy, the general climate of employment and poverty should be addressed in Kerala. The implementation of recent legal reforms, such as the Protection of Women from Domestic Violence Act, 2005, and the Hindu Succession (Amendment) Act, 2005, would make a difference to women's ability to deal with domestic violence. However, amendment of the law is also necessary for taking into account rape and other forms of sexual assault. Campaigns for legal literacy, awareness and legal aid support, including strategies to enhance women's housing and land access in both rural and urban areas, are crucial for the struggle to achieve gender justice and protection against sexual violence. Media, especially films, should play a sensible role while handling or portraying themes on sexual violence. Sexual violence should be covered prominently in all types of media to raise awareness in communities.

Since many cases of sexual violence are not reported due to the stigma and shame attached to it in a patriarchal society like India, there is a need to change community norms that perpetuate and condone sexual violence. A concerted effort is required to address men who sexually abuse women. The problem of sexual violence needs to be acknowledged publicly and discussed openly by policy makers. Clearly, a combination of medical, psychosocial support and legal aid is extremely important to provide adequate care and support to the victims of sexual violence. The health sector can play an important role by providing sensitive and appropriate help to survivors of sexual violence. Health care providers need to be trained in treating victims of sexual violence.

The Government of India, under its women's programmes, has a few schemes to cater to the needs of victims of violence (short-stay homes) and for the provision of rehabilitation services to women in difficult circumstances (Swadhar). In both these schemes, there is substantial underutilisation of funds in the Tenth Plan. This defeats the objectives and concerns with which the schemes had been launched (Government of India, 2005). Better and effective utilisation of funds is key for the success of these schemes.

Sexual violence against women and other gender-based violence violate women's human rights and fundamental freedoms. It is our responsibility to protect and promote these rights and freedoms. Planners and policy makers should be committed to fulfil this role. The evidence from this study that women's ownership of immovable property reduces sexual violence within marriage is too strong to ignore.

References

Agnes, F. 1992. 'Protecting Women Against Violence? Review of a Decade of Legislation, 1980–89', *Economic and Political Weekly*. Vol. 27, No. 17.

———. 1995. *State, Gender and the Rhetoric of Law Reform*, Mumbai: SNDT Women's University.

Bakshi, P.M. 1994. 'The Offence of Rape and Certain Medico-Legal Aspects', New Delhi: A Study by the National Commission for Women.

Beckerman, N. 2002. 'Intimate Sexual Violence in the United States: Social Work and Family Therapy Interventions' in *The Journal of Social Aggression*, Vol. 8.

Campbell, J.C. and K.L. Soeken. 1999. 'Forced Sex and Intimate Partner Violence: Effects on Women's Risk and Women's Health', in *Violence Against Women*. Vol. 5.

Campbell, J.C. and P. Alford. 1989. 'The Dark Consequences of Marital Rape', in *American Journal of Nursing*. Vol. 89.

Devika, J. and P. Kodoth. 2001. 'Sexual Violence and Predicament of Feminist Politics in Kerala', *Economic and Political Weekly*, August 18.

———. 1999. 'Making Sex Violent: Love as Force in Recent Hindi Films', in *Violence Against Women*. Vol. 5.

———. 1995. *Culture in Action: Family Life, Emotion and Male Dominance in Banaras, India*, Albany: State University of New York Press.

Dreze, J. and A. Sen. 1989. *Hunger and Public Action*, Oxford: Claren on Press.

Dutton, M.A. et al. 2005. 'Patterns of Intimate Partner Violence: Correlates and Outcomes', in *Violence and Victims*, Vol. 20, No. 5.

Eapen, M., and P. Kodoth. 2003. 'Family Structures, Women's Education, and Work: Re-Examining the High Status of Women in Kerala' in S. Mukhopadhyay and R. Sudarshan (eds.), *Tracking Gender Equity under Economic Reforms*, New Delhi: Kali for Women.

Eby, K.K. and J.C. Campbell. 1995. 'Health Effects of Experiences of Sexual Violence for Women with Abusive Partners', in *Women's Health Care International*. Vol. 14.

Gandhi, N. and N. Shah. 1992. *The Issue at Stake: Theory and Practice in the Contemporary Women's Movements in India*, New Delhi: Kali for Women.

George, A. 2002. 'Embodying Identity through Heterosexual Sexuality: Newly Married Adolescent Women in India', in *Culture, Health and Sexuality*, Vol. 4, No. 2.

George, A., and S. Jaswal. 1995. 'Understanding Sexuality: An Ethnographic Study of Poor Women in Bombay, India', in *Women and AIDS Research Program Report Series No. 12*, Washington DC: ICRW.

Government of India. 2005. *Mid-Term Appraisal of 10th Five Year Plan (2002–2007)*, New Delhi: Planning Commission.

Government of Kerala. 2006. *Human Development Report 2005: Kerala*, Kerala: State Planning Board.

Heise, L. 1998. 'Violence against Women: An Integrated Ecological Framework', in *Violence Against Women*, Vol. 43, No. 3.

INCLEN. 2000. *Domestic Violence in India 3: A Summary Report of a Multi-site Household Survey.* Washington DC: ICRW and CEDPA.

Jejeebhoy, S.J., I. Shah and S. Thapa (eds.). 2005. *Sex Without Consent: Young People in Developing Countries*, London and New York: Zed Books.

Jewkes, R. 2002. 'Preventing Sexual Violence: A Rights-Based Approach', in *Lancet*, Vol. 360.

Joshi, A., M. Dhapola and E. Kurian. 2001. 'Experiences and Perceptions of Marital Sexual Relationships among Rural Women in Gujarat, India', in *Asia-Pacific Population Journal*, Vol. 16, No. 2.

Khan, M.E., J.W. Townsend, R. Sinha and S. Lakhanpal. 1996. 'Sexual Violence within Marriage', in *Seminar*, Vol. 447.

Kodoth, P. 2005. 'Fostering Insecure Livelihoods: Dowry and Female Seclusion in Left Developmental Contexts in West Bengal and Kerala', in *Economic and Political Weekly*, June 18.

Koenig, M., R. Stephenson, S. Ahmad, S.J. Jejeebhoy and J. Campbell. 2006. 'Individual and Contextual Determinants of Domestic Violence in North India', in *American Journal of Public Health*, Vol. 96, No. 1.

Maitra, S. and S.L. Schensul. 2004. 'The Evolution of Marital Relationships and Sexual Risk in an Urban Slum Community in Mumbai', in R.K. Verma, P.J. Pelto, S.L. Schensul and A. Joshi (eds.), *Sexuality in the Time of AIDS*, New Delhi: Sage Publications.

Majumdar, B. 2004. 'An Exploration of Socio-Economic, Spiritual, and Family Support among HIV-Positive Women in India', in *Journal of the Association of Nurses in AIDS Care*, Vol. 15, No. 3.

Panda, P. 2003. 'Rights-Based Strategies in the Prevention of Domestic Violence', Working Paper No. 344, Centre for Development Studies, Thiruvananthapuram, Kerala.

———. 2004. 'Domestic Violence Against Women in Kerala'. Discussion Paper No. 86, Kerala Research Programme on Local Level Development, Centre for Development Studies, Thiruvananthapuram, Kerala.

————. 2006. 'Domestic Violence and Women's Property Ownership: Delving Deeper into the Linkages in Kerala', in International Center for Research on Women (ed.), *Property Ownership and Inheritance Rights of Women for Social Protection: The South Asia Experience, Synthesis Report of Three Studies,* Washington DC: ICRW.

Panda, P., and B. Agarwal. 2005. 'Marital Violence, Human Development and Women's Property Status in India', in *World Development,* Vol. 33, No. 5.

Patel, V., B.R. Kirkwood, H. Weiss, S. Pednekar et al. 2005. 'Chronic Fatigue in Developing Countries: Population Based Survey of Women in India', in *British Medical Journal,* Vol. 330, No. 7501.

Ramasubramanian, S., and M.B. Oliver. 2003. 'Portrayals of Sexual Violence in Popular Hindi Films, 1997–99' in *Sex Roles,* Vol. 48, Nos. 7/8.

Santhya, K.G., and S.J. Jejeebhoy. 2005. 'Young Women's Experiences of Forced Sex within Marriage: Evidence from India', in S.J. Jejeebbhoy, I. Shah and S. Thapa (eds.), *Sex Without Consent: Young People in Developing Countries,* London and New York: Zed Books.

Singh, K. 2004. 'Violence against Women and the Indian Law', in S. Goonesekere (ed.), *Violence Law and Women's Rights in South Asia,* New Delhi: Sage Publications.

Sodhi, G., and M. Verma. 2003. 'Sexual Coercion among Unmarried Adolescents of an Urban Slum in India', in S. Bott, S.J. Jejeebhoy, I. Shah et al. (eds.), *Towards Adulthood: Exploring the Sexual and Reproductive Health of Adolescents in South Asia,* Geneva: WHO.

World Health Organization (2002). *World Report on Violence and Health,* Geneva: WHO.

6

Implications of Ageing with Special Reference to Women

ANUPAMA DATTA

M ost of us think about elderly women as an over-assertive member of the family whose main occupation is to ensure that the life of the daughter-in-law becomes miserable. The subtle message is that she is the wielder of patriarchal authority in the family and is most often an instrument of patriarchal exploitation of younger women. This image no doubt has its basis in reality, but is that all there is to the elderly women in our society? Are these not the same women who willingly accepted all the disadvantages of illiteracy, malnutrition, dispossession of property, and lack of access to resources when they were young? Life might not have been a bed of roses for many of them when they were young, and if that was the case then how have they turned out to be manipulative aggressors? There is an urgent need to look beyond this stereotypical image and find out the real status of elderly women in India in view of their increasing longevity and the changing social realities.

Issues concerning elderly women in India are an area of increasing concern for many reasons. Firstly, in 2002, the sex ratio (men per 100 women) for the 60+population was 91:100 and it reduced to 81 in the 80+ population. Around 75 per cent men in the age group of 60+ were currently married as compared to 42 women in the same age category.[1] Life expectancy at the age of 60 years (2000–2050) was 16 years for men as compared to 18 for women. The implication of this is feminisation of the ageing population. In the coming years, these women will form a segment of society that will be completely dependent on members of their family and/or community for survival. Their dependence will be qualitatively different from that of ageing males for the simple reason of socially and culturally induced dependence on males.

According to Census 2001, 7.4 per cent of the population in the country is over the age of 60 years, which is an increase over 6.8 per cent in 1991. The proportion of older males has increased from 6.7 per cent in 1991 to 7.1 per cent in 2001, whereas the proportion of older females in the same duration has gone up from 6.8 per cent to 7.8 per cent.

In rural areas, the proportion of older persons has increased from 7.1 per cent (1991) to 7.7 per cent (2001). The proportion of older females in rural areas increased from 7 per cent to 8.1 per cent, whereas that of older males increased marginally from 7.2 per cent to 7.4 per cent in the same period. In urban areas, the trends are more or less the same, but the proportion is somewhat less. Around 6.7 per cent of the elderly lived in the country's urban areas, according to the 2001 Census; the corresponding figure for 1991 was 5.7 per cent. The percentage of older males increased marginally from 5.6 per cent in 1991 to 6.2 per cent in 2001, but the female population increased from 6 per cent to 7.2 per cent (ORGI, 2004). These trends also testify to the feminisation of ageing in India, though the pace is slower than that in developed countries.

Most women in India live in the shadow of their male relatives through-out their lives—father, husband, son, nephew brother, or uncle. In most cases, they do not earn money, and even when they do, their employment is often guided by family considerations so that most of them take up casual employment or under-employment so that they can shoulder their family responsibilities. Labour force participation in the 60+age group also reflects the secondary economic status of women in India; 59 per cent men as compared to 18 per cent women are included in the labour force. It is easy to defraud such women as their world view, in most cases, is limited to family and their kin group. Similar is the case with ownership of property. Most of the women do not own property, and even when they do, they do not manage it. They are completely dependent on the male members of the family for the fulfilment of all their basic needs. They cannot even go to the local doctor without a male relative accompanying them, even when they are fit to move around. With age, this dependence increases. Besides, it is culturally accepted that women are the nurturers and caregivers for the family and, in the process, neglect themselves. This can have terrible implications for elderly women as they tend to neglect their genuine needs. Effective steps should be taken urgently to ensure their healthy ageing and reduce the burden of ill health on the family and on the health care system.

Problems Faced by Older Women

The problems that elderly women face are more or less the same – health, economic and emotional insecurity, abuse and at times, crime. Combinations of various socioeconomic factors change the resulting disabilities. However, some challenges are common to all and this includes health and emotional insecurity.

Elderly women face specific health problems; they are prone to arthritis, osteoporosis, and hypertension, cervical and breast cancer, anaemia, dementia and, most of all, depression. It was revealed that 93 per cent older women suffered from depression. In the same study, it was found that about 88 per cent elderly women suffered from multiple geriatric problems and this increased their dependence on others. Nearly 23 per cent women were completely dependent, and 60 per cent were partially dependent on their caregivers (Kumar, 2000). The challenge in this case is doubled by the fact that women generally tend to underplay their health problems. They do not consult doctors unless the symptoms become obvious. In some cases they neglect their health due to preoccupation with taking care of their husbands. Illiteracy and lack of awareness makes matters worse. Those who visit medical facilities generally go to the primary health centres or hakims. The social emphasis on sacrifice by the mother and wife leads to nutritional deficiencies in women, which could create major health risks in old age.

Irrespective of class, qualification, educational background and marital status, elderly women face an emotional void in their life. Almost all women in India lead a family-centric life – their world revolves around their family; when they get old, they get sidelined by the same family because it no longer requires their services. As their children grow up and marry, their position and status in the family deteriorates even further. The elderly lady loses her status in the family due to the assertion of her right by the daughter-in-law to manage the household as she wants. Differences of opinion on seemingly minor matters like observance of religious taboos on food; lifestyle etc. might become irreconcilable. They are considered to be 'too interfering' and 'too demanding' by the family and often confined to a corner of the house. It is common to find elderly women complaining about blaring music, meat eating on certain auspicious days, etc.

Here, differences are observed according to the class and marital status of elderly women; in households where they have adequate resources and their husband is still alive, their 'idiosyncrasies' are 'tolerated'. But in the absence of either of these factors, they are either ignored completely or told to lie in a corner of the house. In some households, where the elderly are economically secure, this could lead to separation of the elderly from their adult children, but in lower middle class families, where the economic condition of the elderly is not so sound and they are partly dependent on their children, it becomes a perpetual source of bickering.

The specific problems faced by various sections of society may be described through the following cases. Rich, educated women may be economically self-sufficient or even have plenty of assets, but could still face problems of emotional insecurity and physical vulnerability. Such women are open to threats of crime and fraud by their own relatives or children. Single elderly women are particularly vulnerable. Imagine a situation where there is an 80 something older women living alone who has to depend on two young servants, or a landlady who has a rogue tenant. Such women would be a very 'attractive' target for miscreants as she would be too weak to resist and they would get away before help reached her. Newspapers have carried many such reports in the past couple of months, about elderly ladies being attacked and killed in the posh localities of Delhi.

Threat of abuse or security is not only from outsiders, but from the family itself. Imagine this: A 75 year old widow whose husband has left her a plush house in South Delhi and who has enough movable assets to see her through the twilight years of her life. Her children might think that she should share it all with them while she is still alive, they might think that she does not need a big house and so much money and so they start harassing her to part with it. What choice does she have? Complain to the police, knock the door of the court? But the significant question here is does she have the courage to do all that or the physical energy to follow up a case in court? All this is in addition to the agony of being harassed by the children she has nurtured all her life. The plight of women living in small towns and other areas could be worse. For, if children use fraudulent means to take away property, such women cannot move the Supreme Court, which is far away in Delhi.

Higher middle class professionally qualified women, who have worked as doctors, teachers and lecturers during their younger years and retired at the mandatory age of 58/60 years, are also economically secure and have well settled children. They may have some health problems that could be looked after and may be only minor irritants, but they have a big emotional gap in their lives. The family members may be so busy in their own affairs that they have no time to talk to them or to take them to a doctor/or a friend. They do not have any substantial role to play in their own house as the grandchildren are taken care of by professionals and the household chores are performed by paid help. They have nothing meaningful to do in life. So, they feel useless, ennui sets in and many of them face psychological problems due to this status and role loss.

Being an elderly woman without resources is bad enough, but some are unfortunate enough to be widows, in which situation they are most at the mercy of adult children. Their health and other needs become secondary to the needs of other members of the household. Nobody wants to 'waste' time or money on taking them to a doctor. They are often accused of blowing things out of proportion, of being too touchy about minor things in life, too adamant to change to the needs of changing times. Such women tend to suppress their real urgent health and nutritional needs and at times face severe depression. Most of the time, they feel they have become a piece of useless furniture! The quality of life of such women most often deteriorates and they neither have the will nor the means to change it. They cannot complain about this neglect to anyone for fear of destitution. In urban areas, community pressure is anyway insignificant. So, these elderly women have to bear their lot in silence.

Many elderly women find themselves forlorn in the world once they have done their job as home-makers. Their children immigrate to cities or foreign countries and they have to take care of their ailing husband in their old age, with only friends, relatives or neighbours to fall back on for help. Their life is not only devoid of the joys of grandparenthood, but also of the emotional support of their own children. The stress of caregiving in old age can tell on their own health, which, more often than not, they neglect. Mrs G had five children, all well settled in life, but all of them lived separately. Mrs G's husband had enough money to see them through their old age. Unfortunately, her husband fell ill and was bedridden for eight long years. Mrs G had to take care of him single-handedly. The children were only willing to shell out money to employ servants and professional help, which Mrs G refused. Needless to say that today she is a disillusioned person who is suffering from severe depression. However, to find meaning in life, she has started teaching poor girls in the neighbourhood.

This brings us to another major issue in the lives of older women, i.e. the role of caregiver to an ailing spouse for long periods of time. In worse cases, elderly women have no family member to support them, sometimes because their children have immigrated. This has many implications for the health of women. It challenges their physical capacity and causes tremendous stress, which could lead to serious psychological problems. Such women are anxious about the loss of their husband and thoughts of what will happen to them if they meet with the same fate. Who will take care of them? Community surveys have proved that, in general, women require more help with activities of daily living (ADL), but unfortunately, they are less likely to get such help. Men have less difficulty, but more people providing such help.

Psychological well-being is another major challenge which women face in old age and which becomes intractable because most people do not consider medical intervention necessary for it. However, all psychiatric books and mental health books establish gender differences in each concept of psychiatric symptoms, frequency, type, cause of disorder; appropriate treatment, adjustments needed, response to the post-treatment phase and long-term outcome.

The disability associated with mental illness in women is very high. It is more so when there is co-morbidity, which is invariably true for most women. The disability may take the form of physical problems like weakening vision, diabetes, breast cancer, cervical cancer, blood pressure, arthritis or any painful condition. Since women have more co-morbid conditions, the disability they suffer is also high.

The other reason to focus on the mental health of older women is because of its relation to the social support system and living conditions. Living alone is a risk for suicide and depression. Older women live alone because of widowhood, even if they are in a family, and often they are lonely.

Irrespective of sex, there are three major mental health concerns – dementia, delirium and depression. Dementia is basically a disease of longevity, so the longer you live, the greater the probability that you may have dementia and women out-survive men. In Alzheimer's, which also leads to dementia, there seems to be a gender specific gene. So, women are more at risk for Alzheimer's as well. Women are more prone to the conditions of delirium because they are more sensitive to drug effects and to toxicity. Depression is the commonest mental disorder found in older people and the incidence of depression in older women is very high. There are some interesting facts about depression:

- The lifetime risk for depression is 7–12 per cent in men and a massive 25 per cent in women.
- Community based surveys show that women across all ages, across all countries and in all cultures, are more prone to depression than men. And the reason for the higher depression in women has been attributed to socialisation practices and gender roles.
- More than one-third of depression in women goes untreated because it is not properly diagnosed. Depression has a way of masquerading as several other things, for example, physical problems, physical illness, and somatic complaints.

- Women who are providing care to a sick or disabled spouse are six times more likely to suffer from depression than non-caregiving spouses.

Surveys show that women report lower self-satisfaction, and more psychological distress across life span, and that they have more chronic ailments and several different types of symptoms. Over and above this, if the women have a gynaecological morbidity, it exacerbates or augments the disability. There is a direct correlation between gynaecological morbidity, depression and other psychological problems. The symptoms have a more disabling influence.

Some ways of tackling this problem of mental health, or even physical health, as there is a direct relationship between the two, are:

- Adopt a life-cycle perspective. Take care of the girl child today so as to have healthier older women tomorrow.
- View women's conditions in the sociocultural context in which they live, whether they have access to resources, whether they can access health facilities, whether they are counted at all in the statistics.
- Be responsive to the multiple sources of operation. Do not just count women's health in terms of whether they are healthy or not healthy, but examine the factors that influence their health.
- Recognise the diversity of context of women to appreciate the differences in the needs of urban from rural women, class, groups like marginalised groups, dalits, tribals, etc.
- Only when women's family roles are disturbed do fanilies wake up to the fact that they may have a psychiatric problem. Take this fact into consideration and raise awareness about these issues.
- Improve the general or social condition of women. The health of women cannot be improved in isolation, especially mental health. Physical illness, disability, presence of disability, extent of disability, economic insecurity, widowhood, poor social network – all these are factors that influence mental health at all stages, especially during old age.
- The real challenge of implementing the National Programme for Older Persons (NPOP) is in providing universal access to mental health services. Care programmes for the elderly could piggyback on the ICDS programme as it reaches rural, urban and tribal areas. Make geriatric care at least the primary referral and identification part of the ICDS scheme.

- Develop culturally acceptable methods to create certain provisions that people may use with ease. There is resistance against day care centres from conventional families. At the same time, make efforts to change mindsets by using Anganwadi workers, mobile medicare units, etc.
- Add a mental health component to all health care programmes. At least, a bit of screening and a bit of referral must be added. This would accrue additional benefits at no extra cost.
- Sensitise community mental health workers to ageing issues because they usually focus on able-bodied young people in the labour force, ofter ignoring older persons.
- Community education programmes are very crucial in addressing cultural factors and improving the general social status of women.
- Form older women's groups and women's self-help groups. These can go a long way in improving mental health because loneliness is a real acute problem. They can also help change mindsets.
- Make efforts to change the mindsets of not only people, especially men, but also of medical personnel, especially in the absence of geriatric medicine, of mental health workers and of women themselves.
- To plan for health delivery, first of all, we need sex de-segregated data, and there is need for sex-segregated data on every count and on every parameter, data on the social basis of mental illness, research on older women's perceptions and perceptions of the health and service system.
- Build positive mental health in women. Positive mental health is directly related to improved social resources; women's groups' *satsangs* or *mahilla mandals* may work to improve the social resources preventive practices, educate women on how to improve themselves, how to keep active and stress management and effective educational methods.

Older Women in Rural Areas

There is a special case for analysing the challenges that face older women living in rural areas. According to the NSSO data, 85 per cent of elderly women are economically dependent on relatives for partial or full support (NSSO, 2006). Even those who are independent are usually working in low-skilled, low-paid jobs like agricultural labour, domestic work, etc. These jobs do not provide enough during the productive years, and in old age, there is no income security for most such women. They have to earn till they can just to survive. Another related feature is that of mobility. The same NSSO report stated that in rural areas, the ratio of older women with difficulty in movement or confined to bed increased with age and 32.6 per cent of women over the age of 80 reported these problems.

Another notable feature is that of family support for older women. The NSSO survey found that in states such as Tamil Nadu and Uttaranchal, more than 15 per cent older women lived alone.

Policy makers and service providers like NGOs should devise special programmes for older women living in rural areas so that their economic and health security is effectively addressed.

Policy Intervention

In the section entitled Principle Areas of Intervention and Action Strategies, the NPOP released by the Government of India in the year 1999 acknowledges and addresses concerns of elderly women. The NPOP states that in India, in 1991, there were four times as many widows as compared to widowers; it acknowledges the vulnerability of single older women as few persons are willing to take care of non-lineal relatives and destitute widows. It is sensitive to the fact that older persons, particularly women, become soft targets for criminals and victims of fraudulent dealings and physical and emotional abuse within the household by family members, who could take away their money and property. Widows' rights of inheritance, occupancy and disposal are at times violated by their own children and relatives. It is important that protection be made available to them. It therefore, makes a commitment that introduction of special provisions in the Indian Penal Code to protect older persons from domestic violence will be considered and machinery provided to attend all such cases promptly. It also promises to review tenancy legislation so that the rights of occupancy of older persons are restored speedily (NPOP, 1991).

Concrete Steps that Could be Taken

In order to address the issues of economic insecurity of elderly women, rather than an outright welfare approach, the government should adopt a rational approach that is a right mix of enterprise and welfare. Women in the age group of 60–75 years who are willing to work should be encouraged to form cooperatives and earn their living. NGOs could assist such women to develop their skills and get credit on reasonable terms from micro-credit schemes. However, the toughest challenge would be to convince older women that they still have the potential to learn new skills and start an enterprise. So, again, NGOs and social workers should be entrusted with this task as they have better communication skills to deal with hardened attitudes. Those who are incapacitated and very old, say, 80 years and more, may be considered for outright help and given money so that the family does not treat them as a burden.

This approach of encouraging enterprise will not only help older women financially, but also give them an opportunity to develop cordial relations with fellow women workers, which would lessen their dependence on their own family. A fellow worker could take an ailing older woman to a local doctor, they would be able to talk to each other about their problems and probable solutions. Solving each other's problems may lessen the feeling of uselessness in them.

Care should be taken to simplify administrative procedures so that illiterate women are also able to take advantage of these schemes. NGOs should be enlisted to give wide publicity to these schemes.

The curriculum for geriatrics and gerontology for medical/paramedical and support services faculties should be sensitive to the health and nutrition concerns of women. The medical fraternity should be able to address the specific health concerns of older women. NGOs and primary health centre staff should be encouraged to spread awareness among women about these issues and the importance of healthy ageing. This is very important as women tend to neglect their health.

The security concerns of older women are of particular importance as they may not be able to deal with such situations adequately. There should be changes in the Indian Penal Code keeping in mind the disabilities older women face. Moreover, there should be collaboration between NGOs and the local police to prevent such crimes, whether perpetrated by the family or by outsiders. NGOs could run a helpline and inform the local police about any such reported crimes, harassment or abuse. The police and volunteers should also carry out a regular round of the identified families of the areas where older persons, particularly women, live. The Delhi Police has introduced such a scheme of regular visits by policemen to the identified houses of senior citizens on a limited basis. The beat officers in the area have been directed to make a list of senior citizens and help ensure a secure environment for them. Under the plan, the local Station House Officer (SHO) visits such households every first Saturday of the month and the beat constable visits once a week on Sundays. The Delhi Police has listed so far 3,325 senior citizens living alone, under the scheme, and it claims that more than 3,200 of these have been visited by the police. The beat constables have been instructed to maintain close contact with the senior citizens' neighbours, the local resident welfare associations and ensure proper verification of their servants and drivers. The police will provide the older people with the addresses and telephone numbers of NGOs they can call in an emergency. The South District has launched the Police at Your Doorstep Scheme, in which senior police officers meet older people during their morning walks.[2] The Delhi Police will soon start a helpline for senior citizens living alone.[3]

Steps taken by the government, NGOs and security agencies go a long way in reducing threats to older women, but the family still remains the most important institution in an Indian woman's life. She nurtures it with all her capacity throughout her 'productive years' in the hope that when she gets old and frail, these very members will take care of her. However, in the context of industrialisation the family has undergone some changes, and its structure and functions are no longer the same. However, it would not be practical to advise older women to sever all ties with their family and expect nothing from their children. Therefore, one needs to work on the policies and programmes that support families to take care of older women. Counselling of both the young and the old to adjust to each is necessary and new methods of conflict management should be taught to people so that they live in their own families without becoming a nuisance to each other.

Special programmes should be devised for rural elderly women, particularly those who are poor and backward. The effort should be to include them in micro-credit and self-help group programmes so that they can save money and take credit to start micro-enterprises.

Health care, particularly, preventive health care programmes should target older women in rural areas to decrease the morbidity level in old age. Curative health care should be available at the block level as they may find it impossible to go to tertiary health care institutions at the district level.

In this regard, it is important to take a cue from other countries and try and examine the possibility of adapting those programmes to Indian conditions. A few examples are given below:

In 1991, Malaysia[4] launched menopause management services for older women as part of its life-span approach to reproductive health. This programme developed an educational booklet on menopause, its symptoms and its long-term health risks. It encourages menopausal women to actively manage their own health. A prominent role was given to NGOs to ensure the reach of these messages to broader audiences at public forums. Besides, regular screening was conducted for breast and cervical cancer at clinics and in public outreach programmes for underserved and marginalised groups.

The programme identified and responded to the following challenges to ensure success:

- Client motivation: To attract older women to new health care services and sustain their interest, materials and activities that raised their awareness of the health problems associated with meno-pause and ageing were developed. Providers encouraged the con-tinuity of care by informing women about the long-term benefits.
- Affordability: Drugs were made affordable to all segments of the population.

In Thailand,[5] grandmothers who are frail and in poor health them-selves have to deal with the physical effort, emotional stress, and social stigma associated with caring for people with HIV/AIDS. The Grandma Cares projects tries to make their job easier by giving them the skills and support they need to handle the role of caregiver and by training other family members to help. The programme involves a one-day training session on home-care skills covering topics such as universal precautions and nutrition and demonstrates practical nursing skills. This gives the participants an opportunity to exchange stories, express their feelings, and ask questions. The programme was designed to provide regular, ongoing support, which continues after training. It also encourages the community to share in the caregiving role

Notes

1. www.un.org.esa/population/publications/ageing/graph.pdf
2. *The Times of India*. New Delhi: May 1, 2003.
3. *The Hindustan Times*. New Delhi: May 1, 2003.
4. www.rho.org
5. Ibid.

References

Bagchi, Kalyan (ed.). 1997. *Elderly Females in India: Their Status and Suffering*, New Delhi: Society for Gerontological Research and HelpAge India.

Bali, Arun P. 2001. *Care of the Elderly: Changing Configurations*, Shimla: Indian Institute of Advanced Study.

Chen, Martha Alter (ed.). 1998. *Widows in India: Social Neglect and Public Action*, New Delhi: Sage Publications.

Dey, A.B. (ed.). 2003. *Ageing in India: Situation Analysis and Planning for Future*, New Delhi: WHO and Ministry of Health and Family Welfare, Government of India.

Kumar, Vijay S. 2000. 'Elderly Women in Rural India: Need for Health Policy Intervention' in P.C. Bhatta (ed.), *Lecture Series in Geriatrics*. New Delhi: Health Care Promotion Trust, pp. 274–277.

Meenai, Zubair. 2003. *Empowering Rural Women: An Approach to Empowering Women Through Credit Based Self Help Groups*, Delhi: Aakar Books.

Ministry of Social Justice and Empowering. 1999. *National Policy on Older Persons.* New Delhi: Government of India.

National Sample Survey Organisation. 2004. Morbidity, Health Care and the Condition of the Aged. NSS 60th Round, January–June 2004. New Delhi: Ministry of Planning and Programme Implementation, 2006.

ORGI. 2004. *Report and Tables on Age*, Vol. 1, New Delhi: Government of India.

Roy, P.K. 2000. *The Indian Family: Change and Persistence,* New Delhi: Gyan Publishing House.

Singh, Arun K. 2000. *Empowerment of Women in India*, New Delhi: Manak Publishers.

WHO and International Network for the Prevention of Elder Abuse. 2000. Missing Voices: Voices of Older Persons on Elder Abuse: Research Report.

7

Gender Equality in Education
Assessing Gains and Reviewing Challenges in Rajasthan

SHOBHITA RAJAGOPAL

The National Policy on Education (NPE), 1986, was announced two decades ago and the subsequent Programme of Action, 1992, laid stress on 'Education for Women's Equality'. It emphasised that "education will be used as an agent of basic change in the status of women and in order to neutralise the accumulated distortions of the past, there will be a well-conceived edge in favour of women. The National Education System will play a positive interventionist role in the empowerment of women." The focus was both on education, social equality and empowerment.

In the past two decades, various national policies and plans have reflected a vision of progress and there has been an increase in the spaces available for women in India. But there exists a paradox – on the one hand there are significant gains, on the other, gender-based inequalities are evident in almost all spheres and do not need to be specially established. The culture of patriarchy and the neglect of the girl child determine both the quantity and quality of entitlements and investments made in girls. Translating the goals of gender equality into reality has been slow and the girl child emerges as an extremely vulnerable category, cutting across social groups as well as geographic locations.

In the education sector, the cumulative experience shows that there is a keen desire to educate children even among the most disadvantaged and marginalised and, given the right environment, parents are willing to educate girls. There is also a certain degree of agreement about constraints on education and about the strategies that work.

However, despite increase in literacy rates in the decade of the 1990s, closing the gender gap in education remains a challenge in many parts of the country and continue to impede universal elementary education efforts. The official estimate for out of school children in the age group of 6–14 was 35 million in 2000, the majority of which were girls (National Plan of Action, 2003, as quoted in Ramachandran, 2004). The National Family Health Survey (NFHS) reveals that nearly 40 per cent of the girls in the 11+ age group in rural India were not attending any educational programme in 1998–99. Further, even if they were attending school, a vast majority of them drop out before completing the requisite eight years of education. The drop-out rates for girls at the primary and elementary level continue to be high, i.e., 33.7 and 53.5, respectively. The situation of girls from the Scheduled Caste (SC) and Scheduled Tribe (ST) groups is even more serious. Almost twice as many girls as boys are pulled out of school or never sent to school in order to assist in household chores.

The recent National Curriculum Framework, 2005 flags the importance of including and retaining all children in school, and enabling all children to experience the dignity and confidence to learn. It further draws attention to the importance of school ethos and culture, classroom practices of teachers, learning sites outside the school and learning resources, all issues that are extremely important in relation to reducing gender inequalities in education.

The Annual Report of the Ministry of Human Resource Development (2004–05) reaffirms its commitment to providing Education for All and states that the National Programme for Education of Girls at the Elementary Level, a component of the Sarva Shiksha Abhiyan (SSA) will provide additional support for girls education in educationally backward blocks and that in the 10th Five-Year Plan, an amount of Rs 1,064.80 crore has been earmarked for this programme.

Further, the report of the CABE Committee on Universalisation of Secondary Education (2005) points out that given the targets of achieving Universal Elementary Education (UEE) by 2010 and the anticipated progress in universalising elementary education, there is a need to take proactive measures to plan and provide for universal secondary education. It is evident that universalising secondary education is only possible when all girls passing out of elementary school enters secondary school.

The present paper focuses on presenting an overview of education in Rajasthan and analysing the specific realities with reference to different levels of education. It is divided into three sections. Section I presents the development context of Rajasthan, including crucial indicators related to the status of women and girls. Section II presents a detailed analysis of girls education in Rajasthan to understand the gender dimensions in educational access, attainment and the challenges ahead. It also looks at the various policy initiatives undertaken by the state to promote girls' education. Section III looks at the direction ahead and offers some suggestions.

I
Profiling the Context

The state of Rajasthan is the largest state in India, situated in the North-west of the country, with a geographical area of 3,42,239 square kilometres. A great part of Rajasthan is arid and semi-arid and forms a major part of the Thar desert. The vastly varied geographical and eco-logical dimensions of the state, i.e., large desert areas, scattered settle-ments and poor communication systems, make it difficult to deliver basic services of health, education and potable water to people. Frequent drought due to scanty and irregular rainfall exposes households with a fragile livelihood base to various uncertainties, risks and stress which have a direct impact on children's access to resources of health and education and development opportunities.

The profile of the state indicates that while some development indi-cators have shown improvement in the last decade, i.e., sex ratio (adult) and literacy, other indicators are not so positive. The Census of India 2001 recorded a population of 56,507,188 in the state. It indicates that Rajasthan has maintained its record of registering one of the highest population growth rates in the country since independence. The total fertility rate in the state was high at 3.25 in 2001 and this has resulted in a compound growth of the population at 2.51 per cent between 1991 and 2001. The infant mortality rate in the state has not improved as much as it has in most other states (IDS, 2006). Rajasthan's ranking among Indian states is ninth according to the Planning Commission's Human Development Report of 2001. The northern districts of the state are seen to be performing better on the human development scale; at the bottom end are the southern districts, which are also predominantly tribal (IDS, 2006). The gender development index (GDI) is also indicative of the range of gender inequalities prevalent in the state.

One of the most crucial indicators of status of women in any society is the sex ratio. The Census of India 2001recorded the overall sex ratio in Rajasthan at 922 as compared to 910 in 1991. This has been both 'significant...and the highest ever recorded since 1901'. Most of the districts in the state have shown an increasing sex ratio in the period from 1991 to 2001, except Sirohi where the sex ratio decreased from 949 to 944. However, this increase in overall sex ratio conceals a very high and significant decline in the sex ratio in the age group of 0–6 years. Rajasthan, like other states in northwestern India, belongs to the category in which an adverse sex ratio is a crucial concern.

The child sex ratio in the state was recorded at 909 in 2001 as compared to 916 in 1991. (Child sex ratio is defined as the number of girls per thousand boys in the age group of 0–6 years). The decrease of seven points at the state level is serious. Out of 32 districts, 21 districts reported a decline. None of the districts has recorded a child sex ratio favouring girls. This pattern is comparable to the all-India level, where the child sex ratio has declined by 18 points from 945 to 927.

Sex ratios are worst in the western and northern regions as compared to the southern and southeastern regions. This decline has been attributed to factors like strong son preference in most communities, and practices of female infanticide and female foeticide. It is clearly indicative of the low value and secondary status of the girl child in a state where patriarchal norms and practices continue to operate. Modern technologies like amniocentesis are used for sex selective abortions and have exacerbated discrimination against the girl child.

The health situation in Rajasthan is characterised by poor availability of health services, poor nutrition among children and women, and high infant and maternal mortality rates. Many interrelated factors impinge upon and shape the health and nutritional status of girls and women. Because of the low value attached to girls from birth, health care, even when it is available, is not accessible and does not reach a large proportion of girls and women. Girls are often discriminated against in distribution of food and nutrition. The 'culture of silence' around reproductive health issues prevents them from accessing information related to their own bodies. According to NFHS 2, more than one-third (36 per cent) of women have a body mass index (BMI) of below 18.5, which indicates a high prevalence of nutritional deficiency. For the 88 per cent of women in the state who were tested for haemoglobin levels, 49 per cent had some degree of anaemia (NFHS 2, 1998–99). Several programmes are being implemented in the state on reproductive and child health, but the current health situation in Rajasthan indicates that goals of universal health care are yet to be realised and that there are substantial shortfalls in the efficacy of the public health system in the state.

Violence against women in Rajasthan is closely linked to their subordinated status. Practices like female infanticide and female foeticide are extreme forms of violence, indicating devaluation of girls in any society. In a study conducted recently in the districts of Barmer and Jaisalmer, interviews with rural women revealed several methods of female infanticide that continue to exist. Often the family members instruct the midwife to suffocate the infant with a small bag containing sand the moment it is confirmed that the infant is a girl; or the neck of the infant is pressed under the foot of the wooden bed. The midwife is paid a small sum of money for this act (Mathur, 2004).

The practice of child/early marriage is common in the state. Child marriages take place on certain auspicious occasions like Akha Teej, Peepal Punio and Phulera Duj. The common perception and interpretation is 'instead of having to spend on the wedding of each daughter repeatedly, when the oldest daughter of the family is married all the younger ones are 'married', too. This saves money. Marrying the child young and having the *gauna* (the time when co-habitation begins) later splits the expenditure. Child marriage inevitably leads to withdrawal of girls from school and has several intergenerational consequences. Every year, the Department of Women and Child of the state government organises campaigns against child marriages. But experience indicates that police action against the families performing child marriages is often counter-productive.

Another area of crucial concern is trafficking of young girls/women from the state. Several communities sanction sex work in Rajasthan, which makes women more vulnerable to trafficking. The subordination of women, along with the social construction of their sexual identities make them more vulnerable to this form of exploitation. More often, various forms of male dominance have pushed women into this profession and men tend to legitimise this trade within their own community in terms of tradition. In a recent exploratory study, Trafficking of Women and Children in Rajasthan, it is revealed that inter- as well as intra-state trafficking is a common phenomenon in Rajasthan. Many girls are trafficked from poor families of different parts of the country into Rajasthan. Also, Rajasthan is one of the main source areas for trafficking of women and girls for sex work (IDSJ, 2003).

The need to ensure participation of girls in the educational process assumes greater significance, given the existence of deeprooted prejudices and the gender discriminatory practices faced by women and girls in the state.

II
Understanding Gender Dimensions in Education

This section presents a detailed analysis of the situation of girls' access to educational opportunities, enrolment and achievement both at the primary and secondary levels. It also focuses on understanding the various initiatives taken by the state to promote girls' education.

Gains in Literacy

Rajasthan made considerable progress in improving its literacy status in the last decade. According to the Census of India 2001, the overall literacy rate rose to 61.03 per cent as compared to 38.55 per cent in 1991. The net increase in literacy rate during the decade, 1991–2001, is 22.4 per cent, the highest in India. Rajasthan is also one of the states where the absolute number of non-literates reduced in 2001. Women's literacy increased more than double from 20.44 per cent in 1991 to 44.34 per cent in 2001, though the gender gap continues.

Table 1: Comparison of State Literacy Rate with National Levels

Year	Rajasthan			India		
	Persons	Males	Females	Persons	Males	Females
1971	19.07	28.74	8.46	34.45	45.95	21.97
1981	30.11	44.77	14.00	43.56	56.37	29.75
1991	38.55	54.99	20.44	52.21	64.13	39.69
2001	61.03	76.46	44.34	65.38	75.85	54.16

Note: 1971 literacy rates relate to population aged five years and above, whereas 1981 1991, 2001 relate to population aged seven years and above.
Source: Census of India, 1971/91/2001.

The districtwise figures indicate that Barmer and Jalore, the only two districts to have a single digit literacy rate for women in the country in 1991, improved their status in 2001.

The improvements in overall literacy rates of women seem to be encouraging. The cumulative gains of various innovative educational programmes like the Women's Development Project (WDP), Shikshakarmi Project (SKP), Lok Jumbish (LJ), District Primary Education Programme (DPEP) and Total Literacy Campaign (TLC) can be seen in the achievements in literacy in the state.

According to the Annual Report 2004–05 of the Department of Education, 6,158 literacy camps were organised, wherein 1.54 lakh women were imparted literacy skills.

Girls' Participation in Schooling

Box 1: Laxmi

14-year-old Laxmi of Sanjanwia village in Banswara belongs to a poor tribal family dependent on agriculture and wage labour. Laxmi was enrolled in the primary school in the village and completed her primary level with a first division. She was extremely keen on continuing her studies, but could not due to her mother's illness. She discontinued her studies because she had to take on her mother's household responsibilities. Today, Laxmi spends her time doing all the household chores, i.e., cleaning/sweeping the house, milching cattle, collecting cow dung, fetching water and cooking. Laxmi also goes to the primary school to prepare the mid-day meal for the students there and is paid Rs 7.50 per day. Laxmi says that if she had not dropped out of school she would have completed her education and become a teacher and would have helped her father to pay off the family's debts.

Understanding Childhood Poverty in Rajasthan, Field Reports, IDSJ, 2004

The case of Laxmi is not unique but is the reality of a large majority of girls in Rajasthan. Almost any discussion on educational access and educational backwardness invariably begins with stories of unequal access, persistence of caste prejudices and situation of girls and women. The female disadvantage in basic education, a part of their historical legacy, also links up with the deeprooted features of gender relations in the state as discussed earlier. The gender division of labour, which relegates most adult women (including those with relatively good education) to domestic work, diminishes the perceived 'returns' of investment in female education. The prevailing norms of village exogamy and patrilocal postmarital residence imply that these returns (along with other benefits of female education) flow primarily to their future in-laws rather than to their parents. A few recent studies have also explored gender and equity questions and the picture that is revealed is disturbing (Probe, 1999; Wazir, 2000; Vaidyanathan and Nair, 2001; and Ramachandran, 2004).

Schooling Facilities and Infrastructure

Access to schooling for a girl is strongly influenced by the availability of a school within reach. In Rajasthan, there has been considerable expansion in the number of schools in the state, as a result of various educational initiatives such as the Shikshakarmi Programme, Lok Jumbish, DPEP and Rajiv Gandhi Swaran Jayanti Pathshalas (RGSJPs). The norm of having a educational facility within one kilometre of a habitation has largely been met. According to official reports there are 34,743 primary schools, 28,414 upper primary schools and 17,966 Rajiv Gandhi Swaran Jayanti Pathshalas functioning in the state. In 2004–05, out of a total of 2,445 schools that were upgraded to upper primary schools 179 were girls' schools (GoR, 2005).

At the secondary level, there are a total of 7,068 secondary schools and 3,638 senior secondary schools functioning in the state. Of these, 3,676 and 2,329 are government schools. The number of secondary schools and senior secondary schools for girls in the government sector are 363 and 399 respectively.

The mushrooming of private schools in rural areas has been an issue of debate in the state. The need for regulating these institutions has also been felt. But for a large proportion of girls, especially from poor and disadvantaged households, government schools are the only possible educational options.

While great progress has been made in the provisioning of elementary schooling in the state in the past decade, in many areas, villages are still divided into separate hamlets. Children from one hamlet find it difficult to reach the school in another hamlet because of the distance between the hamlets, especially during the rainy season. The issue of distance also gains significance from the point of view of girls as distance may inhibit their access to schooling. This is particularly so in the case of upper primary and secondary schools. The distance norms for opening new upper primary schools need to be reviewed.

School infrastructure has received attention in the past few years. The annual report of the Department of Education indicates that under the DPEP Phase I, as many as 719 new school buildings, 7,285 toilets and 1,905 additional classrooms were constructed. Around 1,215 hand-pumps have also been installed in school premises. Under the SSA, 1,571 new primary schools and 1281 new upper primary schools have been constructed along with 6,987 additional classrooms, 9,991 toilets and 1,241 headmaster rooms. Drinking water facilities have been provided to 3,345 schools (GoR, 2005). Further, the DISE report prepared by the department indicates that out of a total of 230,003 primary and upper primary government schools, 53,533 schools require minor and major repairs.

However, several research studies/surveys show that school infrastructure is far from adequate despite all the work undertaken. A large number of schools with five sections still have two rooms and a verandah. The condition in the tribal districts is poor and many schools are in need of repair (Nambissan, 2001; Majumdar, 2001; and IDS, 2000).

The issue of toilets has been fairly debated in the educational discourse. Ramachandran and Sahjee (2004) point out that in the microstudies taken up in DPEP states, the availability of toilets was perceived as being unimportant, at least at the primary stage. Only the teachers mostly used the toilets. Discussions with children revealed that they did not see toilet facilities as an encouraging or inhibiting factor in school attendance. On the other hand, the availability of drinking water was an important issue. In water scarce regions like Rajasthan, the question of keeping toilets clean is important. Field observations reveal that many of the newly constructed toilets are kept locked by the teachers. In the context of older girls, efforts to manage menstruation and hygiene would be an important area of intervention.

In the context of universalising secondary education, it is evident that the state is yet to prepare itself to meet the infrastructure demands at this level. The annual report of the Department of Secondary Education indicates that in 2005–06, 481 government upper primary schools were upgraded as secondary schools.

Enrolment and Attendance

Meeting the goals of the UEE demands that the gender gap be bridged in enrolment and achievements. The problem of enrolment disparity persists in Rajasthan, where the percentage of enrolment at the primary and upper primary stages is less than the national average. According to the latest official reports of the Government of Rajasthan, the total enrolment of children in elementary education (Grades I-VIII) in 2004–05 is 126.65 lakhs. The total enrolment of girls is 44.7 per cent. The enrolment of girls at the primary level is 46.2 per cent and of boys is 53.8 per cent. At the upper primary level, the enrolment of girls is 39 per cent as compared to 61 per cent for boys (GoR, 2005). While enrolment has been steadily rising, there is a significant gap in enrolment between boys and girls at the upper primary education level, which further confirms that upper primary education continues to be largely inaccessible to most girls.

The total enrolment of SC children is 24.54 lakhs. The percentage of boys enrolled is 56.2 and that of girls is 43.8. The total enrolment of ST children at the elementary level is 19.20 lakhs. The percentage of boys is 57.4 and girls is 42.6. The position of girls among the disadvantaged groups is also clearly visible.

The total enrolment of children in secondary and senior secondary schooling, in the age group of 14–17 years, is 18.66 lakhs, with one-third students being girls. This high level of gender disparity at the secondary level points out that girls tend to disappear from the education scenario past the age of 14 years, at a crucial age when aspirations can be channelled into opportunities. Nambissan (2001) in her study on disparities in schooling in the Alwar and Jhadol blocks of Rajasthan points out that in Jhadol only 35. 6 per cent children were enrolled. Boys predominated among the enrolled children: 45 per cent of boys to 25 per cent of girls were enrolled. A large majority (61 per cent) had never been enrolled. The pattern was much the same in Alwar district, though the percentage of enrolment of girls was twice as much. Enrolment rates also varied sharply among social groups. Enrolment rates of girls were lower than boys in all social groups, but strikingly so among Muslims (25 per cent) and Dalits (33 per cent).

The study, 'Understanding Childhood Poverty in Rajasthan', points out that given the nature of gender roles in the state, more girls than boys are out of school in the two districts taken up for study, Banswara and Tonk. In the 11-14 age group, around 60 per cent of boys and 25 per cent of girls in Banswara, and 80 per cent of boys and 45 per cent of girls in Tonk, were enrolled in school. Attendance on a 'normal' day shows that absenteeism is high. If we look at actual enrolment in school, it is evident that girls' enrolment continues to be lower than that of boys. The reasons cited by the teachers in Banswara for poor attendance of children were that the children accompany parents on short-term migration to the neighbouring areas of Ratlam for soyabean cultivation. Some of the older children were helping their parents with agricultural work (Bhargava, Mathur and Rajagopal, 2005).

Another report on the district that fall in the Dang area (Karauli, Dholpur, Baran, Jhalawar, Bundi, Kota and Sawai Madhopur), shows that out of a total of 441,900 children aged under 15 years, 63.8 per cent who are enrolled in elementary schools, 65.2 per cent are boys and 61.9 per cent are girls. The enrolment ratio works out low as compared to the all-Rajasthan average. The factors contributing to low enrolment include lack of infrastructure facilities and quality education (Sharma and Sharma, 2005). In nine districts, more than 40 per cent girls had never been enrolled in any school (Planning Commission, 2006).

Recent interactions with community leaders in the Mewat region reveal out that 30–40 per cent of enrolled children do not attend school and the percentage of girls among such children is more than 60 per cent.

Government data indicates that the gross enrolment ratio in primary schools is more than 107 per cent. However, field experiences show that a large number of children remain enrolled in the register, but do not attend school. It is also evident that enrolment statistics which are compiled from school registers through official sources are not checked directly for accuracy or validity. Nor do they reflect actual attendance or participation. The state government has been organising Praveshutsavs (intensive enrolment drives) at the beginning of the school term to enrol children in the 6–14 age group. These enrolment drives are organised by the teachers with help from the community. However, enrolment does not mean regular attendance, nor is it a guarantee that a child will continue in school. A large number of girls continue to be out of school or fall into the category of never enrolled.

Retention and Dropping Out

While there is ample evidence to show that parents can be motivated to send children to school, regular schooling requires a commitment and modification of lifestyle and gender roles to enable boys and girls to go to school.

One of the major problems confronting elementary education is the low level of retention in schools. Retention is defined as the number of children remaining in school till the end of a specific time period as a proportion of the number who enrolled at the beginning of the time period. A large percentage of children who enter Class I drop out before completing Class V. Social assessment studies carried out for DPEP districts in 2000 indicated that the retention rate for boys was 46.20 per cent and that for girls was 41.89 per cent (IDSJ, 2000).

Retention rates continue to be abysmally low in the state. Government data shows a retention rate of 60.15 per cent and a dropout rate of 39.85 per cent (GOR, 2005). However, recent studies indicate that the government estimates are often inflated. A study on retention in DPEP schools found the overall retention in DPEP–Phase I schools to be 43 per cent. There was no significant difference between retention of boys and girls (Sharma, Methi and Khan, 2003).

A survey in 2004–05 of 74 schools in Rajasthan shows a retention rate of 36 per cent (i.e., only 36 per cent of 1008 children entering Class I in 1999–2000 completed Class V in 2003–04) though 82 per cent children are shown to be enrolled in schools. In one village in Kotra block of Udaipur district, only three children passed out of Class V in 2003–04 from among the 113 enrolled in 1999–2000. In sample schools of the present study of children enrolled in Class I in 2000–01, only 36 per cent reached Class V in 2004–05. The study also identified various factors affecting grade to grade transition and retention in schools. Availability of infrastructure, i.e., toilets, sufficient classrooms, drinking water facilities and playgrounds, play a major role in the high enrolment, attendance and achievement levels of children. Besides, teachers' behaviour and attitude towards children contributes to low dropout rates among children. Teacher absenteeism is another reason for children dropping out from school. Livelihood constraints remain, by far, the most important factor: Children are forced to migrate with parents and/or work for a living. Children have to fetch water, fuelwood and work the family owned land and livestock. The livelihoods in the state are vulnerable to drought and the employment opportunities are poor, shifting the burden onto children to work for survival. There is no attempt to link livelihoods and schooling (Bhargava and Balana, 2005).

The dropout rates for girls after the primary stage is higher than for boys for all castes, but significantly higher for girls from scheduled castes and scheduled tribes. Nambissan (2001) points out that one of the main reasons why girls drop out was involvement in household work. Schooling was not considered by some parents to be socially desirable for older girls. Similarly, a number of parents from the Meo community were not in favour of co-education. The objection appeared not so much to male teachers as to older girls studying with boys.

Teachers

The total number of teachers at the elementary level is 1.76 lakhs, of which 25.7 per cent are women. To give a boost to girls' education, 8,485 women para-teachers have been appointed in government primary schools. The problem of teacher absenteeism and irregularity and single-teacher schools continues to persist.

At the secondary level, out of a total of 25,217 teachers in government schools, the number of women teachers is 4,589. Discussions with Department of Education functionaries reveal that there are a large number of posts lying vacant, and the selection and appointment process is so long and arduous that when there are policy announcements of upgrading and opening of new schools, there are no teachers in place.

A recurrent policy recommendation for improving girls' participation in schooling has been the appointment and presence of women teachers. In the Shikshakarmi Programme (SKP) implemented by the state government from 1987, consistent efforts were made to train and appoint Mahila Shikshakarmis to encourage girls' enrolment. The SKP experience shows that the appointment of women teachers facilitated a large number of girls enrolling in school (Rajagopal, 1999). While there is unanimity on the impact of women teachers, researchers and observers point out that a local person whom the community trusts and who is regular can make a significant impact. Conversely, frequent teacher absenteeism makes parents apprehensive about leaving their daughters unattended, especially in areas like Rajasthan (Ramachandran, 2004).

While lack of teacher motivation and lack of positive reinforcements have been seen as a major cause for poor teaching-learning in schools, an important aspect related to women teachers is the support provided to them within the mainstream system itself. There is a definite need to improve the status, conditions and career development opportunities of women. Given the state government's stated aim of improving girls' education, some issues which gain significance are: providing safety of school environment, understanding the multiple demands on women's time, provision of childcare services, minimising male domination in school management and assignment of decision-making jobs.

Quality of Schooling

The quality of classroom transaction in government schools or alternative schools/centres are important for both 'sustaining' and 'pushing' children in/from school. Even where children come from similar household backgrounds, their rates of survival through primary school are different. Reasons for this could be failure on the part of the school environment to keep the children motivated enough to come to school, lack of infrastructure and teaching and learning aids, or overcrowding in the classroom. The inability of teachers to generate interest in students about a subject clearly raises issues about pedagogy, especially for first generation learners. Fear of punishment has often been cited as another reason for non-participation in schooling, especially of poor children and girls (IDSJ, 2000).

The Annual Status of Education Report (ASER), 2005, notes that in Rajasthan 59 per cent children and 45.6 per cent children studying in Class V could read the story administered during the assessment and solve division and subtraction, respectively.

A study, 'Classroom Observation in Formal and Alternative Schools in DPEP', reveals that the average teacher-student ratio was 1:45, the teacher-student ratio in the Rajiv Gandhi Swaran Jayanti Pathshalas and alternative schools was adverse. In the 660 schools covered in the study, most of the teachers were trained teachers, but the desired effect of training could not be observed during the actual teaching process. Only 10 per cent teachers could link chapters to the existing knowledge of students and facilitate understanding through the use of local contexts. About 50 per cent teachers did not make any attempt to link the chapters or to explain with examples. Very little effort was made to explain difficult concepts through contextually relevant examples. The teachers also did not make an attempt to see whether the children finally understood the concepts. For 30 per cent teachers, using Teaching Learning Materials (TLM) was a mere formality. Most of the teachers had not been able to internalise the concept of TLM (Sandhan, 2004).

The childhood poverty study indicates that even the Shikshakarmis, or local teachers, who were trained in using child-friendly methods, have started resorting to conventional ways of teaching and classroom practices. No efforts are being made by the teachers to address the specific needs of the children or link what is learnt in school to their lives outside the school. In the RGSJPs in Banswara, the levels attained by children are poor because of the irregular attendance of teachers. The children in the 'ungraded' classes (Class I and II) could not read the alphabet or count. The teacher defended herself and insisted that the problem lay with the children as they speak a different dialect and do not understand Hindi. She also stated that most of the men in the village were drunk and that she felt insecure. In the RGSJP in Bairwon ki Dhani in Tonk, the general awareness levels of the children were high and it was clear that the teacher took a great deal of interest in teaching them. The teacher had made efforts to increase the enrolment of children in the school by establishing door to door contacts (Bhargava, et al., 2005).

It is obvious that education for all cannot be achieved without improving quality. Given that an overwhelming majority of poor children especially girls, go to government schools and among them the poorest, it is pertinent that decent learning conditions and opportunities exist and the standards of teaching and learning improve. Quality education also has to move beyond certification as the expected outcome

Incentives for Girls

Various incentives have been part of the official policy to promote girls' education. These include free distribution of textbooks for girls enrolled in the elementary stage, exemption of fees, and cash awards. The annual report of the Department of Secondary Education (2005–06) indicates that the following incentives are being given to promote girls education in the state.

- Free education will be provided to girls from Class I till graduation level.

- Free textbooks will be distributed to girls studying in government schools in Class I-XII
- 20 per cent reservation of seats out of 8,340 seats in teachers' training colleges for BEd and Shiksha Shastri courses. In addition, 6,450 seats in women teacher training colleges are also available.
- To promote secondary and senior secondary schooling for girls from rural areas, six girls' hostels, accommodating 50 girls each, have been established in the regional headquarters.
- The Balika Shiksha Foundation was established in 1994–95 to provide financial assistance to girls from economically poor backgrounds for higher and technical education.
- The Gargi Award has been instituted for girls attaining 75 per cent in the Board examinations – a cash prize of Rs 1,000 per year for two years. In 2005–06 this award was given to 10,804 girls.
- To facilitate transport for girls studying in Class IX-XII, free bus passes were announced in January 2006.

Very few studies, however, are available to show how these incentives have actually benefited girls.

Factors Impacting Girls' Access to Education

There is a considerable consensus in literature on the reasons for the lag in girls' participation in education as compared to boys' and for the higher dropout rates of girls. Some factors are related to institutional policies and practices, others associated with social customs, beliefs and attitudes about women's roles, responsibilities and capabilities.

These are often categorised as 'supply' versus 'demand' side constraints. However, a combination of these factors is actually at work in a given situation. The process of separating them in different categories is largely a methodological device for analysis. It is not always possible to provide a sense of the relative importance of each factor taken in isolation from the rest.

Some of the factors that continue to impede girls' schooling in Rajasthan are:

- **Social Construction of Gender:** As in many other parts of the country, the construct of the 'mini woman' leads the majority of girls to be groomed as 'homemakers'. The gender roles prescribed by society encourage participation in domestic duties as a priority. This means that there is a distinct difference in the educational aspirations for boys and girls. Marriage becomes a central consideration for girls and education is therefore not a priority. In the study on childhood poverty, interactions with parents on the desired level of education revealed that in both the districts studied, most parents desire more education for boys than they had themselves, but they desire less education for girls. The differences are glaring. In Tonk, for example, all parents desire boys to study above the primary level, but 44 per cent want their girls to study to no more than the primary level. Even when the father is literate, girls' education is not a priority and girls may not be enrolled in schools. Social assessment studies carried out for the various DPEP districts also point to the same (IDSJ, 2000).

There is a lot of pressure on girls to drop out from school when they attain puberty, especially those attending co-educational schools. There are concerns for their security given their physical vulnerability. Also, child marriages continue to be very popular among several backward castes and lead to the withdrawal of girls from school. Though these young girls are formally sent to their marital homes only when they reach puberty, often, in-laws refuse to allow their young daughter-in-law to study even if she is residing with her parents. Further, girls from marginalised families and from larger families have fewer opportunities than girls from the higher caste families and smaller families.

- **Engagement in Work:** Involvement in domestic work is an intrinsic part of childhood, especially for girls in the state. Looking after siblings, grazing cattle, fetching water, cooking and cleaning are tasks carried out by girls. Nambissan (2001) notes that a large number of children (29 per cent) were engaged in unpaid work in the household (cultivation, livestock rearing, domestic and survival tasks). Such unpaid tasks are usually invisible and receive little recognition. The childhood poverty study has shown that girls spend 33–50 per cent more time than boys in these activities in all income and age groups. This deprives them more of educational opportunities than boys. Parents also prefer that girls start working early.

Working for wages is also a reality for many children. A study undertaken by a local non-government organisation (NGO) reveals that children are found working in carpet weaving, bidi rolling, gem polishing, embroidery, mining and tie-and-dye work. Nearly half of the child workers had never been enrolled in school and were illiterate. The proportion of girls (54 per cent) in this category was higher than that of boys (46 per cent). Of those who had been enrolled in the formal school system, 31 per cent had dropped out at the primary school level (CECOEDECON, 1999). Given that livelihoods are insecure, especially during periods of distress the choice between schooling and economic activity may be real and tough for many poor households.

- **Processes within School:** Teachers' attitudes are often a deterrent to girls' education, Discrimination takes other hidden forms and are often reflected in the attitudes of teachers. Higher caste teachers continue to consider scheduled caste children as 'worthless', refuse to touch them, make them feel unintelligent and inferior, target them for physical and verbal abuse, use them for menial chores (PROBE, 1999; Sainath, 2001). Nambissan (2001), in her study on social disparities in schooling in rural Rajasthan, notes that teachers appear to have definite views on children coming from different caste/communities. A recent study on inclusion and exclusion in schooling in two districts of Rajasthan, reveals that teachers carry the caste biases existing in society into schools. Teachers do not drink water from the hands of Dalit students. Dalit girls are made to clean the school premises and used utensils. The teacher makes the girls sit separately from boys and the Dalit students sit at the back of the class. The study points out that a 'hidden curriculum' seems to pervade the cultural environment in the school (Vishakha, 2002).

There are several cases reported of girls having been sexually exploited by teachers. The case of the girl student who was raped by a teacher in village Dhabich in Jaipur district was taken up by local NGOs in November 2000. It came to light that the same teacher had victimised other girls in the school. The school environment was not supportive and, subsequently, the parents sent the girl away from the village. Such instances act as a deterrent to girls continuing their education.

Quality in education is an important aspect in any discussion on education. It is central to ensuring that gender equality is achieved. Commonly, quality in education refers to the scholastic achievement of children. A more refined interpretation is to look at the process through which the child has achieved education to ensure future learning competencies. This approach therefore focuses on the self-learning opportunities given to the child through interaction with educational materials as well as learner to learner interactions. Educational processes should forge links with the lived reality of the child. Quality education must ensure that whatever is being learnt outside the school is fed into what is being learnt at school to develop a consolidated understanding. Gender equality as a major concern fits in here (Jain and Rajagopal, 2002).

• Political and institutional factors relate to government policies practices and institutions which overtly or covertly promote gender biases and affect women's participation in the educational system. While there is immense rhetoric about gender equality in policy, it has proved to be much more intractable. Resistance in bureaucracies are much more sustained than anticipated. Mainstreaming gender in education is yet to become a collective goal with transformational agenda.

It is apparent that forms of patriarchal and economic control, multiple roles and cultural norms, which have a bearing on girls' access to education, have to be addressed in a sustained manner and at various levels to bring about visible changes and a social transformation.

Policies and Programmes Promoting Girls' Education

As a result of the NPE, several innovative programmes were implemented in the state of Rajasthan which demonstrated a range of positive interventions and helped move towards bridging the gender gaps in education. The Shikshakarmi Programme (SKP), initiated in 1987, offered a possible approach to problem-solving in educational delivery and demonstrated a paradigm shift in educational planning by utilising and developing locally available human resources for education. Special efforts were made to increase girls' enrolment in the programme by appointing Mahila Shikshakarmis, Mahila Sahyogis and opening Mahila Prashikshan Kendras and Anganpathshalas. A major educational intervention, the Lok Jumbish Project (1992), worked towards universalising primary education. Concerns of gender equity were consciously woven into the programme activities.

The District Primary Education Programme (DPEP) being implemented since 1999 also has a gender focus. The Janshala Programme addressed the needs of urban deprived children. The Sarva Shiksha Abhiyan (SSA) was launched in 2003. The main objective of the SSA was to achieve the goal of universal primary education by 2007 and elementary education by 2010. It provides for strategies to increase enrolment through people's participation, building physical infrastructure and enhancing the professional capacities of teachers. In Rajasthan, all educational initiatives have been brought under this umbrella programme.

The Rajasthan Policy for Women (2000) and the Draft Child Policy (2005) both emphasise the need to address the needs of the girl child. The women's policy announcement generated hope amongst various groups working for women's advancement in the state and it was seen as an instrument for bringing gender issues centrestage in development planning. However, an analysis of initiatives taken after four years of the policy, indicates that action has largely focussed on *integration* rather than adoption of *transformative* strategies, which seek to address not only the manifestations of gender inequality, but also their underlying causes (Rajagopal, 2004).

The state policy for children has specific components on childcare, health and nutrition education and child safety and protection measures. However, the policy ignores the intergenerational aspects of deprivation.

In addition to the above alternative learning centres, residential camps/bridge courses, Bal Melas, Balika Manches and women's meetings have been organised under the aegis of the SKP and DPEP programmes. Gender training of functionaries has also been carried out in DPEP districts. In the National Programme for Education of Girls at the Elementary Level which is part of the SSA, gender units have been established in all the districts of the state. Around 47 Kasturba Gandhi Balika Vidyalayas have been started in the state, where 2,739 girls have been enrolled. A number of non-government organisations have been working on promoting girls' education in the state. The interventions, though on a small scale, show us that there is demand for education and skills even in those regions and communities that were considered resistant to girls' education. These groups have undertaken diverse sets of activities in different parts of the state and these experiences point towards the definite need to incorporate these learnings into policy.

III
Directions Ahead

The foregoing analysis reveals that despite several interventions, the situation of women and girls continues to be marginalised in the state. Beginning with an adverse sex ratio, the health indicators show that issues such as child marriage, early pregnancy, social norms and attitudes have changed little through generations. The long-term intergenerational consequences of poor health are quite alarming. Poorly nourished and overworked girls face early marriage and have children quickly, which further leads to poor health, low self-esteem and low awareness. The recently released UNFPA World Population Report 2005 states that globally, in the next 10 years, more than 10 crore girls will be married before the age of 18 years, and that for a large number of girls, adolescence is a period when freedom is curtailed and they are forced to face violence.

Though successive government policies have acknowledged the need to address the education of girls in the state and innovative programmes have been implemented, sociocultural factors, along with factors within the education system, are critical variables in differential school participation and outcomes. The larger development issues of availability of fuel, fodder and water also need to be addressed in the context of girls' education. The consequence of poor education leading to intergenerational poverty is self-evident.

There are several issues that need to be addressed:

- The lack of an integrated approach for addressing gender inequalities in crucial sectors like nutrition, health and education is evident. The women's policy, reiterated that the special needs of girls have not been taken forward. There is little evidence of collaborative effort among the various departments, i.e., Women and Child Development, Health and Education.
- There is a need to systematically identify the hard to reach regions and social groups where girls' education is still a problem. The social assessment studies in the DPEP carried out by the IDSJ (2000), identified these groups in various districts, but the information was hardly used in the district planning exercises. Microplanning exercises have proven to be an organised method for planning and provisioning education.
- There is a lack of systematic and reliable data on net enrolment, learning achievements, transition from one stage to another and completion of each level of education disaggregated by gender and social groupings. Enrolment figures collected through the departments have a tendency to be over-reported or under-reported. The situation at the secondary level is particularly wanting.
- There is little information on how gender issues are being addressed in the various teacher-training programmes and the impact of these on teaching-learning processes in schools.
- The various innovative programmes wherein efforts were made to address gender imbalances have been discontinued and have raised questions about the sustainability of such programmes.
- It is also evident that the state needs to clearly plan the agenda for universalising secondary education. At present, the network of secondary schools is poor and it is extremely important to assess the demand and make provisions for delivering good quality secondary schooling to children in the state.

Gender equality is integral to the idea of educational equality, since gender equality entails the removal of deep-seated barriers to equality of opportunity and outcome. Both field experience and research show that there are no short cuts to addressing problems of unequal access, equity and gender disparity. Redressal of the problem of gender bias necessitates multiple level interventions at the policy and implementation level. Some recommendations that flow from the above in the context of Rajasthan are:

- At the policy level, coordinated efforts need to be made to bring the issues of girl child nutrition, health and education centre stage. An intergenerational perspective would help in designing effective strategies. There is a definite need to create a predictable forum (with the participation of policy makers, academia and NGOs), which would meet every quarter to review the understanding and implementation of the quality education strategy, which incorporates the gender perspective at all levels. This forum would provide an opportunity to review and refine strategies that create a basic pool of cumulative knowledge.

- It is evident that the absence of upper primary facilities is creating greater inequalities in the system. If this issue is not addressed upfront, it will prevent a large number of girls from continuing their education. A mapping exercise should be initiated in the state to assess the availability of upper primary and secondary schools.

- The need to improve the quality of teaching-learning is self-evident. An in-depth review of the outcomes of current teacher training modules to generate a fuller understanding of how quality education can be linked to equality in society will help generate clarity on the issue in the minds of teachers. This, in turn, will be manifested in appropriate pedagogic choices made by them in a contextually relevant manner.

- Given the fact that government schools are the only facility within the reach of girls from poor households, the state has to take the responsibility of ensuring good quality government schools at all levels, which function regularly. An effective monitoring system has to be in place to check teacher absenteeism and irregularity. Making schools 'safe' and 'girl friendly' is essential, too.

- The curriculum is key to good quality education. It is important to regularly review what girls are being taught about themselves in formal schooling, whether educational institutions allow girls effective participation and whether the existing situation of girls and women is enhanced or diminished by the schooling they receive.

Life skills education should become an intrinsic part of the curriculum.

- Engaging with civil society is essential, as it is evident that communities and women's groups can play an important role in supporting girls' participation in schooling. Listening to parents about their expectations is vital for the designing of realistic interventions.
- There is a need for in-depth research and documentation on understanding what has worked and what has not worked in different contexts and conditions for girls in the state. There is a need to identify success stories and evaluate their potential replicability.

Conclusion

In Rajasthan, addressing gender gaps in education, health and nutrition necessitates sustained engagement at various levels. Any approach towards engendering development and education in particular, must recognise the connections between universal education, social justice and equity. Any educational intervention for girls must facilitate them and other women to increase their capacity to analyse and define their own subordination as well as alter a given situation.

References

BARC. 2005. *Gender Budgets*. Jaipur: Budget Analysis Research Centre.

Bhargava P., K. Mathur and S. Rajagopal. 2005. 'Understanding Childhood Poverty in Rajasthan'. CHIP Working Paper 16, UK: SCF and Childhood Poverty Research Centre.

Bhargava, P. and M. Balana, 2005. 'Meeting Common Minimum Programme (CMP) Promises on Education in Rajasthan: A Report', Jaipur: Institute of Development Studies.

Bhargava P., and R. Sharma. 2004. 'Retention Rate among Children at Primary Level in 9 DPEP (Phase II) Districts in Rajasthan', Jaipur: Institute of Development Studies.

CECOEDECON. 1999. 'Baseline Data for Child Workers Opportunity Project 1999–03: A Report', Jaipur: CECOEDECON.

Census of India. 2001. *Provisional Population Totals*, Directorate of Census Operations.

Government of India. 2002, *National Human Development Report 2001*, New Delhi: Planning Commission.

———. Annual Report of the Ministry of Human Resource Development (2004–2005), New Delhi: MHRD.

————. 2005. *Report of the CABE Committee: Universalisation of Secondary Education,* New Delhi: Ministry of Human Resource Development.

Government of Rajasthan. 2000. *Rajasthan Human Development Report,* Jaipur: Government of Rajasthan.

————. 2001. *Pragati Prativedan, Primary Education, Literacy and Satat Shiksha,* Jaipur: Panchayati Raj Department.

————. 2001. *Annual Report,* Department of Education, Government of Rajasthan.

————. 2005. *Pragati Prativedan,* Jaipur: Department of Primary Education, Government of Rajasthan.

————. 2006. *Annual Report,* Jaipur: Department of Secondary Education, Government of Rajasthan.

————. 2005. Data for Elementary Education (DISE, 2005), Department of School Education.

Institute of Development Studies. 2003. 'Trafficking of Women and Children in Rajasthan'. Report prepared for NHRC New Delhi. Jaipur: IDS.

————. 2000. 'Social Assessment of DPEP', Integrated Report, Jaipur: IDS.

————. 2006. 'Human Development Report, Update', Jaipur: IDS and Government of Rajasthan.

Jain, S., and S. Rajagopal 2001. 'Gender Analysis of UNICEF Education Programmes in UP and Maharashtra', Jaipur: Sandhan.

Majumdar, M. 2001. 'Educational Opportunity in Rajasthan and Tamil Nadu: Despair and Hope' in A. Vaidyanathan and P.R. Gopinathan Nair (eds.) *Elementary Education in Rural India: A Grass-Roots View,* New Delhi: Sage Publications.

Mathur, K. 2004. *Countering Gender Violence,* New Delhi: Sage Publications.

Nambissan, G.B. 2001. 'Social Diversity and Regional Disparity in Schooling: A Study of Rural Rajasthan' in A. Vaidyanathan and P.R. Gopinathan Nair (eds.), *Elementary Education in Rural India: A Grass-Roots View,* New Delhi: Sage Publications.

National Family Health Survey (NFHS 2) 1998–99, Rajasthan. 2001. Mumbai: International Institute of Population Sciences and ORC Macro.

NCERT. 2004. *Elementary Education in Rural India,* New Delhi: NCERT.

Planning Commission. 2006. 'Rajasthan Development Report', New Delhi: Planning Commission/Academic Foundation.

Pratham. 2005. 'Annual Status of Education Report (ASER)', Mumbai: Pratham.

PROBE. 1999. *Public Report on Basic Education in India,* New Delhi: Oxford University Press.

Rajagopal, S. 1999. 'The Shikshakarmi Programme: Closing the Gender Gap in Education' in N. Kabeer and R. Subramanian (eds.), *Institutions Relations and Outcomes: Framework and Tools for Gender Planning*, New Delhi: Kali for Women.

————. 2004. Mainstreaming Gender and Development: Policies, Programmes and Outcomes: A Perspective from Rajasthan. IDSJ Working Paper 138, March.

Ramachandran, V. 2000. 'Literacy, Development and Empowerment: Conceptual Issues' in R. Wazir (ed.), *The Gender Gap in Basic Education: NGOs as Change Agents*, New Delhi: Sage Publications, pp. 115–149.

————. 2004. *Gender and Social Equity in Primary Education: Hierarchies of Access*, New Delhi: Sage Publications.

————. 2003. 'Community Participation and Empowerment in Primary Education: Discussions of Experiences from Rajasthan' in R. Govinda and R. Diwan (eds.), *Community Participation and Empowerment in Primary Education*, New Delhi: Sage Publications.

Sainath, P. 2001. 'This is the Way They Go to School'. *The Hindu*, November 28.

Sandhan. 2004. Classroom Observation in Formal and Alternative Schools, Nine DPEP (Phase-II) Districts, Jaipur: Sandhan.

Sharma, M.L., S.N. Methi and A.R. Khan. 2003. 'Retention in Formal and Alternative Schools in 10 DPEP Phase I Districts: A Research Report'. Jaipur: Worldview Hindustan Foundation.

Sharma, P.R. and R.S. Sharma. 2005. Daang Area Development Project: Benchmark Survey, 2005, IDSJ Research Report 179.

State Institute for Educational Research and Training. 2005. 'Universalisation of Secondary Education, Proposals for Facilities for Girls' Education'. Udaipur: SIERT.

Vishakha. 2002. *Char Deewaron ke Beech Ghuti Shiksha*. Jaipur: Vishakha.

Wazir, R. 2000. *The Gender Gap in Basic Education: NGOs as Change Agents*. New Delhi: Sage Publications.

8

Women's Work and Indian Labour Markets

Preet Rustagi

This paper addresses the relevance of 'feminisation' as a term for Indian labour markets within the context of women's work and their labour market participation over time in India. The spectrum of women's work range from the unpaid, household domain to the paid employment spheres, from illiterate, unskilled workers to educated, skilled and technical personnel. The multi-layered and segmented structures of the labour markets are affected differently by the changing macro policy regimes. Traditional sexual division of labour and gender-based stereotypes seem to persist amidst some slow and gradual alterations that serve as a silver lining for gender transformation or even equality. These few positive changes can at best preserve the hope that gender equality or transformation is possible and feasible even in the Indian context. However, such observations remain highly exclusive and limited, with the majority scenario displaying persistence of women facing discrimination in the labour market processes in terms of job access, skill and human capital development, upward mobility within job hierarchies, nature of work contracts, working conditions and remuneration.

Women's work in its broader sense remains unrecognised and hidden in standard economic categorisations and valuations. Only some aspects of the work put in by women are accounted for as their labour. The enumeration of women as a workforce, therefore, remains an undercount, missing out many women and much of their work. The lower participation of women is both an offshoot of these reasons as well as due to the overwhelming burden of domestic responsibilities which almost entirely fall upon the women within the household.

Increasing coverage or better enumeration of the female workforce itself can lead to a situation of feminisation of the labour markets.

Alternatively, the supply and demand side factors need to be examined to understand whether there are more women entrants or a greater demand for female labour. The changing nature of employment can also serve as a factor in enhancing or displacing female labour participation vis-à-vis an earlier period of time or men. The traditional sexual division of labour continues to be operational with some alterations occurring over time. There is increasing pressure upon women to enter paid work in certain sections among the poor and impoverished for survival while another section of women who are educated and professionally qualified also choose or opt for employment in regular, formal sector jobs. The increasing numbers of poor, needy women entering the labour force is a supply side factor, just as educational qualification induces enhanced labour supply of women for regular employment.

What is happening on the demand front? Are there more employment avenues in general or is there a demand hike for women's employment? Women can also be demanded in preference over men for certain specific labour supply characteristics or as cost-saving measures where they can be hired at lower wage rates. Alternatively, it is also possible that the additional labour supply of women gets absorbed in activities which may often work against their own interests due to their lower bargaining power in these circumstances.

The trends in economic growth are indicative of the potential for the overall employment scenario. Higher growth patterns are expected to propel more employment avenues. However, quite on the contrary, the situation for India has been highlighted for its low or no job creation—categorising the country's economic growth as jobless development (see Bhattacharya and Sakthivel, 2003; Kundu and Sharma (eds), 2001, among others).

On the supply side, entry into the labour force is influenced by the overall population growth rate, which has been declining steadily. The greater impetus on education also witnessed a lowering down of the total rate of growth of the labour force. In spite of this seeming lowering down of pressure on jobs, the rate of unemployment for India is growing. A similar scenario for women is because of the poor employment generation that forecloses the possibility of feminisation of the labour markets.

This paper is divided into seven sections. After the brief introduction, the first section discusses the labour force participation rates of men and women across rural-urban locations by age groups over time based on the 50th and 55th NSS rounds. Over this period 1993–94 to 1999–2000, both the labour force and workforce participation rates have registered declines, with the rural areas being worse. While a part of this decline is a positive development among the younger age groups as they are an outcome of educational pursuits, there is no obvious explanation for the older groups. An expected rise in unemployment rates is noted over the 1990s among males and females in rural and urban locations, except for urban females.

The second section focuses on the feminisation debates that have risen and waned over a couple of decades to re-emphasise the sustained and consistent patterns of work and labour utilisation of women that are only gradually shifting their gender-based divisions, hierarchical structures and power relations. The condition of women workers therefore continues to remain vulnerable and under the influence of gender stereotypes. What signifies feminisation of Indian labour markets? Any kind of increase in the employment share of women or does it need to be further clarified? An increase in women's employment amidst an overall decline in the rate of growth of employment without changing the nature and conditions of work is only partially laudable in as much as it is generating paid work. The nature of such work remains contractual, casual, and maintains women's vulnerabilities, demanding that 'flexicurity' be given serious thought.

It is only organised sector employment which is relatively secure, but it is both minuscule and marginal in terms of the share of women working within this sector. Further concern for work within this sector has been regarding the increasing informalisation within the organised sector, termed as 'organised informalisation' by Kundu (1997). The share of women within organised sector employment has remained steady and shows marginal improvement, although the rate of increase in total and women's employment has been declining over time. The third section looks at the small but secure employment offered in the organised sector for women. Both the public and private sector employment avenues are covered. Despite the gradual increases observed in public sector jobs for women, the gender stereotyping and hierarchies are quite resilient and slow in changing. The significant thing to note here is that these rising employment trends for females accompany replacement of men from these secure avenues. Significant numbers of organised sector workers have been retrenched and eliminated in the process of economic restructuring, privatisation and cuts in public expenditure. The repercussions on society at large as a result of these trends are discussed in this section.

The bulk of the employment is in the unorganised segments of the workforce. Trends towards work organisation through a range of mechanisms, contractualisation, outsourcing and home-based work have been noted by many studies which indicate the reasons for women's participation in such activities and also address the implications of these patterns for women as well as labour market processes. This is addressed in the fourth section. The women reported as workers as per the usual status (principal and subsidiary statuses), when cross-tabulated by their current daily status, displays the high degrees of visible underemployment and erratic, seasonal or intermittent participation of women in the labour market. This poses even more serious questions for the feminisation of labour markets in India.

Even with technological innovation and capital intensive mechanisation, the labour markets in India have not displayed an upward mobility among workers in terms of better avenues of employment, higher wages and more secure and non-discriminatory jobs for larger numbers of people. On the contrary, even high paid jobs are insecure and the larger bulk of employment generation is among the rungs of workers who seem to be facing a downward spiralling of wage returns. The use of female labour in many such activities is serving precisely this purpose of preventing upward movement of wages and dissuading all forms of organisation among workers. Thus, flexibility seems to be closely inter-spersed with feminisation just as elements of cheap, low cost labour. Therefore, the appropriateness of using the term 'feminisation' for the Indian labour markets is questioned while elucidating the few contexts in which it could be considered relevant.

Since women's labour supply is influenced by their socio-culturally defined roles and responsibilities in the domestic domain and the repro-ductive functions they perform, we examine the proportion of females who are involved in household duties according to their usual principal status (UPS) based on the 50th and 55th rounds of the NSS. There have been views about the women's work in unpaid spheres intensifying as an offshoot of rising prices, falling incomes and declining social sector spending of the state in the post-reforms era. These dimensions of women's intensifying work situation can either be captured through qualitative studies or through time-use surveys (which have been undertaken only on a pilot basis in India). The discussion reveals that women are involved in household duties since there is no other household member to under-take these duties. What is pertinent here, however, is that a large propor-tion of these women are willing to hire their labour services for full or part time work, if available at their home. Thus, women are desirous of earning income and have expressed their willingness to work, provided work is available on their terms. Very few among these women are found undertaking economic activities on a subsidiary basis. These issues are covered in the fifth section.

Finally, the paper summarises the debate on feminisation by highlight-ing the different strands and segments of the Indian labour markets and the changes noted therein, which displays no feminisation of the labour force or workforce except in certain activities, with persistent concentration of women in the stereotypical spheres of the labour markets. Other phenomena discussed in the paper include feminisation of male workers in certain occupations and tasks; displacement of men by women in regular organised sector employment; feminisation of unemployment, especially among graduates and qualified women, and underemployment, which is not a new development for Indian labour markets, which have always utilised female labour in times of peak demand in agriculture or as seasonal or part-time workers in self-employed activities.

The nature of employment is becoming increasingly insecure. Therefore, even if feminisation were occurring amidst poor livelihood opportunities that cannot qualify as 'decent work' or 'work with dignity', such forms of labour indicate heightened degrees of vulnerabilities. The demand for labour rights (in terms of minimum wages, proper working hours, rest periods, working conditions, social security measures, and so on) for all workers together with protection of women worker rights need to be re-emphasised along with the issue of shared household/domestic responsibilities.

Labour Market Participation by Age, Gender and Location

The Indian labour markets function as multi-structured and multi-layered institutions across rural-urban locations, organised-unorganised and public-private sectors. The workers are classified as self-employed, regular or casual workers within primary, secondary or tertiary sector activities. In terms of their educational status, the labour force may be at different levels of attainment from illiterates to higher levels of education or professional qualification. These human capital endowments influence the labour market participation significantly. Even women stand to gain by entering at higher echelons of job hierarchies and thereby wielding some power.

Diverse segments of the labour market are differentially affected by the changes occurring in the overall economic environment. The changing policy regimes influence the extent of unpaid and paid work undertaken and the interlinkages and interconnectedness of institutional processes across the ranges of activities that are simultaneously, seasonally or periodically carried out. The rural workforce differs from the urban workers, the literate and better educated women face very different situations from the illiterate women working as unorganised contractual workers. While some women may be benefiting from employment avenues generated in the 1990s, a large segment of women may be facing

declining opportunities, shrinkage in quantum of contractual work and
even lowering of already poorly paid wages.

The changing economic policy regimes over the 1980s and 1990s have
generated vigorous and prolonged debates regarding its expected employment and income gains along with their distributional and sectoral
dimensions. At the macro level, there are ample signals of heightening
and intensifying inequalities and jobless growth patterns by the turn of
the century (Ghosh, 2003; Bhattacharya and Sakthivel, 2003; Stiglitz,
2002; Bhalla, 2000; Kundu and Sharma (eds), 2001, among others).

The annual rate of employment growth has been declining sharply
from 2.4 per cent (over 1987–88 to 1993–94) to less than 1 per cent (in
1993–94 to 1999–2000) (see Table 1). Therefore, in spite of the decline
in labour force growth, the unemployment rate (current daily status
basis) increased from 5.99 per cent in 1993–94 to 7.32 per cent in 1999–
2000 (Bhaumik, 2003) (the unemployment rate being unemployed as a
percentage of the labour force).

Table 1: Rate of Growth of Population, Labour Force and
Employment (Percentage per Annum)

Period	Rate of Growth of Population	Rate of Growth of Labour Force (UPSS)	Rate of Growth of Employment (UPSS)
1983 to 1987-88	2.14	1.74	1.54
1987-88 to 1993-94	2.10	2.29	2.43
(1983 to 1993-94)	2.12	2.05	2.04
1993-94 to 1999-2000	1.93	1.03	0.98

Source: GoI, 2001; p. 19, Table 2.3.

A larger proportion of people desirous of undertaking paid work
remained unemployed. This is an indication of low job creation as well
as mismatch between the kind of jobs being demanded and those for
which avenues exist. While educationally qualified women demand appropriate jobs in the organised, and better paid segments of the labour
market, there are others who do not opt for certain categories of employment due to preferences governed by their personal or social status.

The usual status labour force participation includes principal and
subsidiary statuses, that is persons who have worked regularly for some
time and those who have either sought work or were available for work
for some time during the reference period. The labour force refers to the
population which supplies their labour and includes both the employed
and unemployed. In 1999–2000, 54 per cent males were in the labour

Table 2: Labour Force Participation Rates and Worker Population Ratios: India (%) (Usual Status)

	1993-94	1999-2000
Labour Force Participation Rates		
Rural Males	56.1	54.0
Rural Females	33.1	30.2
Urban Males	54.3	54.2
Urban Females	16.4	14.7
Worker Population Ratios		
Rural Males	55.3	53.1
Rural Females	32.8	29.9
Urban Males	52.1	51.8
Urban Females	15.5	13.9

Source: NSSO, 2000.

force in both rural and urban areas, while among females, the labour force participation rate (LFPR) was 30 in rural areas and 15 in urban areas. In the period from 1993–94 to 1999–2000, for all categories of males and females, rural and urban LFPRs declined (see Table 2).

The matter of significant concern in this context is the reduction in the LFPR themselves over the 1990s. This is occurring among both males and females and for both rural and urban locations. The decline noted for rural areas is far steeper as compared to urban locations, especially among the men (see Table 2).

Explanations for this decline are linked to the educational pursuits which perhaps delay entry into the labour force, especially among adolescents (Sundaram, 2001), and also socio-economic changes post-reforms which affect time and work dispositions across paid and unpaid economic activities (Hirway, 2002).

Higher educational pursuits imply positive investment in human capital development, which is found to have beneficial impacts for the individuals themselves and the economy at large. The educational status of the Indian labour force has been undergoing gradual improvements over time (see Table 3). Upward educational mobility is more prominent in the case of men, with 17 per cent of them being educated upto secondary levels and above in rural areas, while 43 per cent fall in the corresponding urban set for 1999–2000. Urban females having secondary and above education levels in the labour force have also exhibited similar improvement in educational status from 26 per cent in 1993–94 to 32 per cent in 1999–2000.

The inequality in educational status across different categories of women can be realised from the prominent 74 per cent and 41 per cent

Table 3: Percentage Distribution of Labour Force by Educational Status

Category	Illiterate	Literate but Upto Primary	Middle	Secondary	Graduate and Above	Total
Rural Males						
1987-88	48.3	29.6	11.6	8.4	2.1	100
1993-94	43.2	28.2	13.9	11.3	2.8	100
1999-2000	39.6	27.4	16.0	13.5	3.4	100
Rural Females						
1987-88	82.3	12.0	3.2	2.0	0.4	100
1993-94	78.0	14.2	4.4	2.8	0.6	100
1999-2000	73.9	15.7	5.8	3.6	1.0	100
Urban Males						
1987-88	19.6	30.5	16.4	21.8	11.7	100
1993-94	17.8	25.3	17.6	24.7	14.5	100
1999-2000	15.9	21.9	18.8	26.4	16.9	100
Urban Females						
1987-88	51.8	19.0	7.3	12.3	9.6	100
1993-94	45.9	19.0	8.9	14.0	12.2	100
1999-2000	41.2	17.0	9.7	15.7	16.4	100

Source: NSSO, 2000. Figures relate to usual status of individuals and population aged 15 years and above.

illiterate women in rural and urban areas, respectively, even in 1999–2000 (see Table 3). Clearly, the labour force consists of one segment of women with improving education status levels, and another segment that remains illiterate. These attributes affect the participation of women in the labour market significantly in terms of the nature of work they are hired for, the wages they are paid and their working conditions.

In order to further elucidate the situation, an examination of the age group specific data is undertaken. The older age groups, which are not offset by educational pursuits as much as the relatively younger age groups, also reflect the declining tendency among women more than for male LFPRs (see Table 4).

An examination of the age group specific LFPRs by sex and location across board displays a decline (see Table 4). Among the younger age groups, this indicates that there is a beneficial shift towards improving educational status as supported by the rising student population ratios up to the secondary and higher levels (Sundaram, 2001) (see Table 3 for percentage distribution of labour force by educational status over three NSS rounds). Among females, this is noted more in urban areas than in rural areas, where the decline over the 1990s is more significant.

Table 4: Age-Specific Usual Status Labour Force Participation Rates: India (per 1,000)

Age Groups	Rural Males		Rural Females		Urban Males		Urban Females	
	1993-94	1999-2000	1993-94	1999-2000	1993-94	1999-2000	1993-94	1999-2000
5-9	11	7	14	7	4	3	4	2
10-14	139	93	142	96	71	52	47	37
15-19	598	532	371	314	404	366	142	121
20-24	902	889	470	425	772	755	230	191
25-29	980	975	528	498	958	951	248	214
30-34	988	987	587	557	983	980	283	245
35-39	992	986	610	579	990	986	304	289
40-44	989	984	607	586	984	980	320	285
45-49	984	980	594	566	976	974	317	269
50-54	970	953	543	515	945	939	287	264
55-59	941	930	468	450	856	811	225	208
60+	699	640	241	218	443	402	114	94
All	561	540	331	302	542	542	164	147

Source: NSSO, 2000.

The decline in LFPR as well as workforce participation rates (WPRs) beyond the 25 years' age groups, which are not offset by increases in educational participation, reflect lowering employment avenues obviously, but also hint at more non-recognised and vulnerable participation that is not amenable to being netted (Hirway, 2002). The fact that unemployment rates have not risen as much (see Table 4) and have in fact fallen for urban females supports this suggestion that, probably, urban women have had to be involved in activities which are intermittent and interspersed with unpaid, domestic responsibilities of household care and related activities.

The age-specific unemployment rates display a rising trend among all categories of males across rural and urban locations. In case of females, the rural scenario is the same as for men; however, the urban situation differs with a distinct lowering of the unemployment rate from 8.2 to 7.1 over 1993–94 to 1999–2000 (see Table 6). Unemployment rates among educated females are reportedly higher as compared to that among educated males. It is in the category of educated persons with graduation and above that the gender disparity is even more stark (NSSO, 2001: NSS Report No. 458).

Thus, it may be stated from the overall Indian labour market situation, in terms of labour force participation and even workforce participation, that there is little feminisation. A perusal of long-term trends of WPRs women as provided in Table 7 does not reveal any significant departure from the extent of female participation in earlier periods. A regional or sectoral analysis may exhibit certain patterns of work involvement by women, which are not ruled out. However, that is not the focus of this paper, which seeks to hypothetically explore the possibilities of pro- and anti-feminisation trends based on country level broad data analysis and specific observations from the dynamics noted in labour market processes.

Feminisation: Meaning and Relevance

Women's work participation has been changing over time. The factors propelling such alterations have been debated in the literature (Standing, 1989,1999; Cagatay and Ozler, 1995; Papola and Sharma, 1999, among many others). The position of the term 'feminisation' within these debates is sought to be examined in this paper for its relevance and appropriateness. After the use of the term by Guy Standing in the 1980s in the global context, its application subsequently for Indian labour markets has been contested and debated (Banerjee's 'bogey of feminisation' in

Table 5: Age-Specific Usual Status Worker Population Ratio: India (per 1,000)

Age Groups	Rural Males		Rural Females		Urban Males		Urban Females	
	1993-94	1999-2000	1993-94	1999-2000	1993-94	1999-00	1993-94	1999-2000
5-9	11	6	14	7	5	3	5	2
10-14	138	91	141	96	66	49	45	36
15-19	577	503	364	304	356	314	123	105
20-24	859	844	456	409	674	658	180	155
25-29	957	950	525	491	904	883	224	194
30-34	983	979	585	555	964	960	301	235
35-39	989	984	608	579	983	975	301	285
40-44	987	983	606	586	981	974	320	283
45-49	983	980	594	566	973	969	317	267
50-54	970	953	542	515	942	935	286	262
55-59	942	929	467	450	856	809	226	207
60+	699	639	241	218	442	402	113	94
All	553	531	328	299	521	518	155	139

Source: NSSO, 2000.

Table 6: Age-Specific Unemployment Rates by Sex for India

Age Groups	Rural Males		Rural Females		Urban Males		Urban Females	
	1993-94	1999-99	1993-94	1999-99	1993-94	1999-99	1993-94	1999-99
15-29	4.9	5.1	3.2	3.7	10.8	11.5	19.6	16.6
30-44	0.4	0.6	0.4	0.4	1.1	1.4	2.8	2.8
45-59	0.1	0.1	0.2	0.2	0.4	0.4	0.4	0.5
All	2.0	2.1	1.4	1.7	4.5	4.8	8.2	7.1

Source: NSSO, 2000.

Table 7: Workforce Participation Rates by Sex and by Sector for India

Year	Rural		Urban	
	Females	*Males*	*Females*	*Males*
1972-73	31.8	54.5	13.4	50.1
1977-78	33.1	55.2	15.6	50.8
1983	34.0	54.7	15.1	51.2
1987-88	32.3	53.9	15.2	50.6
1993-94	32.8	55.3	15.5	52.1
1994-95*	31.7	56.0	13.6	51.9
1995-96*	29.5	55.1	12.4	52.5
1996-97*	29.1	55.0	13.1	52.1
1998*	26.3	53.9	11.4	50.9
1999-2000	29.9	53.1	13.9	51.8
2000-2001*	28.7	54.4	14.0	53.1
2001-2002*	31.4	54.6	13.9	55.3
2002*	28.1	54.6	14.0	53.4

Source: National Sample Survey Organisation, different years; CSO, 2005.
Note: Figures for all the years are based on usual status approach and includes principal status and subsidiary status workers of all ages.
*Based on thin sample.

1997; the participation of women in export processing units and the popularisation of the term to simply mean more women in any sector or labour activity; for a review of the debates, see Shaktivel and Bhattacharya, 2002).

The primary usage of the term arose in the global context with larger numbers of women entering the labour force and the visibility of women workers in specific jobs. As Standing stated when he revisited the theme: "Feminisation arises because available employment and labour options tend increasingly to characterise activities associated, rightly or wrongly, with women and because the pattern of employment tends to result in an increasing proportion of women occupying the jobs." He also decomposed the term to specify its constituents: "a type of job could be feminised, or men could find themselves in feminised positions ... "when" certain jobs could be changed to have characteristics associated with women's historical pattern of labour force participation" (1999: p. 583).

Any examination/consideration of whether Indian labour markets are getting feminised needs to look at both women's and overall employment. Is there an increase in women's participation occurring? And if so, is it in the context of overall employment increase or amidst declining job opportunities? The different contexts under which female labour employment occurs lead to distinct scenarios and therefore need to be differentiated. For instance, women's work participation increasing under circumstances of scarcity of labour supply amidst higher demand for labour is distinct from other work participation which are a result of supply side compulsions of poverty or vulnerability. These situations may differ in terms of the bargaining position and can also have implications for wages.

What is meant by feminisation of labour markets? When we refer to labour markets, we are speaking of the demand and supply dimensions as well as the actual employment outcome visible or noticeable. In other words, to elucidate, higher demand for female labour will result in greater participation of women in the labour markets subject to their services being available. There are different dimensions relating to whether the demand for female labour has increased, or whether the levels of absorbing women in the workforce have risen, or whether it is an aspect of more women being available for work (never mind the rate at which they offer such services at this juncture).

On the other hand, feminisation of the labour force refers to the increasing supply of female labour services. Since, labour force refers to all those desirous of undertaking work as well as the unemployed, increasing women in the labour force is one type of feminisation. Under what circumstances is this occurring? Is it amidst an overall increase in the labour force or under conditions of a declining male labour force? It could also be an instance of relative increase. More importantly, the causal factors for the increase in labour force differ depending upon the socio-economic level to which the women belong. Resource poor women will enter the domains of paid labour as a result of their need for monetary resources, as a survival measure, while there may be others who are able to break away from the restrictions laid upon their participation as visibility of women in public spheres in general increases.

Another dimension of feminisation relates to the traits and attributes of labour activities/tasks/jobs/services. Apart from the existing tradition influenced sexual division of labour practised and prevalent in the labour markets (such as transplanting, weeding and not ploughing in agriculture; certain manufacturing tasks and clerical/administrative services; nursing, teaching, domestic servants, and so on), all modern or evolving activities (such as new jobs in the IT sector, call centres, media, entertainment and hospitality sectors, and so on) also get influenced by gender roles to an extent. Having stated this, it needs to also be emphasised that there are transitions occurring either with the introduction of technology or automation; with changes in employment scenarios; or any other factors. Certain jobs known to be women oriented or almost exclusively being carried out by females are witnessing change as men begin to enter these occupations, such as nursing, primary school teachers, tailoring, in the hospitality and entertainment sectors, and so on. This is often referred to as feminisation of male workers in the literature (the term is often used even in medical and cultural contexts) of the field.

The processes leading to such change may be clear in cases of technological change or remuneration hikes that result in males entering otherwise gender segregated domains within labour markets. Some of these processes, however, may not be as obvious, but may be linked to a complex set of processes in turn, which influence the opportunities set or remuneration packages and attract men into these domains. For instance, men entering nursing is motivated by the tremendous potential for emigration that is possible in the profession. There may be a further set of gender concerns operative in cases where women may not opt for such options, thereby propelling men into such spheres as well.

However, the bulk of labour market occupations continue to display gender divisions with marginal changes, if any. These alterations are not yet visible in country level data sets, except in some spheres. For instance, the increasing international out-migration of women is one such information. Most jobs where women concentrate are based on certain gender segregation principles, which is illustrated in Table 8.

The gender ideologies prevalent under patriarchal structures assign lower value to investment in women's education since there is more

Table 8: Occupations in which Female Workers were More than Male Workers in 1991 India

Description	NCO Group	Number of Workers (Figures in Hundred)		Percentage of Females
		Females	Males	
Bidi Makers	784	14,210	6,198	70.00
Domestic Servants	531	4,603	2,798	62.00
Nurses	084	2,440	306	89.00
Ayahs, Nurses and Maids	530	1,131	210	84.00
Teachers, Pre-primary	154	1,094	550	67.00
Midwives and Health Visitors	085	359	242	60.00
Mat Weavers	945	835	414	67.00
Food Preservers	775	644	414	61.00
Housekeeping Service Workers NEC	539	330	262	56.00

Source: CSO, 2005.
NEC: Not elsewhere classified.

emphasis laid upon their entry into the marriage market. Even the rising educational status of girls sometimes is dictated by improving their prospects for marriage. This certainly influences the disciplines taken up for study and so on. It also affects the nature of their participation in the labour market. The next section discusses the minuscule organised employment segment that is reflective of certain elements of tranformation.

Women's Employment in the Organised Sector

Organised sector employment is a small proportion of around 7 per cent with the bulk of workers in the unorganised sector. Total employment in the organised sector in 2003 was 270 lakhs, of which women were 18 per cent (i.e., 50 lakhs) (GoI, 2006). The growth in employment in the organised sector is almost stagnant, if not declining. However, the share of women's employment within these secure segments of the workforce is seen to be gradually rising from 14 per cent in 1992 to 18 per cent in 2003 (see Table 9).

Table 9: Women's Employment in the Organised Sector

Year	Women Employment (in Lakhs)	Total Employment (in Lakhs)	Percentage of Women's Employment to Total Employment
1992	38.89	270.55	14.4
1995	42.27	275.25	15.4
2000	49.22	279.59	17.6
2001	49.49	277.89	17.8
2002	49.35	272.05	18.1
2003	49.68	270.00	18.4

Source: CSO, 2005; GoI, 2006.

The private sector is a small employer in terms of the overall employment it generates, as compared to the public sector. However, the number of women employed within the private sector tend to be almost as substantial as those employed by the public sector. The proportion of women employees constitutes a larger share among the private sector when compared with that of the public sector gender composition of employees. This has been the case through the decade or more. The share of women in the private sector ranges from 19 per cent in the early 1990s to close to a quarter of all employees by the turn of the millennium (see Table 10).

Table 10: Share of Women's Employment to Total Employment
in the Organised Sector in India

(Figures in Thousand)

Year	Public Sector			Private Sector		
	Women	*Total*	*% age of Women*	*Women*	*Total*	*% age of Women*
1992	2,467.0	19,209.6	12.8	1,522.7	7,846.1	19.4
1993	2,476.7	19,326.1	12.8	1,549.7	7,850.5	19.7
1994	2,564.6	19,444.9	13.2	1,589.3	7,929.9	20.0
1995	2,600.4	19,466.3	13.4	1,627.5	8,058.5	20.2
1996	2,634.5	19,429.3	13.6	1,791.9	8,511.6	21.1
1997	2,727.6	19,559.1	14.0	1,909.4	8,685.5	22.0
1998	2,762.7	19,417.8	14.2	2,010.9	8,747.9	23.0
1999	2,810.7	19,414.8	14.5	2,018.4	8,698.2	23.2
2000	2,857.0	19,313.7	14.8	2,065.8	8,646.0	23.9
2001	2,859.2	19,137.5	14.9	2,090.1	8,651.7	24.2
2002	2,886.7	18,773.4	15.4	2,048.7	8,432.1	24.3
2003	2,905.0	18,580.0	15.6	2,064.0	8,421.0	24.5

Source: DGE&T, various years; GoI, 2006.

In the period from 2001 to 2002, however, private sector employment witnessed a drop by 2 percentage points (see Table 11). There were 29 lakh women in the public sector and another 21 lakh in the private sector in 2001. While the public sector recorded a slight increase of 1 per cent in the period, the private sector saw a decline of about 42,000 from 2001 to 2002. However, by 2003, the number of women in the private sector actually rose by 16,000. What is of interest is that the proportion of women among total employees remains steady and is in fact rising over time in spite of the overall decline both in public and private sector employees.

It is largely in this segment of the organised labour market that the visibility of women in urban locations tends to lend credence to the

Table 11: Women's Employment in Public and Private Sectors

Sector	Employment (as on March 31) (in Lakhs)		% Change 2001/2002
	2001	*2002*	
Public	28.59	28.86	+1.0
Private	20.90	20.48	−2.0
Total	49.49	49.35	−0.3

Source: DGE&T, 2002.

arguments of feminisation of the labour markets. The proximity and visibility of the unorganised sector workers, especially in certain occupations within the services sector, is another factor that will be discussed subsequently.

The larger masses of women organised sector workers are employed in gender stereotypical occupations, such as clerks, teachers, nurses, and other service providers. There are a number of studies that have examined the location of women within organised sector hierarchies to find that more women hold positions at the lower rungs (Srivastava, 1999; Banerjee, 1999).

The point to note here is that women's share is increasing at the cost of men's secure employment. While this may be seen as gender equating to some extent, there are limitations to the positive outcomes of such trends. In the work sphere, this compels the need for addressing gender relations and who wields power and authority. On the social front, loss of secure jobs to the breadwinners may destabilise the prevalent equanimity and cause intensification of hardships to some sections of women. While women may be considered as empowered economically with access to earnings, there are limitations to their levels of autonomy.

Industry distribution of organised sector workers reveals that the bulk of women are located in the services sector, followed by manufacturing activities. The latter, however, is declining in terms of employment (see Table 12). Reduction of women's employment in the primary sector is also noted. Within most of these activities, women are generally involved in manual, lower paid, low status activities.

Table 12: Distribution of Women in Organised Sector Employment by Industry

NIC Code	Industry	Women's Employment (in Thousands) as on March 31		% age change 2001/2002
		2001	2002	
0	Agriculture, Hunting, Forestry and Fishing	512.8	463.4	−9.6
1	Mining and Quarrying	64.0	62.3	−2.7
2 & 3	Manufacturing	1,030.0	1,016.1	−1.4
4	Electricity, Gas and Water	46.0	46.7	1.4
5	Construction	67.3	67.5	0.4
6	Wholesale and Retail Trade and Restaurants and Hotels	46.6	47.6	1.7
7	Transport, Storage and Communication	182.9	186.4	1.9

Contd.

Contd.

8	Financing, Insurance, Real Estate and Business Services	245.0	256.1	4.5
9	Community, Social and Personal Services	2,754.5	2,789.4	1.3
	Total	4,949.3	4,935.4	−0.3

Source: DGE&T, 2002.

A look at the 1991 distribution of main workers in different occupational categories reveals the highest share in production and related workers and labourers (see Table 13). The educational status improvement is reflected in the share of professional, technical and related workers in female employment, which was about 19 per cent. In the service sector, women are involved in teaching, banking, health work and personal services. Some of these jobs have relatively better acceptance among families and society at large as they are in line with the gender stereotyping of employment.

The manufacturing sector, which has been another major source of employment, has witnessed drastic changes in the form of production

Table 13: Distribution of Main Workers other than Cultivators and Agricultural Labourers according to Different Occupational Categories, 1991

Code	Occupation	Percentage Distribution		% age Share of Female Employment in Different Occupations
		Females	Males	
0–1	Professional, Technical and Related Workers	24.9	75.1	18.6
2	Administrative and Managerial Workers	4.4	95.6	0.9
3	Clerical and Related Workers	9.4	90.6	6.7
4	Sales Workers	6.6	93.4	8.0
5	Service Workers	19.5	80.5	11.9
6	Farmers, Fisherman, Hunters Loggers and Related Workers	24.0	76.0	9.1
7–8–9	Production and Related Workers, Transport Equipment Operators and Labourers	13.1	86.9	42.6
	Others	8.9	91.1	2.2
	Total	100		

Source: CSO, 2005: based on Census of India, 1991.

organisation with large factories/industries giving way to smaller units or contractual production through outsourcing. This is the segment within the unorganised sector that would be expected to increase with the export orientation of growth. Employment avenues for women in garments, gems and jewellery, footwear and electronics have been noted in India and most of South Asia, too. A host of assembling, labelling and packaging tasks have generated employment for women and men. Sometimes, these jobs are contracted through the organised sector into informal segments.

Women's Participation in the Unorganised Sector

Among the unorganised segments, the largest proportion of workers are involved in primary sector activities. Women are mostly involved as household labour with little power of decision-making. Even ownership of resources is denied in most cases. Gender-based segmentation and segregation of tasks is common and wage differentiation among male-female workers is the rule rather than an exception.

Without going into great details on this segment, we can say that there are few alterations in the participation of women within agriculture given the overall stagnation and underemployed nature of involvement for many in this sector. The rural sector predominantly offers primary sector activities for both males and females, while in urban areas, services employ the larger share (see Table 14). The changing trends are noted in the methods adopted for hiring labour, labour utilisation mechanisms, outsourcing, home-based, piece-rated contractualisation, all of which introduce insecurities and heighten the vulnerabilities of the workers.

Table 14: Distribution of Usual Workers by·
Broad Industrial Groups (Per 1,000): All (PS+SS)

NSS Rounds	Primary		Secondary		Tertiary	
	Males	Females	Males	Females	Males	Females
Rural						
1987-88	745	847	121	100	134	53
1993-94	741	862	112	83	147	56
1999-2000	714	854	126	89	160	57
Urban						
1987-88	91	294	340	317	569	389
1993-94	90	247	330	291	579	463
1999-2000	66	177	328	293	606	529

Source: NSSO, 2000.

The bulk of the Indian workforce is self-employed both in urban and rural areas (see Table 15). The trends of casualisation are clear from the table for rural and urban, male and female usually employed workers. The increase visible among regular employees especially among women, needs to be considered with some degree of scepticism, since the analysis of the usual status workers by their current daily status shows high levels of visible underemployment (Shaktivel and Bhattacharya, 2002).

Table 15: Distribution of Workers by Category of
Employment: UPSS (Per 1,000)

NSS Rounds	Self-Employed		Regular Employees		Casual Labour	
	Males	Females	Males	Females	Males	Females
Rural						
1987-88	586	608	100	37	314	355
1993-94	579	585	83	28	338	387
1999-2000	550	573	88	31	362	396
Urban						
1987-88	417	471	437	275	146	254
1993-94	417	454	421	286	162	162
1999-2000	415	453	417	333	168	214

Source: NSSO, 2000.

Studies have highlighted the reasons why women's labour is sought as their cost-effectiveness and almost never emphasise upon the productivity of their work. Women are sometimes hired at casual male wage rates on a regular basis to replace regular male workers (Ghosh, 2001). Unni and Uma Rani (2003) have analysed industries and their employment patterns to show that top growth industries with good quality employment grew with a slightly declining share of women workers. The share of women increased mainly in the non-performing industries with low quality employment (Bose, 1996; Ramaswamy, 1999).

The hype being created regarding the new technology based sectors and their potential for employment is another periodic phase generating work for a small segment of educated urban women and men. The initial absorption of women seems to be phased out as requisite male labour supplies become available, since gender stereotypes continue to affect labour markets and employers prefer male workers to female workers if they have to bear the social security benefits for their employees. In other words, women are preferred in the lowest parts of production chains and in the poorest paid jobs. If men are available to work at similar rates, then they will be replaced by men.

Table 16: Distribution of Persondays by Current Daily Status (per 1,000)

| | Current Daily Status | | | |
	Employed	Unemployed	Not in Labour Force	All
Rural Males				
1987-88	926	27	47	1000
1993-94	909	40	51	1000
1999-2000	897	53	51	1000
Rural Females				
1987-88	638	26	336	1000
1993-94	663	30	306	1000
1999-2000	676	41	283	1000
Urban Males				
1987-88	938	37	25	1000
1993-94	949	27	25	1000
1999-2000	942	27	31	1000
Urban Females				
1987-88	716	37	247	1000
1993-94	766	24	210	1000
1999-2000	791	22	187	1000

Source: NSSO, 2000; Shaktivel and Bhattacharya, 2002.

On the women's labour supply side, increasing burden of household work prevents women from being in the labour force for a continued period through the year. The large proportion of women in the labour force by current daily status even among those who have reported working status as per UPSS category reflects this phenomenon very clearly, as shown in Table 16. The reasons for this behaviour may be both due to non-availability of work for continuous stretches of time as well as the women not being able to undertake work due to domestic responsibilities.

Women's Unpaid and Potential Labour

The preponderance of domestic duties as women's natural role constrains and affects the extent and nature of their work participation. In addition to this, the reproductive responsibilities of bearing and rearing children also gravitate to the women's domain entirely, thereby affecting the age specific patterns of women's work availability as seen in the earlier section. These roles performed by women are viewed as vulnerabilities and insecurities confronting female work participation.

Policy makers and employers alike have assigned lower value to female labour due to these functions. They view them as secondary earners and thereby do not hesitate in meting out discriminatory treatment to them. Female labour supplies are often erroneously treated as temporary, non-serious and/or an outcome of certain contingency-ridden phases in the lives of individual families and, therefore, the concerns over the wage payments made to them, equal returns for equal work are undermined. These notions towards female employment need drastic alteration to recognise women too as equal workers. Employers have often been noted as preferring young unmarried girls in export-oriented industries and factories to ensure higher commitment to productivity and efficiency and higher turnover rates as these young entrants, it is assumed, will soon get married and quit.

How many women are exclusively or predominantly engaged in household duties as per the usual principal status in India, in rural and urban areas? The number of females engaged in domestic duties per 1000 females in rural areas have declined from 382 in 1993–94 to 358 in 1999–2000, while urban locations reflect a reverse trend of more women undertaking unpaid, non-recognised, non-economic activities over the same period – from 449 to 453 women (see Table 17).

In urban areas, where 45 per cent women were involved with household maintenance in 1999–2000, the age groupwise analysis reveals that the share of women rose among the 30–59 years age groups. Nearly 50 per cent among those women who are principally involved in home-making reported the reason for doing so as there being no other household member to undertake these responsibilities (NSS 55th round). Only a small proportion of them are involved in subsidiary activities.

It is noteworthy that even among these segments of women, in 31 per cent urban and 26 per cent rural cases, the women expressed their willingness to undertake work within the household premises. Kalpagam (1999) stressed on the need for income earning among housewives as a means of empowering them and improving their economic status. The

Table 17: Number of Women Engaged in Household Duties per 1,000 Females (Usual Principal Status): All India

Age Groups	Rural		Urban	
	1999-2000	*1993-94*	*1999-2000*	*1993-94*
0-14	66	99	38	51
15-29	565	592	589	601
30-44	547	565	761	755
45-59	550	562	716	711
60 & Above	399	430	440	460
All	358	382	453	449

Source: NSSO, 2000.

stress on formation of self-help groups through governmental and non-governmental efforts ought to focus on these sections of women in addition to those who are underemployed or unemployed.

The sustenance of these initiatives is dependent critically upon the market conditions and demand for the goods and services being supplied by the self-help groups. One indication of the low level of demand for their labour, which is a structural and endemic issue pertaining to the overall economic activity levels in the country, is the low level of women's involvement in subsidiary status activities as noted among those involved in household duties.

Concluding Observations

The labour force and workforce in India have been experiencing a decline over the 1990s and this is also true among females in both rural and urban areas. Clearly, therefore, there is no feminisation of the labour force occurring for the country as a whole. As for labour market feminisation, if examined in its different segments within public and private sector organised employment, there is an increase in the share of women in total organised sector employment. This is a positive outcome of the enhancing educational attainments among women in the population, especially in urban locations.

The increase in organised sector employment for females, in addition to being a positive outcome of improved educational status, is also an indication of gradual changes in the attitudes of parents and society regarding women's job mobility. These alterations in mindsets are motivated to some extent by the increasing visibility of women and their occupying prominent positions, sometimes in people's lives in a very localised context, and at other times, in more public domains such as in the media and so on. This change may be marginal in magnitude, but is nevertheless significant for gender transformation.

There is little to contest in the fact that women's participation in the unorganised sector is more due to economic compulsions rather than any change in work ethos. However, even in the unorganised sector, there is some element of demonstration effect operational. When migrant populations from rural areas find restraint in mobility for work, from family members for instance, the proximity of other families who send their women to work and the obvious gains they experience at times acts as a motivating factor in changing age-old restrictions imposed on women's entry into paid work. The availability of work in proximate areas may also serve as an attraction for women to enter the labour market.

However, the traditional sexual division of labour continues to persist in the location of women in manual, low paid jobs with limited upward mobility within job hierarchies. Employers' preferences for female workers are most often a result of gender differentiation of wages, which facilitates in minimising costs. The persistence of gender discrimination stemming from patriarchal influences within households and in the labour markets is witnessed.

Women workers seem to face more flexible forms of labour utilisation. The seasonality and temporary nature of their work participation, together with underemployment in self-employed work, is highlighted in a comparison between the usual status of employment and the current daily status reported. This reiterates that labour market processes are gravitating towards more insecure and vulnerable labour utilisation forms in general and women's situation is no better.

The slight increase in the share of organised sector employment noted over the years is a positive development, but its gender equalising impact has to be examined with caution. Since women's participation is occurring amidst overall declining employment avenues, implying displacement of men, the implications of such change for society at large can take the form of inter-personal conflicts within households, which can extend to the society at large.

To sum up, feminisation of the labour force and workforce as a whole is not occurring although certain sectoral and regional dimensions may reveal a different picture, which is worth exploring. The organised sector and the regular employment domains seem to be witnessing some elements of feminisation. However, these can barely serve as a silver lining for the gradual alterations and gender transformations occurring. These phenomena merely emphasise that enhancing human capital endowments of the labour force can potentially improve labour market participation for women. To what extent such participation is made feasible and what its potential is for dispelling the patriarchal hold over women's labour needs further in-depth enquiry, which has not been undertaken here.

In conclusion, it may be stated that the term holds limited relevance and significance in analysing women's labour market participation since the structures in the labour markets as well as in households have not been substantially adjusted to improve the conditions for it. Given that the overall job situation is not improving, it poses further constraints on such change. Equal treatment for women as workers is still a long way off. The quandary regarding domestic responsibilities needs to be addressed if an ambience for women's equal participation is to be created.

References

Banerjee, Nirmala. 1997. 'How Real is the Bogey of Feminisation'? in *Indian Journal of Labour Economics*. Vol. 40, No. 3.

———. 1999. 'Women in the Emerging Labour Market' in *Indian Journal of Labour Economics*. Vol. 42, No. 4.

Bhalla, Sheila. 2000. *Behind Poverty: The Qualitative Deterioration of Employment Prospects for Rural Indians*, Working Paper No. 7. New Delhi: Institute for Human Development.

Bhattacharya, B.B. and S. Sakthivel. 2003. 'Economic Reforms and Jobless Growth in India in the 1990s' in *Indian Journal of Labour Economics*, Vol. 46, No. 4.

Bhaumik, S.K. 2003. 'Unemployment in India in the Post-Liberalisation Era' in *Indian Journal of Labour Economics*. Vol. 46, No. 1.

Bose, A.J.C. 1996. 'Subcontracting, Industrialisation and Labouring Conditions in India: An Appraisal, in *Indian Journal of Labour Economics*. Vol. 39. No. 1.

Cagatay, N., and S. Ozler. 1995. 'Feminisation of the Labour Force: The Effects of Long Term Development and Structural Adjustment' in *World Development*. Vol. 23, No. 11.

CSO. 2005. *Women and Men in India–2004*. Central Statistical Organisation, Ministry of Statistics and Programme Implementation, Government of India.

DGE&T. Various Years from 1999 to 2002. *Employment Review*. Directorate General of Employment and Training, Ministry of Labour, Government of India.

Ghosh, Jayati. 2001. 'Urban Indian Women in Informal Employment: Macro Trends in the Nineties' in Kundu and Sharma (eds), *Informal Sector in India: Perspectives and Policies*, New Delhi: Institute of Human Development and Institute of Applied Manpower Research.

———. 2003. 'Changes in the World of Work' in *Indian Journal of Labour Economics*. Vol. 46, No. 4.

GoI. 2001. Report of the Task Force on Employment Opportunities, Planning Commission, Government of India, July.

———. 2006. *Economic Survey 2005–06*. Government of India.

Hirway, Indira. 1999. 'Economic Reforms and Women's Work' in Papola and Sharma (eds.), Gender and Employment in India, *Indian Journal of Labour Economics*, New Delhi: IEG and FES, New Delhi.

———. 2002. 'Employment and Unemployment Situation in the Nineties: How Good are the NSS Data' in *Indian Journal of Labour Economics*. Vol. 45, No. 1.

Kalpagam, U. 1999. 'Women, Work and Domestic Duties: Income Planning for Housewives' in *Indian Journal of Labour Economics*. Vol. 42, No. 4.

————. 2001. 'Globalisation, Liberalisation and Women Workers in the Informal Sector' in Kundu and Sharma (eds.), *Informal Sector in India: Perspectives and Policies*, New Delhi: Institute of Human Development and Institute of Applied Manpower Research.

Kundu, Amitabh. 1997. 'Trends and Patterns of Female Employment in India: A Case of Organsied Informalisation' in *Indian Journal of Labour Economics*, Vol. 40, No. 3.

Kundu, Amitabh and A.N. Sharma (eds.), 2001. *Informal Sector in India– Perspectives and Policies*. New Delhi: Institute for Human Development and Institute of Applied Manpower Research.

NSSO. 2000. 'Employment and Unemployment Situation in India, 1999–2000', Report No. 458, 55th Round, National Sample Survey Organisation, Government of India, December.

Papola, T.S., and A.N. Sharma (eds.), 1999. 'Gender and Employment in India' in *Indian Journal of Labour Economics,* New Delhi: IEG and FES.

Ramaswamy, K.V. 1999. 'The Search for Flexibility in Indian Manufacturing: New Guidance on Outsourcing Activities' in *Economic and Political Weekly*. Vol. 34, No. 6.

Shaktivel, S and B.B. Bhattacharya. 2002. 'Feminisation of Indian Labour Force: Evidence from the Literature in *Labour and Development,* Vol. 8, Nos. 1 and 2.

Singh, C.S.K. 2003. 'Structural Rigidity of the Workforce' in *Indian Journal of Labour Economics*. Vol. 46, No. 4.

Srivastava, Nisha. 1999. 'Striving for a Toehold: Women in the Organised Sector' in Papola and Sharma (eds.), Gender and Employment in India, *Indian Journal of Labour Economics*, New Delhi: IEG and FES, New Delhi.

Standing, Guy. 1989. 'Global Feminization Through Flexible Labor' in *World Development*. Vol. 17, No. 1.

————. 1999. 'Global Feminization Through Flexible Labor: A Theme Revisited' in *World Development*. Vol. 27, No. 3.

Stiglitz, J.E. 2002. *Globalisation and Its Discontents*. London: Penguin.

Sundaram, K. 2001. 'Employment and Poverty in the 1990s: Further Results from NSS 55th Round Employment – Unemployment, 1999–2000' in *Economic and Political Weekly*. August 11.

Swaminathan, Padmini. 2002. 'Industrial Labour Force, Higher Education, Gender and Skill Formation: Some Issues' in *Indian Journal of Labour Economics*. Vol. 45, No. 4.

Unni, Jeemol and Uma Rani. 2000. 'Globalisation, Information Technology Revolution and Service Sector in India', *Indian Journal of Labour Economics*. Vol. 43, No. 4.

————. 2003. 'Changing Structure of Workforce in Unorganised Manufacturing' in *Indian Journal of Labour Economics*. Vol. 46, No. 4.

9

Rural Poverty Alleviation and Conservation

Some Recent Evidence from Himachal Pradesh on the Implications of Interventions for Rural Women

PURNAMITA DASGUPTA

This study proposes to investigate the role of common pool resources (CPRs)[1] as a source of sustainable rural income in the context of opportunities created by the development process, such as improved access to markets. Development in the present context is defined as an enhancement of well-being (MEA, 2003). The development process thus involves transition from conditions of ill-being to those of well-being.[2] Scholars have defined human well-being in different ways (Alkire, 2002). Although how well-being is expressed and experienced is context- and situation-dependent, and the concept of well-being is both complex and value-laden, research in under-developed countries across the world (Narayan et al., 2000) has revealed certain universal constituents and determinants of human well-being. These include the basic material needs for a good life, health, security, good social relations, freedom and choice. The MEA contributes in recognising ecological security as another equally important aspect of well-being. The freedom and choice aspect of well-being focuses on the capability to achieve that which

Paper presented at the National Seminar on Gender Issues in Development: Concerns of the 21st Century, May 2006, Council for Social Development, New Delhi.

individuals value doing and being (MEA, 2003). The present study adopts this definition of development, and focuses on the contribution of CPRs in enhancing the well-being of the communities dependent on them. In doing so, it will throw light on the web of interactions that exist between the three dimensions of well-being – the necessary material for a good life, good social relations, and freedom and choice.

In a dynamic perspective, CPRs can generate surplus to be used for reinvestment in physical, social or natural capital. Thus, when households adopt conservation practices (such as planting of trees for future use), CPRs become development drivers. In the context of the present study, CPRs can contribute to the necessary material for a good life by increasing household incomes through sale of CPR-based products. Good social relations are promoted through improvements in gender and family relations and increased social cohesion along with material well-being. The freedom and choice aspects of well-being find expression in the evolution of institutions – institutions that mediate the link between the CPR provisioning service and human well-being. Institutions can be defined in the present context as sets of rules and norms that shape the interactions of humans with others and nature (Agrawal and Gibson, 1999). It is hypothesised that while institutional innovations have a primary impact on the necessary material for the good life aspect of well-being, the impacts on the good social relations and freedom and choice aspects develop simultaneously as a conjoint process, although the evidence may take longer in making its presence felt.

Institutions evolve – and this evolutionary process is a social process that gets determined by various factors. It follows that institutional innovation can redefine or widen the individual's ability to achieve what he values doing or being. For instance, in the case of the evolution of the Kangra Women's Cooperative,[3] the impact in terms of improved family and gender relations is evident at this point in time. But, this end result, occurred through a social process that had many constituents. One of these was an institutional innovation. Gender-based discrimination within the household in accessing the common household fund became evident when women desired to meet the raw material expenses incurred in processing the fruit out of their household funds. This prompted the members of the cooperative to create a new rule about making monthly deposits out of their wages (before taking them home and pooling them into a common household fund) to meet future expenses on raw material. Over time, this impacted in various ways on improving social relations (increased cohesion, increased respect for women).

The Empirical Context: The 'Development Driver' Role of CPRs

In examining the possible "development driver" role of CPRs, the study pertains to situations in which households choose to spend time on collection from the commons for sale and value addition as an income enhancing activity in its own right, as distinct from its role as a safety net in times of distress and/or its role as a provider of agricultural inputs. It would be realistic to assume that all rural households who have access to CPRs in varying degrees would consider the options for generating marketable surpluses from CPR-based activity, in arriving at decisions on optimal allocation of labour to maximise incomes. The motivation for management of the commons would correspondingly be dependent on the returns and the uses to which the commons are put. The availability of markets and the incentive structures for CPR-based products and the ecological limits of the resource base would determine the extent to which CPRs could act as sources of sustainable income.

Improving access to markets and higher returns from Non-Timber Forest-Products (NTFP) based sales could provide the motivating factor for better preservation of the forest. There is room for investigating whether market linkages promote conservation in this context and how. However, what needs to be also kept in mind is that the availability of alternative income opportunities (exit options from farm/CPR to non-farm economic activities, for instance) may adversely affect incentives for collective action based on CPRs, either by raising the opportunity cost of labour or reducing user interest in the resource (Baland and Platteau, 2003). When initial interventions lead to increases in human, social and natural capital, over time, they also provide the means to move away from the resource, particularly if exit opportunities exist, by providing a greater ability to take advantage of these opportunities. The impact on the resource in this case is ambiguous.

The conceptual framework for the study builds on the following empirical understanding. The initial situation is characterised by the presence of a number of low to middle income, small farm households, with access to CPRs, i.e., forestlands and village common land. These forests constitute both village forests and protected forests where the villagers have certain rights to collect products from the forest. In this situation, an external agent (an NGO) provides the motivation and initial financial support for the creation of an institution that brings together women from these villages, with rules for processing and marketing CPR-based products. Economic incentives for the participation in the collective activity for processing and marketing exist, for which labour and collections from the CPR are the major inputs. The institution is made effective through an organisation called Samridhi. The overall state of development in the local economy (roads, infrastructure services – electricity, basic education) helps in the achievement of the goals for which the rules have been worked out. This stage is characterised by higher incomes (and employment) for the households. Economic incentives are now created for conservation. The impacts on conservation are defined in a narrow sense here – simply as an increased incentive to plant trees that would yield inputs for the value-addition activity without interfering with the existing farming system. There is a realisation among the households of the need to plant more trees in order to ensure the supply of raw material in the following years. This is a phase characterised by both higher incomes and conservation impacts in terms of increased tree planting.

Thus, institutional change transforms the structure of incentives within which future strategic decisions are made. The link between institutional change, incentive structures and decision-making is of course well established in the literature (North, 1994; Ostrom, 1990).

However, as demand and profitability for the fruit-based product from the CPR increases, there are two options for the individual to ensure supply. One is to establish property rights over fruit trees growing in the commons or at least (*de facto*) collection rights. This is reflected in the fact that some households are collecting from the village common lands, apart from the government forests. The other alternative is to plant trees on one's own private land. This reduces uncertainty and is less costly than collections from commons presumably, since a fair number of households seem to be exercising this option. Thus, an individual who wishes to maximise expected benefits over costs would compare different ways of ensuring supply and minimise the costs of doing so. In the present case, one would compare the costs of tree planting with the costs of collecting from the commons (government forests, village common lands). The latter could, for instance, be reflected in time costs of collection.

The institutional evolution takes place in the form of encouraging planting of trees. This is preferable since it appears to be more costly to continue/expand collections from the village commons through changes in property rights and so on. Such changes in informal constraints – norms, conventions – occur gradually as individuals evolve alternative patterns of behaviour consistent with their newly perceived evaluation of costs and benefits.

Description of Study Site

In investigating the abovementioned hypotheses, an empirical analysis of household and village level data from Kangra district of Himachal Pradesh was done. The study area comprises villages where households have women who are members of a fruit processing and marketing cooperative called Samridhi Mahila Cooperative Society (SMCS). Samridhi is considered to be a success story in Kangra and is perceived to have improved rural livelihoods along with conserving the environment (Ahal, 1996; 2003). It is seen as a successful agrobusiness consortium and as an example of rural women's empowerment ("Gender Empowerment", Himachal Pradesh Development Report, 2005). Under Samridhi, local women form cooperatives called women's production groups (WPGs) and collect and process fruit into pickles, chutneys and candy. The products are made at village production centres. These products are further processed, checked for quality, packaged and marketed by the 'Apex' located at Thakurdwara, near Palampur town in Kangra district. The Apex represents the headquarters of the cooperative and is managed by the top office-bearers of the cooperative, who are also members drawn from the surrounding villages.

Samridhi had its beginnings in 1996 under the Indo-German Changar Eco Development Project (IGCEDP), which was initiated in 1993 with support from the Government of Himachal Pradesh and the Government of Germany (through the GTZ) in an effort to improve natural resources and forest-based livelihoods in the Changar area. Although the IGCEDP provided support in a number of ways, it gradually withdrew professional support and by 2000 had done so completely, handing over the entire administration and financial responsibility to the SMCS (Sircar, 2002). The SMCS has grown steadily from 16 members in 1996–97 to 182 members in 2000–01, with sales rising from Rs 17,000 to Rs 17,26,671, production from 425 kgs to 22,685 kgs, and total wages paid from Rs 4,250 to Rs 4,16,156 over the same period.

Collection of fruit is mostly from government (protected) forests, although, in recent times, there has been an increase in fruit collected from trees planted on private land as well, which indicates that farmers view the sale of fruit to the production centres of Samridhi as an income earning opportunity. Some smaller amounts of collection also take place from common lands around villages. Among the fruit being collected, the two most important ones are mango (locally called *aam* or *Mangifera indica)* and *amla (Emblica officinalis).*

Findings from the Field

For this study, 15 villages in Kangra district, which had Samridhi members, were surveyed. The sampling technique was simple: With a target sample size of 500, all the member households were selected and the non-member households were distributed across villages in proportion to the total number of households. The 15 selected villages had 182 member households, of which 173 were available at the time of the survey. After making the necessary statistical adjustments, a total of 339 non-member households were surveyed.

Household Income and Expenditure

The survey also collected data on some major items of household expenditure. While the mean monthly household expenditure was Rs 2,374.65, the expenditure on food items averaged at Rs 1,373.45 per month. This can be compared with the reported mean monthly household income of Rs 4,548.76. It was also interesting to observe from the data that while only 95 households reported that they had borrowed money from local money lenders, most of these households are among the better-off households, and more than 50 per cent had borrowed between Rs 10,000 and Rs 60,000 in the last one year. The second head on which a sizeable proportion of monthly expenditure is incurred is on education of children. Expenditure on entertainment is the least at Rs 123 per month. A comparison of the average monthly household income with expenditure shows that expectedly, lower income villages spend proportionately higher amounts of their incomes.

Among the members of the WPG, 82 per cent of the members who reported savings data, stated that their monthly savings varied between 5 per cent and 50 per cent of what they earned, while around 18 per cent save in the range of 60–100 per cent of their WPG income.

Primary Occupation

When we look at the distribution of primary occupations across all the households, we find that the bulk of the workforce, 52 per cent, is engaged in salaried employment. The second major occupation category is assured wage labour with a share of 15 per cent, while petty business/manufacturing and work at the cooperative have a share of 12 per cent, followed by casual labour at 8 per cent. Farm cultivation and collection for self-consumption have a negligible share in the primary occupation of households in these villages. The distribution of average monthly income by different occupation categories shows that salaried employment has the highest returns, followed by petty business/trade/manufacturing, and then by own farm cultivation.

Housing and Asset Ownership

Around 26 per cent of the households lived in *pucca* constructions, 54 per cent had semi-*pucca* constructions, while the rest had *kutcha* constructions.

The 'wealth' status of the households was sought to be captured by constructing a score for each household taking into account the assets owned by the household. Five assets that were found relevant to the study were bicycles, scooters/motorbikes, refrigerator, television and telephone. A household got a score of one for each asset that it owned and 0 for those which it did not. Subsequently, a principal components analysis was done and a score was thereby generated as a proxy for capturing the wealth effect. Across 492 households, the mean value was 1.71, indicating that asset ownership was on the lower side for most households.

Caste Structure

The villages of Kangra district falling in our sample area represent a relatively high aggregate percentage of upper caste households (56.48 per cent) as compared to lower caste households (43.52 per cent).[4] The upper castes are represented by the Rajput, Brahmin, Chowdhry and Dheeman castes, while Koli, Kabir Panthi, Mhasa, Jogi, Doomer, Lohar and Harijan are the lower castes. Out of a total of 15 villages, eight villages are dominated by higher castes, whereas four villages have a higher proportion of lower caste households. Barring Tambar, Daglehr and Dhati, in all the other villages lower caste households have relatively more representation in the WPGs.

Literacy

Out of a total of 492 sample households, 75 per cent were male-headed households, while the remaining 25 per cent were female-headed households. The literacy rate in the sampled Samridhi villages (82 per cent) is higher than the rate for Himachal Pradesh (77 per cent) and slightly higher than that for Kangra district (81 per cent) for the year 2001.

Contribution of CPRs to Economic Well-Being

While the contribution of CPR-based activity to the average household income is quite small, this contribution in the poorer households is quite large ranging from 20 per cent to 40 per cent of their incomes. This suggests that CPRs are still a very important source of income for the poor.

The contribution of CPRs to household incomes was examined by creating a ratio of WPG income to total household income. In the lowest expenditure class, for instance, this ratio (extent of contribution of WPG income) is more than 33 per cent for 53 per cent of the households. The proportion of households with such high contributions from WPG incomes falls steadily as one moves up the expenditure classes. When it comes to the contribution of CPR-based incomes in improving household incomes, it is clear that the less well-off gain more relative to their total incomes from such value-addition activities.

It was also found that better-off households spend relatively less time on collections, both because time costs are lower for collecting from own lands rather than CPRs and also because they may have easier access to disposable income to pay fees to other villagers for collection.

Forest Conservation Activities

All the villagers interviewed felt that the forest area had 'increased' over the last five to ten years mainly due to the government (including the Changar project) and local (villagers involved with Samridhi activities) efforts in conserving forests. Sixty-four per cent of the households reported that they took active measures such as building fences and barriers to protect trees. Around 40 per cent households indicated that they had actively encouraged their neighbours in tree-protection activities. The poor in particular, not only seem to have a heightened awareness of the benefits from conservation activities, but also engage much more in encouraging such activities among the community. A larger proportion of relatively poorer households are involved in such activity both across and within income classes. This suggests that the poor contribute relatively more to the protection of CPR resources as compared to the better-off. Poorer households are also more likely to plant on common lands, while wealthier (land-owning) households plant more trees on their own land.

An econometric analysis of tree-planting behaviour revealed that collection time, educational levels, membership of the organisation, extent of development in the village, and the total land owned by a household impacts significantly on the decision to plant trees.

At the household level, it is individual land holdings that are important, apart from the other significant explanatory variables. Further, it is the better-off in terms of landholdings that would be able to take maximum advantage of the complementarities with market linkages. Taking tree-planting across the entire sample, the probability of planting is higher for the wealthier.

Improving Gender and Social Relations

The institutional evolution process shapes the possible outcomes for the development constituents, of which the economic outcomes are one important component. There arises a need to look at the other constituents which get influenced by the institution and in turn play an important role in influencing the future evolution of the institution. There exists a complex web of interactions between the economic and social aspects of well-being.

A qualitative approach is adopted in attempting to highlight this aspect by analysing a set of semi-structured interviews that were conducted with a few key informants. The informants included Panchayat members of the village (village leaders), school teachers and the office-bearers of the production centres. The interviews capture the perceptions of the people regarding key issues. The following paragraphs report on these and present some representative quotes from the interviews.[5]

The important role played by the project officials initially and the NGO in initiating activities is obvious. Also of interest are the range of perceptions on what motivates an individual to join the WPG. Women stated that they were happy and proud to go out and work and earn some additional income for their families. Social recognition as income earning members of the family, personality development, and the opportunity to be together were the reasons cited for working and forming the groups.

Some quotes:

Seema Devi: "We were very happy to think that *we were recognised as working* women".

Mishro Devi: The most important reasons for the formation of WPG were "interest, satisfaction and *desire of women to go out* and work"; "we took it as *an opportunity to improve our personality* and money was considered as a secondary thing."

Pushpa Devi: "When Samridhi people came to know that we were interested to join they came and trained us. We wanted *to earn money and know about people.*" Sushma Devi: "Both the fruits and the *time of women got wasted earlier,* but when Changar people came and taught us about the usefulness of fruit processing, we started working."

Meera Devi: "Women were interested and excited to be able *to earn money and acquire knowledge.*"

Overall, the groups (and, by and large, the villagers) are very optimistic about future prospects and see themselves as growing with the organisation. They are very enthusiastic about the prospects of getting insurance cover and a share in profits. They look forward to the formation of new groups each year and expansion of their activities as a means to more prosperity in their homes and lives.

Conclusion

The role of CPRs in supporting rural livelihoods through initiation of value-added activities has been well documented. Much less is known about the long-term implications of such value-added activities for the resources themselves and the institutions that govern the use of these resources.

We find that commercial use of forested common lands can increase the returns per unit time spent on collection activity. Improved access to markets, and higher returns from sales, by adding value to forest products, can motivate preservation of the forest. However, on the other hand, alternative income opportunities resulting from economic development can also adversely affect incentives for conserving natural resources. If this happens, the impact on the resource is ambiguous. Further, in terms of welfare implications, it may also lead to distributionally regressive outcomes, with newly emerging opportunities being more accessible to those with greater initial wealth and greater market access (Dasgupta, 2006).

Commercial use of common lands can increase the returns per unit time spent on collection activity. Value-addition at the local level, to the extent that it represents reduced transaction costs or a move towards more optimum rents, implies a welfare improvement. Further, benefits are likely to grow over time from the learning process involved in local entrepreneurial activity. From the point of view of preservation of the resource, it is also likely that the implicit discount rate could be higher for outsiders (as buyers) than for the local community. This implies that there is better preservation of the resource even with commercialisation if value-added activities benefit locals.

In the study area in Himachal Pradesh, commercialisation of CPRs is seen as a means for both economic development and resource improvement. For example, a recent report on the area notes that "the impacts on conservation are now easily available. The *amla* trees in forests and haylands, which were just like a bush to them and were cut for firewood, are today carefully preserved. The right holders are now zealously guarding the mango trees on common lands, which were beginning to be cut and to be made into furniture. Families are now planting lime and other trees on private lands" (Ahal, 2003).

Value-addition of CPR products leads to increased income from CPRs. The increased income from CPRs resulting from such activities in turn contributes to increased protection of trees in CPRs and the creation of institutions, i.e., norms, to protect trees in CPRs. To this extent the conclusion counters popular wisdom that an increase in demand and profitability from CPR products can lead to unsustainable harvests in the short run. Rather, this study shows that where there is a learning process about income earning possibilities, enabled by the creation and evolution of appropriate institutions, there is a dampening effect on the degradation of the CPRs and an increase in conservation activities relating to both private and CPR resources.

Commercialisation of CPR products, however, also leads to tree-planting activities on private land outside the CPRs. In the absence of complete and secure rights over CPRs, this in turn implies that the returns in the long run could benefit households differentially while having ambiguous effects on the CPR itself (Dasgupta, 2006).

The present study finds substantial evidence of the contributions that are made by the CPR-related activity in enhancing well-being of the communities dependent on them, particularly women. These contributions are not always amenable to measurement in quantitative terms, but are an essential part of the development process, particularly in the South Asian context. Improved gender, family and community-level relations occur simultaneously with material well-being if interventions are well formulated and implemented. The achievements of the women's cooperative on these fronts, in the empowerment and education of its women members, is a success story meriting attention in its own right. Although it is intertwined with the income-generating activity in the initial stages, the impacts continue even as the income-enhancing aspect of the value-addition activity gets differentiated within the same community.

In the context of attaining Millennium Development Goals (MDGs) it is clear that the headcount poverty index (HCI) has been declining, but consistently the rural HCI has been higher than the urban one. Also, the decline in either HCI has not been fast enough. Further, it is clear to development economists that there is no reason to expect automatic improvement in the non-monetary indicators of development even in situations where income growth is widely seen as being positive. This seems to be as well accepted today as the fact that there has not been enough trickle down from purely growth oriented approaches. Increasingly, this has in turn led to the adoption of alternative approaches to tackle problems such as community approaches and governance reforms based approaches, the latter not necessarily being inclusive of the former.

It is important to draw insights from the experience of the women's co-operative that may have important implications for our planning for development projects. After all, the attainment of the MDGs, of eradication of extreme poverty and hunger, is critical to the achievement of other goals, including ensuring environmental sustainability. One praise-worthy attempt is the UNESCO's Gender, Science and Technology (GST) Programme, which aims at mainstreaming a gender perspective in development and implementation of science and technology policies, programmes and activities. Building bridges between women in local communities and the 'modern' sector is an important aspect of tackling rural poverty and empowering women living in poverty. The implementation of innovative grass-roots science and technology based programmes through NGO initiatives is an important aspect worth promoting from this perspective (Hermawati, 2006). The important point to recognise is the need for moving towards innovative technology and its transfer, and not limiting it to traditional technologies. The successful implementation of technologies appropriate to poor women would require linkages to financial services and markets. Effective natural resource management, which combines preservation with sustained income generation, requires support in terms of appropriate institutional frameworks such as legally enabling conditions where the state can play a primary role. An appropriate institutional framework would also encourage community partnerships with private agents who may be better able to provide financial and marketing support.

.This is different from the traditional thinking on seeing women as those who bear a disproportionate burden of degradation of the environment and, therefore, the need to protect the commons. The present perspective is more in keeping with the demands of a changing society in rural India. A combination of decentralised production units, with centralised marketing, product promotion, management and training components, seems to have yielded benefits for all concerned. The salient feature has been the involvement of local women in all the stages of the enterprise.

There are many such examples of best practice cases from across the South Asian region including India, the Philippines, China, Vietnam, Indonesia and Mongolia.[6] The key lies in recognising the potential for improving the quality of life of poor women in rural areas through simple initiatives that build on existing knowledge, technology and practices, and with appropriate institutional support (institutional innovation need not depend only on the state, it could be from an NGO or a private individual or a local collective) can translate into processes with major potential. There has been more focus and perhaps rightly so in conditions of extreme poverty, on the more tangible and easily measurable impacts in terms of increased incomes, time savings or improved health outcomes. However, the impacts on improved family and gender relations are outcomes of these processes which may occur in a major way, as repeatedly emphasised by the women in the present case.

Finally, the present study reveals that the experience with commercialisation can be quite context and situation specific. The nature of the commercialisation process and the types of commodities involved are important determinants. The commercialisation process does not occur in a vaccum, but has positives and negatives, not only in terms of eocnomic outcomes, but also social outcomes. Hence, when planning for interventions that sustain and create incentives for maximising economic gains (rents as commonly understood in the CPR context), the social impacts also need to be taken into account.

Notes

1. CPRs are defined here as resources with varying degrees of access on which multiple and often overlapping property rights and regulatory regimes exist. Such rights of access include those defined on different categories of government forests. The de facto access may be limited to some groups and legitimised either by law or convention, customary rights or traditional practices.
2. The World Development Report 2000/2001 defines poverty as the pronounced deprivation of well-being (World Bank, 2001).
3. More details are provided in the section on description of study area.
4. According to the Census of India 1991, there were about 63 per cent upper caste households and about 37 per cent lower caste households in these villages
5. Throughout this section, all names have been changed to maintain confidentiality.

6. Such initiatives include those of food technology, sericulture, floriculture, waste management, medicinal plants, aquaculture, environmental protection. For more details, see Hermawati (2006).

References

Agrawal, A., and G.N. Yadama. 1997. 'How Do Local Institutions Mediate Market and Population Pressures on Resources? Forest Panchayats in Kumaon, India' in *Development and Change*. 28: 435–465.

Agrawal, A. 2001. 'Common Property Institutions and Sustainable Governance of Resources' in *World Development*. 29(10): 1649–1672.

Agrawal, A., and C.C. Gibson 1999. 'Enchantment and Disenchantment: The Role of Community in Natural Resource Conservation' in *World Development*. 27(4): 629–649.

Agarwal, B. 2001. 'Participatory Exclusions, Community Forestry, and Gender: An Analysis for South Asia and a Conceptual Framework' in *World Development*. 29(10): 1623–1648.

Ahal, R. 1996. 'The Unfulfilled Vision: An Account of Village Forest Cooperative Societies of Kangra District, Himachal Pradesh'. Kathmandu, Nepal: ICIMOD.

Ahal, R. 2003. 'The Process Documentation of Samridhi Mahila Cooperative Society'. Draft Report, Personal Communication from Navrachna, Palampur.

Alkire, S. 2002. 'Dimensions of Human Development' in *World Development*. Vol. 30(2), pp. 181–205.

Amacher, G.S., W.F. Hyde, and M. Rafiq. 1993. 'Local Adoption of New Forestry Technologies: An Example from Pakistan's Northwest Frontier Province', in *World Development*. 2(3): 445–453.

Annual Report 2002–2003, 'Samridhi Mahila Sahakari Sabha, Varshik Report 2002–03'. Thakurdwara, Kangra, Himachal Pradesh.

Baland, J.M, and J.P. Platteau 2003. 'Economics of Common Property Management Regimes' in Karl-Göran Mäler and Jeffrey R. Vincent (eds.), *Handbook of Environmental Economics*. Vol. 1, Amsterdam: Elsevier Science.

Besley, T. 1995. 'Property Rights and Investment Incentives: Theory and Evidence from Ghana' in *Journal of Political Economy*. 103(5): 903–937.

Bluffstone, R., M. Boscolo and R. Molina. 2004. 'Does Better Common Property Forest Management Improve Rural Livelihoods? Evidence from Bolivia'. Department of Economics, Portland State University, *Mimeo*.

Bon, E. 2000. 'Common Property Resources: Two Case Studies', in *Economic and Political Weekly*. XXXV (28 and 29) July 15: 2569–2573.

Brasselle, A., F. Gaspart and J. Platteau. 2002. 'Land Tenure Security and Investment Incentives: Puzzling Evidence from Burkina Faso' in *Journal of Development Economics.* (67): 373–418.

Byron, N., and M. Arnold. 1999. 'What Futures for the People of the Tropical Forests?' in *World Development.* 27(5): 789–805.

Census of India. 1991. District Census Handbook (Kangra), Series 9, Part XII A and B. 'Village Primary Census Abstract'. Himachal Pradesh: Director of Census Operations. 617–1363.

Chambers, R. and M. Leach 1989. 'Trees as Savings and Security for the Rural Poor' in *World Development.* 17(3): 329–342.

Chomitz, K. 1995. 'Roads, Land, Markets and Deforestation: A Spatial Model of Land Use in Belize'. Paper presented at the First Open Meeting of the Human Dimensions of Global Environmental Change Community, Duke University, Durham. June 1–3.

Chopra, K., and P. Dasgupta. 2002. 'Common Pool Resources in India: Evidence, Significance and New Management Initiatives'. Final report of DFID-sponsored project on Policy Implications of Knowledge with Respect to Common Pool Resources, undertaken jointly with the University of Cambridge, UK.

———. 2003. 'The Nature of Household Dependence on Common Pool Resources: An Econometric Study for India'. *Working Paper Series No. E/232/2003.* Delhi: Institute of Economic Growth.

Chopra, Kanchan, G.K. Kadekodi and M.N. Murty. 1990. *Participatory Development: People and Common Property Resources.* New Delhi: Sage Publications.

Dasgupta, P. 2006. 'Common Pool Resources as Development Drivers: A Case Study of NTFPs in Himachal Pradesh, India'. SANDEE Working Paper (referred) No. 15–06. Kathmandu, Nepal: SANDEE.

Dasgupta, P., and K.G. Maler. 2004. 'Environmental Resource Economics: Some Recent Developments'. Special Issue, SANDEE Working Paper, No. 7–04. Kathmandu, Nepal: SANDEE.

Dewees, P.A. 1995. 'Trees on Farms in Malawi: Private Investment, Public Policy and Farmer Choice' in *World Development.* 23(7): 1085–1102.

Godoy, R.A. 1992. 'Determinants of Smallholder Commercial Tree Cultivation' in *World Development.* 20(5): 713–725.

Greene, W.H. 2003. *Econometric Analysis.* 5th edition. USA: Pearson Education.

Hermawati, W. 2006. 'Innovative Grass-roots Technology for Women's Empowerment and Sustainable Development: Experience from the Asia-Pacific Countries'. Sixth Conference of the Science Council of Asia, April 17–19, 2006, New Delhi, India.

Himachal Pradesh Development Report. 2005. Planning Commission, Government of India. New Delhi: Academic Foundation.

Jodha, N.S. 1997. 'Management of Common Property Resources in Selected Dry Areas of India' in J.M. Kerr, D.K. Marothia, K. Singh, C. Ramasamy, and W.R. Bentley (eds.), *Natural Resource Economics: Theory and Application in India*. New Delhi: Oxford and IBH Publishing Company, Pvt. Ltd.

———. 2001. *Life on the Edge: Sustaining Agriculture and Community Resources in Fragile Environments*. Delhi: Oxford University Press.

Lybbert, T.J., C.B. Barrett, and H. Narjisse. 2002. 'Market-Based Conservation and Local Benefits: The Case of Argan Oil in Morocco' *Ecological Economics*. 41:125–144.

MEA. 2003. 'Ecosystems and Human Well-Being: A Framework for Assessment, Millennium Ecosystem Assessment'. Washington DC: Island Press. (Chapter 3 – Colin Butler, Robert Chambers, Kanchan Chopra, Partha Dasgupta, et al.).

Narayan, D., R. Chambers, M. Shah, and P. Petesch. 2000. *Voices of the Poor: Crying Out for Change*. New York: Oxford University Press.

North, D.C. 1994. 'Institutional Change: A Framework of Analysis' in *Economic History, No. 9412001*. Articles available at the website of: Economics Working Paper Archive at WUSTL.

North, D.C. and R. Thomas. 1993. 'The Rise of the Western World: A New Economic Thought'. Available at *http://ideas.repec.org/e/pro11.html#works*.

NSSO. 1999. 'Common Property Resources in India'. NSS 54th Round (January 1998–June 1998), Government of India.

Ostrom, E. 1990. *Governing the Commons: The Evolution of Institutions for Collective Action*. Cambridge: Cambridge University Press.

Otsuka, K., A.R. Quisumbing, E. Payongayong and J.B. Aidoo. 2003. 'Land Tenure and the Management of Land and Trees: The Case of Customary Land Tenure Areas of Ghana' in *Environment and Development Economics*. 8: 77–104.

Pasha, S.A. 1992. 'CPRs and Rural Poor: A Micro-Level Analysis' in *Economic and Political Weekly*. November 14, 2499–2503.

Place, F., and K. Otsuka. 2001. 'Population, Tenure, and Natural Resource Management: The Case of Customary Land Area in Malawi' in *Journal of Environmental Economics and Management*. 41(1): 13–32.

Rao, K.K. 2000. 'Vegetation and Non-Timber Forest Products Assessment under JFM in Eastern Ghats of Andhra Pradesh, India'. Visakhapatnam: Dept. of Environmental Sciences, Andhra University, Monograph.

Ravindranath, N.H., P. Sudha and K.M. Indu. 2000. 'Participatory Forestry: Indian Experience in Community Forestry and Joint Forest

Management'. Bangalore: Centre for Ecological Sciences, Indian Institute of Sciences.

Reardon, T., and S.A. Vosti. 1995. 'Links between Rural Poverty and the Environment in Developing Countries: Asset Categories and Investment Poverty' in *World Development.* 23(9): 1495–1506.

Schatzki, Todd. 2003. 'Options, Uncertainty and Sunk Costs: An Empirical Analysis of Land Use Change' in *Journal of Environmental Economics and Management.* 46(1): 86–105.

Shively, G.E. 1999. 'Prices and Tree Planting on Hillside Farms in Palawan' *World Development.* 27(6): 937–949.

Sircar, Surbhi. 2002. 'Eco Income Generation: For Sustainable Livelihoods Generation in the Mountains'. IGCEDP Report, Palampur, Kangra, Himachal Pradesh.

Vira, B. 2002. 'Conceptualising the Commons: Power and Politics in a Globalising Economy'. University of Cambridge: Department of Geography, Monograph.

'Working Plan (Revised) for Palampur Forest Division for the Period 1981–82 to 1995–96'. Volumes I and II, Department of Forest Farming and Conservation, Himachal Pradesh.

10

An Encounter between University Teachers and the Rural Women of Jhargram
The Narrative of a Workshop and the Lessons Learnt

ABHIJIT GUHA

In this paper we have made an attempt to construct the ethnography of an encounter between a group of poor rural women belonging to various tribal and caste populations and a team of anthropologists and historians in the setting of a workshop. Traditionally, the anthropologists observe human behaviour in their naturally occurring contexts for a prolonged period of time and describe the various dimensions of a particular culture in the form of writing for the wider audience. This is known as ethnography. Ethnography involves a kind of storytelling about a particular cultural practice (e.g., performance of a ritual) or a social institution (e.g., matrilineal kinship) in which the ethnographer participates with the people in a particular setting in order to discover the 'insider's view' about their own behaviour and the world around them. Since its inception through the writings of Bronislow Malinowski in the 1920s (Malinowski, 1922), the style of ethnographic writing has undergone, many changes of which the genre developed by Clifford Geertz has gained the most popularity among professional anthropologists in recent times. In this particular style of ethnographic practice, the presence of the people as characters is more important. This style of ethnographic practice was termed by Geertz as 'thick description', in which he incorporated his own interactions with the different human characters in the field (Geertz, 1973). Geertzian ethnography, therefore, differed from the

Malinowskian style in its attempt to unfold the complex layers of meaning of the behaviour and acts of the people while they interact with the ethnographer. The methodology of participation (particularly when conducted to bring about 'development'), however, has recently been critiqued by a group of scholars on the ground that it also sometimes entails a kind of tyranny upon the people among whom the ethnographer works (Cooke and Kothari, 2001). In this paper, we have tried to unfold the changing world views of a group of women while they interacted with researchers who were making an attempt to understand their achievements and aspirations. Additionally, we have also made an attempt to place our own understanding of the events and activities of the people of the locality before the women in the form of writing in the setting of a workshop. All these helped us to discover the meaning of personhood (one may call it womanhood), which the Jhargram women attached to their lives in the context of gradual transformation leading to empowerment of the 'second sex'.

The Background: Two Types of Knowledge Systems

The Centre for Women's Development Studies (CWDS) has been trying to involve Vidyasagar University in action research in the various fields of rural development, where the role of women is traditionally being ignored by the academic disciplines. The basic thrust of the CWDS in this endeavour was to set the stage for a series of encounters in different kinds of settings between the poor rural women (who are undergoing a transformation in the various facets of their material and ideological levels of existence) and the faculties as well as the students of Vidyasagar University, which was established as a non-traditional institution by the Government of West Bengal in 1981. These encounters can be viewed as interactions between two kinds of knowledge systems, which have their own genesis and modes of transmission, yet are dependent on one another.

On the one hand, the poor rural women, through their daily struggle for existence and being part of a wider socioeconomic and cultural formation, have been developing their own strategies for survival as cultural identities. The maintenance and continuation of these cultural identities are dynamic processes wherein the CWDS acts as an outside agency whose employees have been gradually becoming part of the 'inner world' of these poor rural women, who belong to the tribal groups and lower caste groups of Southwest Bengal.

On the other hand Vidyasagar University is a new institution, located in a rural area in Medinipur district. Although young, the university has already been developing its own modes of transmission of knowledge, which are not too different from other established and traditional universities in West Bengal. The university has its social science departments, which include anthropology with compulsory fieldwork, and there is scope for teaching action-oriented courses, although there is little scope for studying rural women's development within the existing framework of the syllabus.

It is against this backdrop that the CWDS initiated a move to involve a few students and teachers of the Department of Anthropology to collect some life historical materials from the rural women of Jhargram subdivision in the middle of 1998. Three teachers of the Department of Anthropology came forward with four postgraduate students (two of whom are inhabitants of the locality where the fieldwork was supposed to be carried out), who agreed to work on this project the ultimate aim of which was to produce a monograph on the dynamics of the various levels of consciousness of the rural women, who are organising themselves to achieve autonomy in the economic, social and cultural spheres of life under the catalytic influence of the CWDS' Jhargram project.

Another related but no less important objective of this project was to make the rural women aware of the importance of oral history and the active role they can play in constructing the history of their region within the wider context of the regional and even national history, which is taught in colleges and universities. For this purpose, one history teacher attached to the CWDS and a student of history of Vidyasagar University also took active part in the discussion with the rural women.

The third objective of the project was to develop an interdisciplinary endeavour towards the collection of oral historical as well as anthropological materials for the vivid portrayal of the material conditions and level of consciousness of the rural women who live at the intersection of various local, regional and national level socio-economic and political forces.

As a first step towards achieving these objectives, a workshop was organised in Jhargram during August 14-17, 1998, to train the five researchers who would employ anthropological and historical methods to collect factual materials on the perception and world view of the rural women who have been organised by the CWDS since 1996.

The Workshop: Breakdown of Traditional Pedagogy

From the beginning, the setting of the workshop was very much unorthodox as 10 rural women, five students and their teachers sat face to face in order to learn each other's viewpoint. The teachers were supposed to deliver lectures on the aims and objectives of the workshop, the history of the CWDS, oral history, the sociodemographic profile of the villages, anthropological perspectives on the status of women and the theory and practice of life history methods with examples drawn from the lives of the women who participated in the workshop.

Initially, the teachers felt a little nervous about how to transmit knowledge from their system to the rural women, none of whom has crossed the level of higher secondary education and most of whom could only sign their names. But with perseverance and humility from both sides, a lot of anthropological and historical findings smoothly crossed the barrier between the 'educated' and the 'uneducated'. More interesting were the reactions of the women towards the so-called academic materials, that were presented before them. But before describing their reactions, we should talk of certain important behavioural expressions of these women, which are now in order.

1. Throughout the tightly scheduled programme of the workshop, which used to start at 10 am and end at 6.30 pm with a one and a half hour break for lunch for four consecutive days, we never found any woman inattentive or leaving the meeting hall. They listened to our lectures with rapt attention and intervened time and again even when they were not invited to do so. Some of the women (especially the younger ones) took notes in their books, which were supplied to them by the CWDS, and assured the Jhargram project supervisor of the organisation that they would submit their views in writing about the workshop.

2. The interventions of these women did not always come up with pointed questions, but look the form of narratives about their own personal histories, local level incidents and, most interestingly, proverbs and their own perceptions about the changing world around them.

3. A common theme, which always ran through the easy and casual drawl of the village women, was their perception of the changing environment around them and their painful struggle for existence from time immemorial. Every now and then, women of different age groups narrated the major events of their life in a dynamic form. Everything flowed from of their description: depletion of forests, preparation of canals, coming of the Left Front government, entry of the market economy and the meetings of the CWDS, which have drawn many of them out of their daily domestic chores

for some time. Things and events never remained static in the eyes of these peasant women. They never seemed to live in a world of 'timeless present', as it is usually conceived in the mainstream anthropological accounts of tribal societies, which are being taught to undergraduate students of anthropology. The dynamic form of the narratives of these women in this sense challenged the basic methodological assumptions of the standard ethnographic texts of the tribal communities of the world.

4. Another lesson that these women taught the teachers and students of Vidyasagar University was their intense desire to apply the knowledge gained from the workshop. This simple desire to find applications of knowledge distinguished the participants of this workshop from the students of universities, where almost similar kinds of inputs, in terms of teaching materials, rarely evoke such responses.

Themes of the Workshop

The abovementioned salient features depict the 'stage' on which the encounter between two types of knowledge systems took place. In the traditional setting of a college or university, anthropology deals with 'subjects', 'informants' or 'respondents' who are never physically present in the classroom even when the classes are taken in the midst of a tribal village. The 'society' or the 'culture' which anthropologists investigate remains 'out there', a kind of 'objective reality' to be discovered by the anthropologists through the application of scientific methods. But here in the Jhargram workshop in the 'oral history of the peasant women's organisation', the 'subjects' of anthropology became active participants in the pedagogy of the discipline. They interacted not only with the findings of anthropology and history, but also with the people who presented the evidence and the concepts and theories of those disciplines. Now we will describe in brief the proceedings of the workshop.

The workshop revolved around three themes: (i) the anthropological method of fieldwork and the various indicators which one should take into consideration in the study of the status of women in tribal societies, (ii) the basic philosophy behind the collection of life historical materials through anthropological as well as oral historical methods which emphasise the role of the ordinary people and events in the construction of history, and (iii) the socio-economic and demographic background of the area and the peasant woman who have become members of the grass-roots level women organisation. Instead of giving a chronological description of the different lectures delivered by the resource persons and the interesting discussions which almost invariably followed each lecture, we will select some significant interactions of the workshop to highlight the uniqueness of this encounter in the form of a 'thick description'. In fact, we have already set the stage for this type of description in the previous sections of this report.

Learning from Peasant Women: The New Pedagogy

One of the most interesting responses from the women was their reaction towards the cultivation of agricultural fields by the tribal women of Northeast India with the help of a digging stick or hoe.

In general, these peasant women, who are involved with all kinds of agricultural work, except ploughing, listened very carefully to the lectures which dealt with archaeological and anthropo-historical research on the origin of agriculture and about the first domestication of plants by the women of the prehistoric period. In one such session, when an anthropology teacher was describing the details of shifting hill cultivation and the tilling of the soil with the digging stick with the help of a diagram of the implement on the blackboard, one woman enquired: "Can't we make a digging stick here?" The teacher, who was equally curious, wanted to know why she desired a digging stick. The women replied, "Even if the implement does not suit this place, we simply want to have it for showing it to our menfolk that women can also till the soil and grow plants on it." So they wanted a digging stick simply for experimental purposes. The teacher had to admit that during his own student life (some 20 years ago) and his teaching career spanning 12 years, he had never come across this type of question even from girl student with a rural background and he agreed to work on the making of this implement for the rural women.

Another illuminating interaction took place when we asked an old woman, Rukshmini Mahato, about her memories of independence Day. Rukshmini was in her late 60s and the day happened to be August 15. At first, she did not realise what Swadhinata Dibash mean. For her, earlier times meant dense forests coming right upto her house, into which the villagers went to collect the essentials of their peasant life. Her father was the headman of the village and had to work hard to earn his daily subsistence. He had some agricultural land, too. Gradually, the forests depleted and life became hard for them. "Are you talking about the *Bamfront* (Left Front) government?" Rukshmini asked, when we continued our queries on her memories of Swadhinata Dibash. "Yes, with the coming of Jyoti Basu's *amal* (regime), things have changed and we got some work. But nowadays, things are becoming very tricky. Nobody can be relied upon!" In the course of our dialogues, someone mentioned Gandhi's name. Suddenly, her eyes lit up (I borrow this phrase from Indu Agnihotri, who was one of the resource persons and understood very little Bengali) and she immediately recognised that name. "Yes I know him. He struggled." Rukshmini did not seem to hesitate in recalling Gandhiji as she did when she tried to recollect independence Day. This old woman had her own unique style of sharing experiences and ideas. She was one of the most vocal participants of the group. Given a chance, she would go on talking in the local dialect about the acute crises of her own family, her intimate relations with her father and husband, prolonged illness and losing of a job, her schooldays, and many other things.

Sometimes, she also expressed her opinions about certain important issues through interesting proverbs. On one such occasion, a serious discussion was going on about the social resistance of the villagers towards the public life of married women, who have joined the peasant women's organisation. Both the tribal and non-tribal younger women were narrating how the senior members of their families showed their displeasure when they went out to attend the meetings of the organisation at Jhargram. One Kapumoni Soren reported that even in 1993, the women who attended such meetings were told by their in-laws to change their dress after coming from those gatherings, since mixing with women and men of different castes and communities was considered to be 'polluting'! While the discussion was going on, Rukshmini suddenly uttered a proverb: "Dhanya Paisare —

Paisa nai jar,
Bithai janam sansare,
Paisa eman balkari,
Kuner boure bair kare"!

A free English translation of this proverb goes something like this:

"Bravo, money —
Those who do not have you
Have come to this world for nothing,
Money has such strength
That it can drag out the wives
From the corner of their family!

Facing the Women Again or How the Text Returned to the Context

Our research project started its journey in the workshop held during August 14–17, 1998, led to the collection of a lot of material on the sociocultural life and the dynamics of empowerment of the women in the villages by our research scholars. Each of us wrote our own articles based on these materials and, according to our previous plan, we again met with the rule women to read the articles before our 'respondents' in another encounter. The second encounter was organised during October 9–10, 1999, at Jhargram.

During the first encounter, we mainly raised questions to the women and listened to their long narratives of struggle and noted down what they said. In the second encounter, after the initial exchanges, we read our descriptions and analyses of the social milieu and the slow building up of the organisation by the women themselves. It was a unique experience of recording the reflections of the women on our anthropological exercise. In the second workshop, nine women came from different villages. The senior-most teacher of our team, Professor Rajat Kanti Das, started with his paper, which was on the anthropological approach and new methods in women's study. The author began with descriptions of the images of matrilineal society constructed by the anthropologists. He placed the anthropological theories of matrilineal society on his own findings among the matrilineal tribes of Northeast India. When he commented "...the anthropological image of empowered women in the tribal societies has to be viewed in a more critical manner...", one Santal women interrupted and started to narrate the story of the purchase of a piece of land by her husband a few years ago. The woman collected some money from her relatives and gave it to her husband, who is a school teacher and an active member of a Left political party. The woman was also a member of the same political party and served as an elected panchayat member. To her utter surprise, the woman discovered that on the day of the registration of the land, her husband excluded her from the team which would go to the land registration office! The team consisted of her husband, one of his friends and her own eldest son. She protested vehemently to her husband, demanding her presence in the team as well as her joint ownership in the land. Her otherwise progressive husband did not agree to include her in the team and a heated exchange ensued between them. The women was however so adamant on establishing her right over their would-be family land that her husband ultimately agreed to take her in the team and she also signed the registration document.

This was the first substantial intervention by a tribal peasant woman on the paper presented by a university teacher. The devotion and interest with which the women listened to the text presented by Prof. Das became clear as soon as he finished. Almost all of them critically reviewed his paper and expressed their frank opinion without any hesitation. They raised the following points.

1. In his description, Prof. Das omitted the incidents of one particular village named Borsol.
2. Although the author did not mention any name, all the women said that they could the person he was talking about. They however did not demand that their names be printed in the book. They realised the difficulties on the part of their organisation.
3. Some women did not like the narration of the life histories of individual women in part. But then some other women also said, "We could feel a rhythm (*chhando*) since Rajatbabu joined the life histories of many women in a single description. Had he described every life history in full, they might have lost their patience in listening to them."
4. The women mentioned another point every now and then. They said, "Everybody will understand the direction in which the events are moving!" They could sense that the publication of the book would strengthen their organisation. One woman expressed in a very lucid manner: " If a minister dies, buses, trams and schools stop moving. Who cares if somebody dies at our Mohulboni? Only her relatives cry. But if our *samiti* member dies, all of us would do something for her. Just on the other day, Sulekha Mahato of Borsol passed away. The *samiti* members raised funds for her family. The same thing happened in the case of Sabitri Patar. We also organised condolence meetings for them. These could not be done had there been no *samiti*. Our *samiti* looks at its members from a different angle. Look at one of our very old members. She is unable to do any work, she cannot see and hear. But she can sing, recite rhymes and tell stories. Some of our members even say 'What is the use of keeping this old lady in our *samiti*?' But we can learn a lot of lessons, listen to many stories of the past, we will listen from her."

After Rajatbabu, Gopal started to read his article. He began by explaining the meaning of 'institution' in human society. Here again, the women interrupted and narrated events of sorrow and crises of their own life. When Gopal made some theoretical points on the inheritance of property and bride price and dowry, one women began to describe the painful story of her own life. There was no male member in her family who could manage and look after the agricultural land when her father and only brother died. Her eldest sister had to be married off at the age of nine just to manage the cultivation of the land her mother owned. Some portion of the land had to be given to the son-in-law as dowry. The cultivation of the total land was, however, being looked after by the affinal kins of her elder sister. Some more land had to be sold again at the time of the marriage of her second sister to pay her dowry.

Another women told a very interesting event in their village. A Santal girl who had given her school final examination chose her husband. The girl's guardian was her maternal uncle since her father had died long ago. Her maternal uncle was a government employee and a well-to-do person. He decided to pay a good amount of dowry in kind as neither the husband nor his parents demanded any dowry in cash. The uncle sent a truckload of furniture and utensils to the father-in-law's house. When the truck reached its destination, which was a Santal village, the village headman and other office-bearers of the traditional village council did not allow the dowry to reach the father-in-law's house since it was not customary for a Santal bridegroom's family to receive marriage payments either in cash or kind. The village headman categorically said to the maternal uncle: "As a Santal, you should know that this is not our custom. Moreover, you may have the capacity to pay dowry in order to show your status, but this may influence the other Santals of our village. We do not want this to be introduced in our village." With such informative interventions, Gopal finished his scholarly article and the women were then asked to give their comments. The comments were again very perceptive. They said: (i) Gopalda explained everything, but he did not describe anything directly. He said the joint family is disintegrating, but he did not cite any example from our villages, and (ii) Gopalda uttered the phrase 'the sorrows of the women', but he neither classified them nor offered any concrete cases. Take, for example, the different kinds of sorrow and pain experienced by women in our villages. A woman feels pain in her childhood when she has to drop out from school; she experiences a different kind of unhappiness when she is forced to marry and her pain is even more different when she is treated inhumanly by her in-laws after marriage. The author did not describe these. Our second workshop ended in this manner.

The Lessons Learnt

Our long lectures on the generation of economic surplus, division of labour on the basis of sex and growth of markets for exchange were so nicely epitomised in proverbs that all of us became spellbound for a moment. Moreover, the interventions of the women during our lectures and reading of the papers were so realistic and illuminating that we had to revise many of our paragraphs by taking their observations into account. How could these illiterate woman assimilate our lectures and discuss them so well? That remains a mystery for us, but undoubtedly, we learnt from these women about how to participate in academic discussions bravely with one's own life experiences and a definite purpose towards the betterment of one's present way of living, which is characterised by inequality in almost every aspect of the public and domestic domain. We academicians really lack this kind of commitment towards life when we participate and organise seminars, workshops and conferences. We have a lot to learn from these poor peasant women of Jhargram.

Acknowledgements

I am greatly indebted to the women of the villages of Mahulboni, Ashakanthi, Borsol and Amlatora, who participated in the workshop and enriched it with their perception and intelligent remarks and critical comments about our research project. I also owe a lot to Vina Mazumdar, Lokenath Roy and Narayan Banerjee of the CWDS, who always tried to drag me out from the traditional anthropological ideology nurtured in universities and research institutes.

Notes

1. The peasant women workers of the *samitis* said that while they want to get the married women of the villages to become members of their organisation, they do not want their unmarried daughters to become members. The reason is that women have to change their residence after marriage. So, if an unmarried woman becomes an active member, the organisation will lose her once she gets married. The women, however, did not express their desire to change this system of post-marital residence during the session in which systems of matrilocal residence among Northeast Indian tribal communities were discussed. These women wanted to cultivate the

land, but did not show any desire to live in a matrilocal residence. They were thus quite pragmatic.

2. An elaborated and much expanded version of this encounter has been published as a chapter in a book titled *Dui Prithibir Uttoran*, edited by Vina Mazumdar (in Bengali) in 2002. A much shorter version of this paper was published in the *Journal of the Indian Anthropological Society* in its Volume 37, published in 2002. The book has been published by Stree Publications, Kolkata, and contains chapters by Rajat Kanti Das, Gopal Krishna Chakraborty and Lokenath Roy on the various aspects of the activities of the peasant women's organisation of Jhargram.

References

Cooke, B. and U. Kothari. 2001. 'The Case of Participation as Tyranny?' In Bill Cooked and Uma Kothari (eds) *Participation: The New Tyranny*. London: Zed Books.

Geertz, C. 1973. 'Thick Description: 'Toward an Interpretative Theory of Culture' in Clifford Geertz, *The Interpretation of Cultures*. New York: Basic Books, Inc.

Malinowski, B. 1922. *The Argonauts of the Western Pacific*. London.

11

Gender Differences among Older Persons

A Study Based on the 2001 Population Census of India

DIPENDRA NATH DAS AND MURALI DHAR VEMURI

Societies recognise four stages in the life of a person that are associated with biological changes in that person. The four stages are: childhood, adolescence, adulthood and old age. At any time, the people living in a society can be attributed to being in one of these four stages. But the number of people who are living in each of these stages depends upon the past demographic events that have occurred in the society and the current prevaling demographic regime. The outcome of the demographic regimes culminates in the aged population, which is often regarded as people who are 60 years and over. Currently, in the midst of a demographic transition, many developing countries including India are experiencing rapid shifts in the relative numbers of children, adult population and older persons. This process of population ageing is primarily determined by trends of fertility and secondarily by mortality rates (Mirkin and Weinberger, 2001). Changes in the aged population can substantially affect the economic and social foundations of societies and consequently new challenges have to be addressed. A higher proportion of older persons implies rising costs of care for the elderly, which may create a conflict of generations (Bose and Shankardass, 2004). Considering the increasing number of aged and their importance in development, the United Nations Second World Assembly on Ageing (Madrid, 2002) unanimously adopted the Madrid Political Declaration and International Plan of Action on Ageing, which emphasises abuse of older people. The assembly noted that it is important to address gender specific issues. However, there has not been enough evidence-based research on the gender aspect of the aged. The present paper is an attempt to bring out the gender differentials in the socioeconomic condition of the aged in India.

The growth of older persons in developing countries is much faster than in the developed countries because of rapid changes in age structure. Therefore, it is more difficult for developing countries to adjust to this phenomenon than developed countries, where this change is slow and spread over a longer time. For example, France took more than 110 years to reach 14 per cent older persons to total population from 7 per cent before 1900. Due to rapid transition, it is estimated that the two most populous countries, China and India, will require only around 25 years to make up a 14 per cent aged population from the present share of 7 per cent (Chakraborti, 2004; Mirkin and Weinberger, 2001). In the world, in 1950, the number of persons aged 60 and more was 205 million, which surged to 606 million in 2000, and may rise to two billion by 2050 (United Nations, 2002). At present, India has more than 12 per cent of the world's aged population. In India, since the early 20th century, as shown in Table 1, both the number and proportion of aged persons has been increasing. In 1911, the number of persons 60 years and over was 13.1 million, which increased to 76.6 million in 2001. The corresponding percentages of aged persons in the total population are 5.2 per cent and 7.4. per cent. Most of the persons who are 60 years and over live in rural areas; aged persons residing in the rural areas of the country are 57.4 million and those in the urban areas are 19.2 million. Data on the population of 60 years and over shows that it doubled in the 50 years since 1911, but its subsequent doubling occurred in nearly half the number of years; the population of people who are 60 years and over doubled in just 25 years and this occurred in early the 1990s. The next doubling of this population is likely to occur in around the same number of years and by 2015, the population of the aged in India may number around 104 million.

An examination of the aged population by sex shows that the population of male aged persons in 2001 was 37.8 million and that of the female aged population was more or less the same, 38.9 million, resulting in a sex ratio of 1,029 females for 1,000 males (Office of the Registrar General, 2004). The latest Population Census of India has revealed that after nearly 60 years, the aged sex ratio is favourable to females. For the first time during the intercensal period of 1991 to 2001, the average annual growth rate of the aged female population is substantially higher than the male growth rate (see Table 2). During 1991–2001, while the male growth rate is 2.52 per cent, the female growth rate is 3.52 per cent.

Table 1: Population for All Ages, 60 Years and Above, Percentage of Aged Population by Sex and Sex Ratio for India, 1911–2001

Years	Population for All Ages (in Million)			Population 60 years and Above (in Million)			Percentage of Aged Population (60 years & Above) to Total Population			Females per 1,000 Males	
	Total	Males	Females	Total	Males	Females	Total	Males	Females	All Ages	Age 60 & Above
1911	252.1	128.4	123.7	13.1	6.2	6.9	5.2	4.8	5.6	963	1,123
1921	251.3	128.5	122.8	13.2	6.4	6.8	5.2	5.0	5.5	956	1,050
1931	279.0	142.9	135.8	11.1	5.6	5.6	4.0	3.9	4.1	950	1,000
1941	318.7	163.7	154.7	15.6	8.0	7.6	4.9	4.9	4.9	945	945
1951	361.1	185.5	175.6	20.4	10.2	10.2	5.6	5.5	5.8	947	998
1961	439.2	226.3	212.9	24.8	12.5	12.4	5.6	5.5	5.8	941	992
1971	548.2	284.0	264.1	32.6	16.8	15.9	5.9	5.9	6.0	930	946
1981	683.3	353.4	330.0	42.4	21.6	20.8	6.2	6.1	6.3	934	964
1991	838.6	435.3	403.4	56.7	29.4	27.3	6.8	6.7	6.8	927	931
2001	1028.6	532.2	496.5	76.6	37.8	38.9	7.4	7.1	7.8	933	1,029
2001-R	742.5	381.6	360.9	57.4	28.4	29.1	7.7	7.4	8.1	946	1,026
2001-U	286.1	150.6	135.6	19.2	9.4	9.8	6.7	6.2	7.2	900	1,038

Source: Census of India, 2001 and Premi, M.K. (2003) *Social Demography: A Systematic Exposition*, Jawahar Publishers and Distributors, New Delhi.

The change that has occurred in the growth rates is a result of the different demographic regimes for males and females. Given these demographic regimes will continue, the future population of older persons is expected to be in favour of females. Population projections show that the elderly population is expected to increase to 179 million in 2031 (Rajan, 2003), with a higher percentage of women among the elderly. Since mortality rates are higher among men than women, older women greatly outnumber older men and the percentage of older women tends to increase with advancing age. Therefore, the concerns about the 'oldest old' should be viewed primarily as concerns about older women (Chakraborti, 2004).

Aging among women has deep-rooted implications that are different from that for men. The biology of females goes through drastic change after menopause. The physical and psychological changes, which could be manageable otherwise, become a problem among low socio-culturally exposed and less empowered women. Social and financial insecurity adds to this normal biological process. The family system in India provides social and economic security to the child and the aged. The prevailing preference for sons in Indian society ensures old age security (Vlassof and Vlassof, 1980). But with increasing industrialisation, urbanisation and, more importantly, increasing migration and mobility among the active population, the family structure is changing. Added to this is the changing value system, which is leading to the breaking up of joint families. Intra-household allocation of duties and resources within the joint family system also sometimes reveals exploitation of the aged (Rabindranathan, 2006). This is true for females, who are engaged through their lives in managing household chores and who have no retirement even in their old age. Many women work even in their old age. They are not only engaged in household chores, but also augment the income of the household by caring for the children so that other family members are free to work. Older women are perceived to contribute more than older men to the family as they continue to be engaged in their traditional role in the domestic area of the household. Rajan et al. (2001) examined the health situation among the elderly in India and found that compared with men, older women were in a disadvantageous position. In the view of Chakraborti (2004), older women faced greater risk of physical and psychological abuse due to discriminatory social attitudes, and harmful traditional and customary practices. Widespread poverty and lack of legal protection exacerbate the situation making older women more vulnerable.

The life cycle of women is socially and culturally designed to make them dependent. Dependence on the father or husband or son is an accepted social norm and this dependency syndrome engulfs the entire life cycle of females. Changes in the norms and the accepted life cycle of women drastically alter the life situation of aged women. Without any support from their husband and son in their old age, aged women easily withdraw from society and lead a life of exploitation. Due to very low labour force participation and wage earning, older women have a precarious economic status and are often totally dependent on others (Palloni, 2001). Among the aged, women become the head of the household mostly on the death of their husbands. Female headship imposes more stress on the family and the socio-economic status of a female-headed households is less than that of a male-headed household (Swain, 2004). The low level of education, lack of skill and limited mobility that already fetter women, impacts aged women when they are widowed and in ill health. The problems associated with widowhood are many. In a traditional patriarchal society, widows have no rights or very limited rights of inheritance. Without inheritance rights, widows find themselves totally dependent on the charity of their husband's relatives (United Nations, 2000). This situation is exacerbated in the absence of a meaningful social security system. Some governments have instituted welfare measures for the elderly, especially widows. Gulati (1993) describes the measures the Kerala state government has initiated.

The above studies have examined the status of the elderly in India on the basis of surveys conducted for specific purposes and they tend to focus on the areas and region of the country of interest. The data collected in the Population Census of India 2001 provides an opportunity to examine the different characteristics of persons who are 60 years and more, especially women, for the country as a whole. In the present paper, we portray the profile of aged women in India. We assess the status of aged females in India, and this can be fruitfully employed to generate programmes and policies for the aged in India.

A Gendered Profile of the Aged Population in India

In recent years, persons who are aged 60 years and over are a significant part of the population of India. As mentioned, the latest Census of India, conducted in 2001, has returned 76.6 million persons who are aged 60 years and over, and this group contains more or less an equal number of males and females: 37.8 million males and 38.9 million females. In 1991, the population of persons 60 years and more was 56.7 million and the male and female populations were 29.4 million and 27.3 million, respectively. An important dimension of the population of persons 60 and over is their rapid growth in number. Table 2 shows the average annual population growth rate for all ages and 60 and over by sex from 1911 to 2001. For the census decade of 1991–2001, the average annual growth rate among these persons is 3.01 per cent. The number of females who are 60 years and more have been growing at a higher rate than males. The male and female growth rate during 1991–2001 is 2.52 and 3.52 per cent respectively, per year. These growth rates are considerably higher than for the entire population, which is 2.01 per cent for males and 2.08 per cent for females during 1991–2001. A fundamental change that has occurred in persons who are aged 60 years and more during the intercensal period is the reversal in the sex ratio. In 1991, the sex ratio of persons 60 years and more was 931 females for 1,000 males (see Table 1). This sex ratio increased to 1,029 females for 1,000 males in 2001. In both years, the sex ratio is higher than that for the general population.

Table 2: Average Annual Population Growth Rate (%) for All Ages and 60 Years and Above by Sex for India, 1911–2001

Years	Growth of Population in % (All Ages)			Growth of Population in % (60 Years and Above)		
	Total	Males	Females	Total	Males	Females
1911–21	−0.03	0.01	−0.07	0.08	0.43	−0.25
1921–31	1.04	1.06	1.01	−1.68	−1.44	−1.92
1931–41	1.33	1.36	1.30	3.37	3.65	3.08
1941–51	1.25	1.25	1.27	2.67	2.40	2.95
1951–61	1.96	1.99	1.93	1.96	1.99	1.93
1961–71	2.22	2.27	2.16	2.74	2.97	2.50
1971–81	2.20	2.19	2.23	2.61	2.52	2.71
1981–91	2.05	2.08	2.01	2.91	3.09	2.73
1991–2001	2.04	2.01	2.08	3.01	2.52	3.52
1991–2001-R	1.76	1.72	1.80	2.60	2.08	3.14
1991–2001-U	2.82	2.79	2.86	4.36	3.97	4.75

Source: Computed from Table 1.

The high growth rate of persons who are 60 years and more is a result of the notable increase in life expectancy. Life expectancy at birth has doubled since the independence of the country: In 1999–2003, the life expectancy at birth was 62.7 years. With increase in life expectancy at birth there has been a corresponding increase in life expectancy at older ages and this is more so for females. In 1999–2003, the male life expectancy at age 60 years and 70 years and over was 16.3 and 10.7 years, respectively. The female life expectancy at these ages was 18.5 and 12.2

years, respectively. The higher increase in life expectancy for females is reflected in the higher number of older females.

Estimates of life expectancy at birth for males and females show that over the years, there has been a shift from higher male life expectancy at birth to higher female life expectancy at birth. In 1970–75, life expectancy at birth for males and females was 50.5 years and 49 years respectively (see Figure 1). But, in 1999–2003, male life expectancy at birth was 61.8 years and female life expectancy at birth was 63.5 years. The change to higher female life expectancy at birth has occurred from 1981–85 and since then the male-female difference has been increasing. (In 1981–85, male and female life expectancy at birth was 55.4 years and 55.7 years, respectively.) Thus, with increasing life expectancy at birth for the total population, there has been a larger increase in female life expectancy at birth.

Figure 1: Life Expectancy at Birth for Males and Females, India, 1973–2001

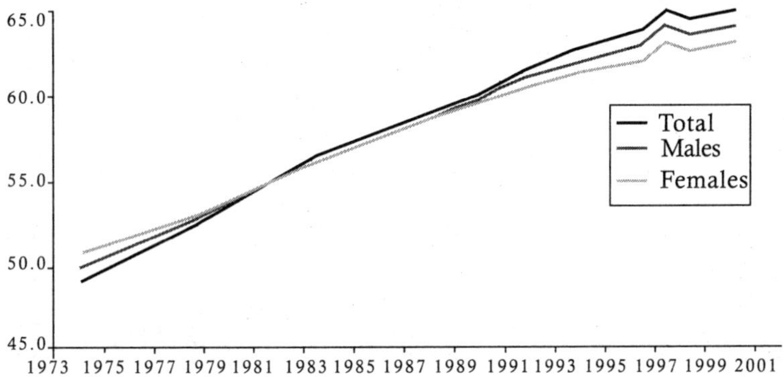

Source: ORGI (2006) SRS Based Abridged Life Tables 1999–2003, Analytical Studies Report No. 1 New Delhi, .

A disturbing fact that emerges from the census is that relating to the marital status of women. As given in Table 3, among all the women who are aged of 60 years and over, 50.7 per cent were recorded as being widowed. This percentage is nearly three times higher than that for males. Among males who are 60 years and above, the percentage widowers is 15 per cent. The percentage of older males and females who are divorced and separated is 0.3 per cent and 0.5 per cent, respectively. A substantial proportion of aged women are the victim of early widowhood because they have lower death rates than men and, on an average, are

Table 3: Distribution of Aged Population according to Marital Status in Rural and Urban Areas by Age and Sex, 2001

Area/Ages	Never Married		Married		Widowed		Divorced/Separated	
	Males	Females	Males	Females	Males	Females	Males	Females
Total								
60+	2.5	1.5	82.1	47.3	15.0	50.7	0.3	0.5
60–64	1.9	1.1	88.0	58.3	9.8	40.0	0.3	0.6
65–69	2.1	1.2	85.1	53.4	12.5	45.0	0.3	0.5
70–74	2.5	1.5	79.6	34.8	17.5	63.3	0.3	0.4
75–79	3.3	1.7	75.2	37.2	21.2	60.6	0.3	0.4
80+	5.4	3.5	65.3	25.1	28.9	71.0	0.4	0.4
Rural								
60+	2.4	1.3	81.6	48.2	15.6	50.1	0.3	0.5
60–64	1.8	0.9	87.3	58.9	10.5	39.6	0.4	0.6
65–69	2.0	1.0	84.6	54.3	13.1	44.2	0.3	0.5
70–74	2.3	1.2	79.3	35.2	18.1	63.2	0.3	0.4
75–79	3.0	1.4	75.1	39.0	21.6	59.3	0.3	0.4
80+	5.0	3.2	65.3	25.6	29.4	70.7	0.4	0.4
Urban								
60+	3.0	2.2	83.7	44.8	13.1	52.4	0.3	0.5
60–64	2.0	1.7	89.9	56.5	7.8	41.2	0.3	0.6
65–69	2.3	1.8	86.9	50.4	10.6	47.3	0.3	0.5
70–74	3.2	2.4	80.9	33.5	15.7	63.7	0.3	0.5
75–79	4.3	2.8	75.5	32.3	19.9	64.4	0.3	0.4
80+	6.9	4.3	65.2	23.5	27.5	71.7	0.3	0.4

Source: Census of India, 2001.

Table 4: Distribution of Head of Households according to Marital Status by Age and Sex in Rural and Urban Areas, 2001

Area/Age Sex of Head of Household	Never Married		Currently Married		Widowed		Divorced/Separated	
	Males	Females	Males	Females	Males	Females	Males	Females
Total								
All Ages	2.5	0.4	83.5	2.8	3.5	6.8	0.2	0.3
60–69	0.6	0.1	74.7	2.3	7.6	14.3	0.2	0.2
70–79	0.6	0.1	68.0	2.0	12.5	16.4	0.2	0.1
80+	23.5	2.7	61.9	4.6	2.9	4.0	0.2	0.2
60+	0.9	0.2	72.5	2.2	9.0	14.8	0.2	0.2
Rural								
All Ages	2.3	0.3	83.6	2.9	3.8	6.6	0.2	0.4
60–69	0.5	0.1	75.3	2.0	8.2	13.4	0.2	0.2
70–79	0.6	0.1	69.1	1.7	13.0	15.1	0.2	0.1
80+	23.2	2.8	62.0	4.6	3.2	3.8	0.2	0.2
60+	0.8	0.1	73.3	2.0	9.6	13.8	0.2	0.2
Urban								
All Ages	3.0	0.5	83.3	2.7	2.5	7.5	0.2	0.3
60–69	0.6	0.3	72.8	2.9	6.0	17.0	0.2	0.2
70–79	0.7	0.3	64.8	2.7	11.0	20.1	0.2	0.2
80+	23.9	2.6	61.6	4.7	2.3	4.6	0.1	0.2
60+	1.0	0.3	70.3	2.9	7.4	17.7	0.2	0.2

Source: Census of India, 2001

younger than their husbands. The age gap between spouses is much higher in India and other Asian countries than in developed countries (Chakraborti, 2004). In their studies, Bumpass et al. have shown that the probability of remarriage, keeping other things constant, is strongly related to sex and age. Women are at a higher risk of not remarrying than men, and older persons have a smaller chance of remarrying than younger people. Consequently, in all ages and more particularly at an older age, widowed and divorced women outnumber widowed and divorced men. Studies have shown that marital status is an important determinant of the well-being of the elderly. Married people are in better health, i.e., they exhibit lower rates of mortality, fewer acute and chronic conditions, lower probability of becoming disabled and less psychiatric morbidity than widowed and divorced people in all ages and of both sexes (Wyke and Ford, 1995). It implies that the larger proportion of elderly women are more susceptible to ill health and conditions of disability than their male counterparts because they are widowed in a higher proportion.

As mentioned, with increase in the longevity of women relative to men, older women may become widowed. This is especially so when widows have a limited chance of marrying again and they may have to shoulder the responsibilities of the household. The census data shows that there are a larger percentage of older females who are widows, who are heading households than that found among male population. Table 4 presents the sex of the head of the household according to marital status for all ages and 60 years and more. In 2001, while female household heads, who are widowed (60 and over) in the country are 14.8 per cent, there are only 6.8 per cent (all ages) such households in the population as a whole. In urban areas, the percentage (17.7 per cent) is higher than in rural areas (13.8 per cent). At higher ages, these differences are sharper; with increase in age, there is a substantial increase in the percentage of widowed women who are heading a household. (An exception is the 80 years and older persons.) There is a need to recognise this section of society when formulating policies and programmes for the aged.

Table 5 shows that among all the persons who are 60 years and more, a larger percentage of females do not work. In the Census of India 2001, while 79.1 per cent of the older women are reported to be non-workers, only 39.8 per cent of the older males do not work. Conversely, those who work in a large proportion are males who continue to work till they retire from their jobs. The population of 60 years and more age group has passed through the social setting where men were traditionally considered to be the breadwinners and women's role was that of housewife. Though males are usually the earning members in a family, the census data is known to not have considered some of work women perform.

Table 5: Distribution of Aged Population by Work Status and Seeking/Available for Work by Age and Sex, 2001

| Age Groups | Total Workers | | Main Workers | | Marginal Workers | | | | Non-Workers | | | |
| | Percentage | | Percentage | | Percentage | | Percentage Seeking/Available for Work | | Percentage | | Seeking/Available for Work | |
	Males	Females	Males	Females	Males	Females	Males	Females	Males	Females	Males	Females
60+	60.25	20.93	87.65	57.30	12.35	42.70	14.53	7.60	39.75	79.07	2.42	1.81
60–69	69.73	26.30	88.24	57.37	11.76	42.63	16.04	7.83	30.27	73.70	3.43	2.20
70–79	49.30	13.32	86.19	56.59	13.81	43.41	11.39	6.52	50.70	86.68	1.82	1.40
80+	34.63	8.57	86.45	58.83	13.55	41.17	11.59	7.78	65.37	91.43	0.94	0.97

Source: Census of India, 2001

Women's work, such as tending animals or collecting cow dung, has been overlooked. This may be more so in the case of older women who perform such activities routinely.

A further examination of the data at different ages for 60 years and more shows that a majority of the males who are working are classified as main workers. In the country, 87.6 per cent of economically active males are returned as main workers, compared with 57.3 per cent of females. However, the opposite is the case for marginal workers: Such female workers are 42.7 per cent of all economically active women while male workers are only 12.3 per cent. A similar picture emerges for those seeking or available for work. A smaller percentage of older females are economically active and of those who are economically active a larger percentage are marginal workers. These differences are present even at older ages, but, as can be expected, male participation in economic activities sharply decreases after they reach 70 years and more (data not shown).

The Census of India 2001 also provides information on the nature of activities that marginal (Table 6) and non-workers (Table 7) undertake. These activities and persons have been categorised as students, household duties, dependents, pensioners and others such as beggars and vagrants. Among non-workers, a high percentage of both males and females are dependents. Among males, 60.7 per cent and among females, 57.4 per cent are classified as dependents. Household duties are carried out, not surprisingly, more by females (35.1 per cent) than males (4.1 per cent). A high percentage of males are pensioners compared with females. While 23 per cent of males receive a pension, only 4.2 per cent of the females are pensioners. As for non-workers, among older persons who are marginal workers, a substantially larger percentage of females (82.7 per cent) perform household duties than males (22.2 per cent). These figures suggest that older women, especially those who are engaged in marginal work, combine household duties with economically active work. The data on pensioners by gender among marginal workers show that a minuscule percentage are beneficiaries of pension. Of the older females who are reported as marginal workers, only 1.6 per cent get a pension as compared with 6.3 per cent males. The data shows that as only a small percentage is deriving the benefit of pension, many persons who are old have to work. Some of those who are drawing a pension are supplementing it with work. These results are especially applicable to older women. A meagre proportion of elderly women have income from pension because of the fact that they have much lower work participation rates than males at all ages, making them economically marginalised and not eli-

Table 6: Distribution of Marginal Workers by Main Activity, Age, Sex and Residence, 2001

Age Group	Students		Household Duties		Dependents		Pensioners		Beggars, Vagrants, etc.		Others	
	Males	Females	Males	Females	Males	Females	Males	Females	Males	Females	Males	Females
Total												
All Ages	9.4	3.3	15.1	78.9	4.3	2.1	0.8	0.2	0.1	0.1	70.2	15.3
60+	0.4	0.2	22.2	82.7	7.4	4.3	6.3	1.6	0.3	0.2	63.4	11.0
60–69	0.3	0.2	21.9	83.6	6.2	3.6	6.5	1.4	0.3	0.1	64.8	11.0
70–79	0.5	0.3	23.3	80.1	9.5	6.4	6.0	2.2	0.4	0.3	60.3	10.8
80+	0.9	0.7	21.1	76.5	11.3	7.8	5.0	1.8	0.4	0.4	61.4	12.9
Rural												
All Ages	10.2	3.3	17.1	79.8	4.4	2.0	0.8	0.2	0.1	0.0	67.4	14.6
60+	0.4	0.2	24.3	83.6	7.6	4.1	6.1	1.5	0.3	0.2	61.4	10.3
60–69	0.3	0.2	24.0	84.5	6.3	3.5	6.3	1.4	0.3	0.1	62.8	10.3
70–79	0.5	0.3	25.2	81.2	9.8	6.2	5.8	2.1	0.4	0.3	58.4	10.0
80+	0.8	0.6	23.0	77.7	11.6	7.6	4.8	1.7	0.4	0.3	59.4	12.1
Urban												
All Ages	4.7	3.8	4.0	65.9	4.0	3.4	0.7	0.4	0.2	0.1	86.4	26.4
60+	0.5	0.4	6.4	68.6	6.1	6.1	7.8	2.5	0.4	0.4	78.9	22.0
60–69	0.4	0.3	6.2	69.8	5.2	5.1	7.9	2.3	0.3	0.3	80.0	22.2
70–79	0.5	0.5	7.0	65.5	7.7	8.7	8.0	3.3	0.5	0.6	76.3	21.4
80+	1.0	0.8	6.4	62.2	9.2	11.3	6.1	2.6	0.6	0.7	76.7	22.4

Source: Census of India, 2001

Table 7: Distribution of Non-Workers by Main Activity, Age, Sex and Residence, 2001

Age Group	Students		Household Duties		Dependents		Pensioners		Beggars, Vagrants, etc.		Others	
	Males	Females	Males	Females	Males	Females	Males	Females	Males	Females	Males	Females
Total												
All Ages	48.7	26.5	1.8	35.8	41.6	33.4	1.7	0.5	0.1	0.1	6.2	3.8
60+	1.2	0.6	4.1	35.1	60.7	57.4	23.0	4.3	0.6	0.3	10.4	2.3
60–69	0.8	0.4	4.8	43.5	52.0	49.3	30.5	4.2	0.7	0.3	11.3	2.2
70–79	1.2	0.7	3.9	25.7	66.0	66.4	18.6	4.5	0.6	0.4	9.8	2.3
80+	2.4	1.5	2.7	18.0	73.3	74.1	12.0	3.7	0.5	0.3	9.0	2.4
Rural												
All Ages	47.0	25.7	1.9	32.7	45.3	37.8	0.9	0.4	0.1	0.1	4.7	3.2
60+	1.2	0.6	4.8	32.7	70.6	60.7	13.6	3.6	0.7	0.4	9.1	2.0
60–69	0.8	0.4	6.0	41.2	63.7	52.6	18.6	3.4	0.8	0.4	10.0	2.1
70–79	1.1	0.6	4.4	23.5	74.2	69.5	11.1	3.9	0.6	0.4	8.7	2.0
80+	2.2	1.3	2.8	15.9	78.7	76.9	7.8	3.4	0.5	0.4	7.9	2.0
Urban												
All Ages	52.8	28.1	1.4	42.1	32.4	24.0	3.5	0.7	0.2	0.1	9.7	5.1
60+	1.2	0.8	2.8	41.0	42.4	49.1	40.3	6.0	0.6	0.2	12.7	2.8
60–69	0.7	0.5	3.0	48.9	35.1	41.5	47.6	6.2	0.6	0.2	13.1	2.6
70–79	1.4	1.1	2.7	31.4	48.3	58.2	34.8	6.1	0.5	0.3	12.2	3.0
80+	3.0	1.9	2.3	23.4	58.4	66.5	23.7	4.5	0.5	0.3	12.1	3.4

Source: Census of India, 2001

gible for a pension. In addition, for women, time taken off from work for child bearing, unpaid family work and part-time work ends their chances of earning a pensionable income (Chakraborti, 2004). After conducting a micro-level study in Pune, Bambawale (1999) reported that women after 60 and before 60 years of age, showed a marginal change in their household duties. In her view, "Retirement is specially difficult for a women because when she retires she is twice as much in the house to cater to as many needs of the people at home" (p. 133).

Towards the final years of life, aged persons experience enervation in physical functioning and acquire physical ailments and disabilities which pose a great challenge for them in carrying out day-to-day activities. Many a time, because of disability, they become fully dependent on others for physical, emotional and financial support. The Census of India 2001 has collected information regarding the disabled status of persons. This data is given in Table 8. Disability has been considered with reference to seeing, speech, hearing, movement and mental health. In the country, among persons who are 60 years and more, the percentage of disabled males is 5.2 and of females is 4.7. Though a marginally larger percentage of older males have been reported to be disabled, the percentage of disabled females is higher for seeing and hearing. Among disabled females 60 years and more, those who have difficulty in seeing is 54.7 per cent and in hearing, is 13.3 per cent. The respective percentages for males are 49.2 and 11.9. Women who are disabled due to restriction in their movement are 24 per cent; the male percentage is 30.8. A similar percentage of males and females, 4.8, have been reported as mentally disabled.

The 52nd round of the NSSO (1998) also collected information on the disability status of the aged in India. The NSSO reports that for the three disabilities, seeing, hearing and moving, a higher percentage of older women report difficulties as compared with men. The data also shows that in rural areas, the situation of the old is worse than in urban areas. In the rural areas, nearly 29 per cent of women report having difficulty in seeing as compared with about 25 per cent men. But, in urban areas, the female and male percentage experiencing difficulty in seeing is 22.5 and 26, respectively. For both hearing and moving, the female percentage having difficulty is higher.

When we compare the percentages obtained from the Census with that of a survey conducted in Delhi, we find that they are somewhat similar. In a survey conducted in 2002, Alam and Mukherjee (2005) found that not only the sensory responses of older women, but their daily activities were also impaired. As revealed by the census, a significantly larger

Table 8: Physical Disability among Aged Persons by Type, Sex and Residence, 2001

% Disabled/Type	Total			Rural			Urban		
	Total	Males	Females	Total	Males	Females	Total	Males	Females
% 60+ Disabled to Total Pop.	4.9	5.2	4.7	5.3	5.5	5.0	3.9	4.2	3.6
Seeing	51.9	49.2	54.7	52.5	49.7	55.4	49.5	47.2	52.1
Speech	3.2	3.3	3.2	4.0	4.1	3.9	3.7	3.9	3.6
Hearing	12.6	11.9	13.3	12.9	12.3	13.5	11.3	10.1	12.6
Movement	27.5	30.8	24.0	27.1	30.3	23.7	29.2	32.5	25.4
Mental	4.8	4.8	4.8	4.4	4.5	4.4	6.3	6.3	6.3

Source: Census of India, 2001

Table 9: Disability among Aged Persons by Type of Disability, Marital Status and Sex

Type/Marital Status	Total		Never Married		Married		Widowed		Divorced/Separated	
	Males	Females	Males	Females	Males	Females	Males	Females	Males	Females
Total	100.00	100.00	4.39	2.00	76.47	35.37	18.53	61.86	0.61	0.77
Hearing	11.87	13.31	2.67	1.21	74.22	31.02	22.47	67.05	0.65	0.72
Movement	30.76	24.01	4.78	2.45	76.36	35.64	18.22	61.10	0.64	0.82
Seeing	49.23	54.73	3.23	1.36	78.07	35.85	18.28	62.19	0.43	0.59
Speech	3.31	3.16	11.69	6.67	71.62	39.59	15.73	52.49	0.96	1.25
Mental	4.83	4.80	12.96	6.19	69.77	37.72	15.37	53.73	1.91	2.37

Source: Census of India, 2001

percentage of older females mention difficulty in reading and hearing. The percentage of older women who have difficulty in reading and hearing is 94.3 and 96.8, respectively, compared with male percentages of 18.2 and 14, respectively. The percentages for older females are rather larger than that given in the census. However, both the census and the survey clearly bring out that a larger percentage of older women suffer from sensory impairment.

The survey data also shows the relatively disadvantageous position of women in activities such as climbing stairs and standing after sitting for a while. For climbing stairs, 86 per cent females reported that they required help and 85 per cent found it difficult to stand after sitting. The respective percentages for men for the two activities were 73 and 69. Older women found it difficult to do routine work such as going to the market. While 65 per cent of the women reported difficulty in shopping, only 49 per cent men reported the same difficulty. The survey data are different from that of the census. When we consider the data on movement of older persons, the census data shows that a smaller percentage of women are affected. The data that has been presented may not be strictly comparable but both sets of data indicate gender differences in disability and that older women are relatively worse off.

A particularly important revelation by the census is the relationship of the disability status of older persons with their marital status. This data, given in Table 9, highlights the disabilities that are particularly found among widows. In all the disabilities considered, widows are proportionately higher than widowers and for certain disabilities, their percentage is more than three times that of widowers. For example, the percentage of widows who have difficulty in seeing is 62.2 and the percentage for widowers is 18.3. A different situation is seen among married people. The percentage of currently married males who have disabilities are more than twice that for females. The percentage of males who have a disability with regard to seeing is 78.1, and that of females is 35.8. Married persons who have disabilities depend on their spouses for help, such help may not be forthcoming for widows. Here again, widows, in addition to leading a life without their spouse, have to overcome the disabilities they face in their old age.

The educational status of aged persons is very important. The wellbeing of life and the scope of skill formation, labour force participation and wage earning are closely linked with education. Distribution of aged persons in terms of level of education by sex and residence is shown in Table 10. As shown, women's level of education lags far behind that of males. Among women aged 60 years and more, only one-fifth are literate, whereas among males, more than half are literate. There is a wide gap in literacy between rural and urban areas. In rural areas, 45.9 per cent males aged 60-plus are reported as literate, against only 13.1 per cent females. Compared with rural areas, the situation is much better in urban areas, with 75.5 per cent and 42.7 per cent aged male and female literacy, respectively. These levels and patterns of literacy over age groups of younger old, adult old and old old are more or less similar by sex and residence. The examination of level of education of these literates shows that three-fourths of the aged women have achieved only primary and below primary levels of education. Males are better with a percentage of slightly over 60. Again in rural areas, though there is a difference between aged males and females, achievements in terms of education are very poor among both the sexes. A huge percentage (87.6) of aged literate women has upto primary education, the majority of them below primary level. There are 72.8 per cent rural aged literate males who have been educated upto the primary level. In urban areas, among aged literates, three-fifths of males and slightly more than one-third of females have been able to go beyond primary education. Education is an important skill through which individuals can win through in difficult situations. It is not less important in the lives of the aged. The scope of earning and importance in decision making are highly dependent on the education level. In India, self-medication is a very usual phenomenon. Elderly people become more dependent on others in the face of ailments and their self-medication is limited by their limited level of education. The situation of aged women is worse because of their dismal educational status. Illiterate and lower educated women, of a lower economic status, are more hesitant in seeking help for their difficulties. The difficulties are more pronounced at the time of seeking treatment, visiting doctors or consulting the doctor over the phone for their ailments, which are common in old age. Thus, it is not wrong to say that aged disabled persons are doubly disabled by lack of education. Chakraborti (2004) says that older people with higher education are generally more open, tolerant and liberal. As the educational level of the elderly improves, intergenerational cultural tensions become weaker and society grows in a more healthy way, leading to a better quality of life.

The above analysis shows the nature of the ageing population and its characteristics as given by the Census of India. The percentage of the aged in the population is only likely to increase in the future. There are four projections for the population of the country available at present. These are the projections that have been prepared by the Office of the Registrar General of India (ORGI) 1996, ORGI 2006, Population

Table 10: Literacy and Level of Education of Aged Persons by Sex and Residence, 2001

Age Groups	Literate		Below Primary		Primary		Middle		Above Middle	
	Males	Females	Males	Females	Males	Females	Males	Females	Males	Females
Total										
60+	53.3	20.5	34.3	43.4	27.4	31.4	11.1	9.8	27.2	15.4
60–64	54.3	21.3	30.8	40.1	27.1	31.7	11.9	10.3	30.3	17.8
65–69	55.0	20.8	34.9	44.6	27.1	31.4	10.9	9.6	27.1	14.4
70–74	49.1	18.3	38.5	47.2	28.4	31.0	10.2	9.0	22.9	12.8
75–79	54.5	21.1	37.9	46.6	28.3	30.4	10.7	9.4	23.1	13.6
80+	48.4	18.0	39.3	50.0	27.9	28.2	11.0	8.9	21.8	13.0
Rural										
60+	45.9	13.1	42.2	56.4	30.6	31.2	10.9	6.6	16.2	5.9
60–64	46.9	13.9	38.1	53.0	30.7	33.0	12.0	7.4	19.1	6.6
65–69	47.5	13.1	43.2	58.3	30.3	30.7	10.6	6.0	15.9	5.0
70–74	41.9	11.5	46.8	59.9	30.8	29.3	9.5	5.7	12.9	5.1
75–79	46.6	13.4	46.8	58.5	30.9	28.4	10.0	6.7	12.2	6.4
80+	41.6	12.0	47.0	59.5	30.1	26.5	10.4	7.0	12.4	7.0
Urban										
60+	75.5	42.7	19.7	31.5	21.7	31.6	11.6	12.7	47.0	24.3
60–64	75.9	44.1	17.3	27.7	20.4	30.6	11.6	13.1	50.6	28.6
65–69	77.1	43.8	19.9	32.4	21.2	32.1	11.4	12.8	47.5	22.8
70–74	72.1	38.5	23.0	35.8	23.8	32.5	11.5	12.0	41.7	19.7
75–79	76.7	42.6	22.4	36.2	23.7	32.1	11.9	11.9	42.0	19.8
80+	70.1	34.4	24.6	40.6	23.8	29.8	12.1	10.7	39.5	18.8

Source: Census of India, 2001

Foundation of India (PFI) (n.d.) and Dyson (2004). These projections are different in their assumptions and approaches. According to the population projections of ORGI 1996, the percentage of population (60 years and more) is expected to increase to 9 per cent in 2016, the last year for which the projections are available. The population of 65 years and more is projected to be 5.9 per cent in 2016. The recent most projections of ORGI 2006 have estimated that the aged population (60 years and more) of India in 2026 will be around 173.2 million, comprising 84.6 million males and 88.6 million females, an old age sex ratio of 1,047. The share of this elderly population to the country's total population is estimated at 12.4 per cent and the share of aged males and females will be 11.7 per cent and 13.1 per cent, respectively. The same ORGI projections have estimated that the population of 65 years and more will be 116.2 million (56.3 million males and 59.9 million females) in 2026, and in age composition, the contribution of this aged population will be 7.8 per cent and 8.9 per cent, respectively, for males and females. The projections prepared by PFI also show that the percentage of old persons (65 years and more) in the population is expected to be 5.9 per cent in 2016. The percentage is expected to increase 7.7 per cent in 2026. The population projections compiled by Dyson are similar to that of ORGI. In 2016, 9 per cent of the population will be aged 60 years and more. The aged population is expected to rise throughout the next decade till 2016, when the percentage of older persons is estimated to be 11.6 per cent. The above projections indicate that the aged population, be it 60 years and more or 65 years and more, will continue to increase and, in another two decades, we can expect more than 10 per cent of the population to belong to this category. The above mentioned characteristics of aged persons in the country will not change drastically unless strong measures are taken to improve the overall situation of aged persons in the country.

The Census of India, 2001 has generated tables that are relevant for studying the aged population of the country. The data that has been presented in this paper has merely provided a general picture of the aged for the country. A similar examination of the data can be carried out for rural and urban areas to bring out the sharp difference that exists in these parts of the country. As is well known, in India, it is important to examine the data according to the states so as to discover the gender differences that came about through social and cultural diversity. An analysis of such data can further our understanding of the nature of gender differences in the country.

Conclusion

With women having a higher life expectancy than men, a higher proportion of women are living upto the age of 60 years and more. The changes
in life expectancy have resulted in differences between women and men
in terms of social, economic and health issues. The census results described above highlight some of the differences. A higher percentage of
women are widowed than men and there has been an increase in female-
headed households. Women work even when they are aged and fewer of
them receive pensions. The data on disability shows that women have
difficulty in performing their day to day activities. In literacy and education level, they lag behind their male counterparts.

While from the census data, we are unable to gauge the extent of the
difficulties faced by aged women as compared with men, the increased
longevity among women has underlined the need for caring for the specific difficulties they face. Due to their biology, more women are now
living into their menopausal years than before and more women now
have to be treated for the associated symptoms. Similarly, according to
anecdotal evidence from doctors, the number of women who suffer from
breast cancer are on the rise, which is partly attributable to the increase
in longevity. We do not have sufficient information for these health
related issues for older women and there is an immediate need to examine
these issues.

The Second World Assembly on Ageing (Madrid, 2002) has cel-
ebrated rising life expectancy as one of humanity's major achievement.
It expects that the number of persons 60 years and more will increase to
2000 million by 2050. It also records that the increase will be greatest
and most rapid in developing countries where the older population is
expected to quadruple during the next 50 years. This demographic transformation challenges all societies to promote increased opportunities, in
particular for older persons to realise their potential to participate fully
in all aspects of life. Population ageing is not gender neutral, therefore,
it recognised the need to mainstream a gender perspective into all policies and programmes to take into account the needs and experiences of
older women and men.

The aged require social security, health security and financial security.
A majority of our aged are from the informal sector, and even among
those from the formal sector, a large proportion is from non-government
institutions. The work profile shows that the majority of our aged are
financially insecure without any pension benefits. The female labour
force is substantially high in the informal and non-government sectors

which leaves them with no pension benefit when they retire. Again the over-dependence of females on male income leaves them in financial insecurity when the spouse dies or retires. The financial insecurity adds to their social insecurity.

The National Policy of Older Persons was framed by the Ministry of Social Justice and Empowerment in 1999 to address the issues of aged persons. The primary objective of the policy is to encourage individuals to make provision for their own as well as their spouse's old age; to encourage families to take care of their older family members; to enable and support voluntary and non-government organisations to supplement the care provided by the family; to provide care and protection to vulnerable elderly people; to provide health care facilities to the elderly; to promote research and training facilities to train caregivers and organisers of services for the elderly; and to create awareness among elderly persons to develop themselves into fully independent citizens. The emphasis, however, appears to be on the preparation of the younger generation for their future aged years. The government has constituted the National Council for Older Persons (NCOP) to advise and aid it on policies and programmes for older people and also to provide feedback on the implementation of the National Policy on Older Persons. However, the NCOP has so far been not very effective in its action and was re-constituted in 2005. There are several national level programmes on the aged in India, i.e., Old Age Social and Income Security (OASIS), Integrated Programme for Older Persons (IPOP), Scheme of Assistance for Construction of Old Age Homes, National Old Age Pension Scheme (NOAP) and Annapurna (which provides food grains). Several state governments have also started different pension schemes for older persons. Conspicuously, in all these programmes and schemes, the gender aspect has not got any individual consideration. Recognising the reality, the policy framework prepared by the government has to also address the needs of aged women, who are the least empowered to manage their life, whatever their economic strata. The policy needs to address the requirement of the present day aged while preparing the younger generation to face old age.

References

Alam, M. and M. Mukherjee. 2005. 'Ageing, Activities of Daily Living Disabilities and the Need for Public Health Initiatives: Some Evidence from a Household Survey in Delhi' in *Asia-Pacific Population Journal*. 20(2): 47–76.

Bambawale, Usha. 1999. 'Aging Issues and Challenges: Gender Bias in the Care of Elderly' in *Social Change*. Vol. 29(1 and 2), pp. 126–137.

Bose, Ashish and Mala Kapur Shankardass, 2004. *Growing Old in India, Voices Reveal, Statistics Speak.* Delhi: B.R. Publishing Corporation.

Bumpass, L., J. Sweet and T.C. Martin. 1990. 'Changing Pattern of Remarriage' in *Journal of Marriage and Family.* Vol. 52, pp. 747–756.

Chakraborti, Rajagopal D. 2004. *The Greying of India: Population Aging in the Context of Asia.* New Delhi: Sage Publication.

Desai, S. and S. Ahmed, 1998. 'Female Headed Households' in N.P. Stromqui (ed.), *Women in the Third World: An Encyclopaedia of Contemporary Issue.* York: Garland Publishing, pp. 227–235.

Dyson. T. 2004. 'India's Population: The Future', in Dyson et al. (eds.) *Twenty-First Century India: Population, Economy, Human Development and the Environment.* New Delhi: Oxford University Press.

Gulati, Leela. 1993. 'Population Ageing and Women in Kerala State, India' in *Asia-Pacific Population Journal.* Vol. 8, No. 1, pp. 53–63.

Mirkin, Barry and M.B. Weinberger. 2001. 'The Demography of Aging Population' in Population Bulletin of the United Nations, *Living Arrangements of Older Persons.* Special Issue Nos. 42/43, pp. 37–53.

National Sample Survey Organisation. 1998. The Aged in India: A Socio-Economic Profile. NSS 52nd Round, July 1995-June 1996. New Delhi: Ministry of Planning and Programme Implementation.

Office of the Registrar General of India. 1996. 'Population Projections for India and States, 1996–2016'. New Delhi: Office of the Registrar General of India.

———. 2004. 'Population Census of India, 2001'. New Delhi: Office of the Registrar General of India.

———. 2006. 'SRS Based Abridged Life Tables 1999–2003'. Analytical Studies Report No. 1. New Delhi: Office of the Registrar General of India.

———. 2006. 'Population Projections for India and States, 2001–2026'. New Delhi: Office of the Registrar General of India.

Palloni, Alberto. 2001. 'Living Arrangement of Older Persons' in Population Bulletin of the United Nations. *Living Arrangements of Older Persons.* Special Issue Nos. 42/43, pp. 54–110.

Population Foundation of India. n.d. Population Projections – 2015. New Delhi: Population Foundation of India.

Rabindranathan, S. 2006. *The Elderly in Urban Indian Families: Conflict in Solidarity.* Delhi: B.R. Publishing Corporation.

Rajan, S.I. 2001. 'Health Concerns among India's Elderly' in *International Journal of Aging and Human Development.* 53(3): 181–194.

Rajan, S.I. et al. 2003. 'Demography of Indian Aging, 2001–2051' in *Journal of Aging and Social Policy.* 15(2–3): 11–30.

Swain, Pushpanjali; 2004. Socio-Demographic and Health Profile of Widows in India, Research Report. New Delhi: NIHEW.

United Nations. 2000. Widowhood: Invisible Women, Secluded or Excluded, Division for the Advancement of Women, Department of Economic and Social Affairs. New York: United Nations.

United Nations. 2002. World Population Aging 1950–2050. Population Division, Department of Economic and Social Affairs, New York.

Vlassof, M. and C. Vlassof. 1980. 'Old Age Security and the Utility of Children in Rural India'. *Population Studies*. 34: 487–499.

Wyke, S., and G. Ford, 1995. Competing Explanations for Association between Marital Status and Health in *Social Science Medicine*, Vol. 34, pp. 523–32.

12

Sensitising Financial Allocations through Gender Budgeting

LEKHA S. CHAKRABORTY[1]

Prima facie, budgets appear to be gender neutral. But budgetary poli cies can have differential impacts across gender due to the systemic differences between men and women in relation to the economy. A gender-sensitive budget aims at examining monetary allocations through the gender lens and also giving a thrust to the statistically invisible care economy. This paper critically examines the approach and methodology of sensitising financial allocations through gender budgeting initiatives in India in an international perspective.

Worldwide there is a growing recognition about the integration of the 'sustainable human development' paradigm into macro-policy frameworks. It takes gender equality along with poverty eradication, environmental regeneration and democratic governance as its cornerstones (Cagatay, Keklik, Lal and Lang, 2000). One of the logical entry points to such a paradigm shift has been gender-sensitive budgeting along with pro-poor budgeting and environment-sensitive budgeting.

Gender responsive budgeting (GRB) is neither making separate budgets for women nor an analysis of the earmarking of funds for programmes targeted exclusively at women in budgets. It is an analysis of the entire budget through a gender lens to identify the gender differential impacts and to translate gender commitments into budgetary commitments (Diane, 1999). It enhances the transparency of and accountability for revenue and expenditure.

The process of gender responsive budgeting refers to: first, a series of policy guidelines and analytical tools, which are expected to be utilised in the budgeting process of all sectoral ministries and organisations to ascertain that gender mainstreaming policies are properly integrated into most sectoral programmes; second, these policies being translated into specific results and outcomes that can be traced; and third, necessary modifications being made in budgeting techniques and procedures to accommodate these changes (Sarraf, 2003). Elson (1999) has suggested seven tools which can be utilised for gender responsive budgeting, viz., gender-aware policy appraisal; gender-disaggregated beneficiary assessments; gender-disaggregated public expenditure incidence analysis; gender-disaggregated tax incidence analysis; gender-disaggregated analysis of the impact of the budget on time-use; gender-aware medium term economic policy framework, and gender-aware budget statement.

The Indian experience of gender budgeting is quite distinct in the global scenario. Though more than 40 countries have initiated gender budgeting, hardly any country has taken a leap forward like India. The experiences most frequently cited are those of Australia, South Africa, the Philippines and India. In Australia, a comprehensive assessment of gender differential impacts of the Federal Budget has been undertaken since 1984. However, this ex-post gender budgeting initiative lost momentum with the change of government in 2001. In the post-apartheid regime of South Africa, though there were ex post gender budgeting initiatives by the Department of Finance, it was rolled back in 1999 after two years of donor-driven initiatives. However, it would not be fair to say that gender budgeting has since been completely given up in South Africa, as a parliamentary-NGO initiative is still active. In the Philippines, gender budgeting started with the GAD (gender and development) budget in 1995. The GAD budget made a provision for earmarking at least 5 per cent of all departmental expenditure on programmes for women in national and subnational budgets, which they referred to as quota-based budgeting. However, earmarking an allocation for women in budgets – say, 5 per cent or 10 per cent – has always been considered to be the second best principle of gender budgeting as it results in the marginalisation of gender issues in the mainstream budget.[2] Evidence for ex ante gender budgeting (identifying the needs of women and then budgeting for them) is rare across the globe; selective attempts were made in a few *Barangays* in the Philippines to identify specific gender needs before budgeting (at the local level); which is similar to the costing exercise for Millenium Development Goal (MDGs).[3]

Gender budgeting has been institutionalised in India since 2005–06. Against the backdrop of the recommendations by the Expert Group on Classification of Budgetary Transactions, Government of India,[4] the finance minister has introduced a statement on gender budgeting in the Union Budget 2005–06, covering 10 demands for grants highlighting the gender sensitivity of the budgetary allocations.[5] In one year's time, the finance minister has been able to enlarge the statement to include 24 demands for grants with an outlay of Rs 28,737 crore. Prima facie, Rs 28,737 crore appears as an unpleasant gender arithmetic, as it constitutes only 5 per cent of the total budget. But this aggregate figure reveals only a partial picture. The maiden attempt of the MoF in institutionalising gender budgeting is much beyond that.

The plan of this paper is as follows: Apart from this introductory, there are sections dealing with rationale of gender budgeting, theoretical framework of gender budgeting, an empirical analysis of gender budgeting and the time-series analysis of the expenditure budgets in India since 1995–96 through a gender lens. The last section concludes and draws policy suggestions.

Rationale of Gender Budgeting

The arguments for public policy stance, in terms of expenditure as the key policy instrument, rest on the fact that the functioning of the market cannot, by itself, activate the signalling, response and mobility of economic agents to achieve efficiency in both static (allocative efficiency) and dynamic (shift in the production frontier) terms (Arndt, 1998). The case of public expenditure proceeds from market failures of one kind or another. Markets fail to secure appropriate signals, responses and mobility because: (i) not all goods and services are traded. Markets cannot determine the prices of public goods; (ii) goods exhibiting externalities in consumption and production force a wedge between market prices and social valuation and the market will not ensure a socially desired supply; (iii) some goods are characterised by increasing returns to scale. In case of such natural monopolies, society can gain from lower prices and higher output when the public sector is the producer or a subsidy is paid to the private sector to cover the losses of producing optimal output; (iv) information asymmetry between the providers and consumers of services such as social insurance can give rise to the problems of moral hazard and adverse selection; and (v) state intervention is necessary also for securing income redistribution.[6]

The existing gender neutrality of macro-indicators ignores the feedback mechanism between gender relations and macro-economic policy. The assumption of labour force exogeneity in the treatment of the care economy in the prevalent macro-economic policy making is dubious. Integrating gender perspective into budgetary policy has dual dimensions: an equality dimension and an efficiency dimension. Apart from the basic principle of promoting equality among citizens, gender equality can benefit the economy through efficiency gains. From the *efficiency* consideration, what is important is the social rate of return of investment in women, and in cases, this can be greater than the corresponding rate for men. There is a growing awareness that gender inequality is inefficient and costly to development.[7]

It is incorrect to say that there is a deliberate built-in gender bias in the formulation of budgets in India. However, as women and men are at asymmetric levels of socio-economic development in India, the existing gender neutrality of budgets can lead to many unintentional negative consequences and thus, the gender neutrality of budgets can in turn translate into gender blindness. Therefore, considering the gender bias inherent in a male dominated society like India – and the evidence of gender discrimination *even before birth* from the trends in juvenile sex ratio[8] and other socio-economic indicators showing how the bias is getting accentuated in many parts of India – it is time that one of the highest policy making authorities in India provided a clear indication that they care for it and what Ministry of Finance can do to redress this acute capability deprivation.

A quick gender diagnosis is given in Table 1, showing India's global position in gender development. India, has a gender development index (GDI) of around or below 0.5, which shows along with Pakistan, Bangladesh, Mozambique, etc., that women suffer the double deprivation of overall achievement in human development.[9] The maternal mortality ratio in India – 540 per one lakh live births as compared to only 16–17 in developed countries – points to the structural deficiencies in access to health care and nutritional disadvantage. The capability deprivation related to education is reflected in the adult literacy rate, which shows that around half of Indian women are still illiterate.

The female economic activity rate (FEAR) is only 42.5 per cent as compared to 72.4 per cent in China and 60.3 per cent in Norway. These figures relate to the economic activity only in the market economy. The point to be noted here is that the magnitude of the contribution of women in the unpaid care economy is alarming. Global estimates suggest that US$ 16 trillion of global output is invisible contribution by the care economy and within that, US$ 11 trillion was the non-monetised, invisible contribution of women. In India, the time-use survey (TUS) conducted by the Central Statistical Organisation (CSO) in about 18,600

Table 1: India's Global Position in Gender Development

	Human Development Index	Gender Development Index	Maternal Mortality Ratio (Per One Lakh Live Births)	Adult Female Literacy Rate	Female Economic Activity Rate (FEAR)
Norway	0.963	0.960	16	—	60.3
Australia	0.955	0.954	8	—	56.7
United States	0.944	0.942	17	—	59.6
China	0.755	0.754	56	86.5	72.4
Sri Lanka	0.751	0.747	92	88.6	43.5
India	0.602	0.586	540	47.8	42.5
Pakistan	0.527	0.508	500	35.2	36.7
Nepal	0.526	0.511	740	34.9	56.9
Bangladesh	0.520	0.514	380	31.4	66.5
Mozambique	0.379	0.365	1,000	31.4	82.6
Ethiopia	0.367	0.355	850	33.8	57.2
Niger	0.281	0.271	1,600	9.4	69.3

Source: UNDP, Human Development Report, 2005.

households in six states from July 1998 to June 1999 – which was a pioneering macro-level attempt not only in South Asia, but also among developing countries – revealed that on an average, a female spent 34.6 hours per week compared to 3.6 hours by a male in the care economy. The inferences from TUS indicating the magnitude of the statistically invisible unpaid care economy work of women are still not integrated into macropolicy making. Gender budgeting provides a thrust to the unpaid care economy.

Men and women frequently have different priorities for budgetary policies and are affected differently by most of these policies due to the gender differentials in the constraints, options, incentives and needs. Men and women face different constraints, assume different socially determined responsibilities and consequently make different social preferences. Legacies of adverse intra-household gender relations inhibit women from playing their rightful role, contributing to the economy, and getting their due share of the economic benefits in many countries, particularly developing ones (NIPFP, 2003). Women therefore are affected by and respond to budgetary policies differently from men. Disaggregation by gender is vital because there are systemic differences between men and women in relation to the economy. Gender budgeting ensures transparency in the budgetary allocation for women and it protects these provisions from reappropriation and thereby enhances accountability.

Theoretical Framework of Gender Budgeting: Capability Approach

Sen's capability approach provides an advanced analytical framework for gender budgeting over mainstream economic welfare criteria and their overemphasis on GDP. It has brought attention to a much wider range of issues on people's well-being than in most earlier economic planning and budgeting.[10] The capability approach provided a channel for an alternative economic development thinking, which went beyond the undue emphasis on economic growth as in the economic planning of the 1970s and its trickle-down effects. It revealed that GDP (economic growth) was never suited to be a measure of well-being as it conceals extreme deprivation for large parts of the population.

In assessing gender-sensitive human development, the orthodox measures of well-being, such as growth of GDP per head or by some distribution-corrected value of GNP per head, used in empirical literature, have inherent limitations in capturing the wider aspects of well-being and the contingent process of development. There can be little doubt about the value of higher real income in opening up possibilities of living worthwhile lives that are not available at lower levels of income (Dreze and Sen, 1995).[11] It is relevant to note the debate of 'growth-led' gender sensitive human development' versus 'support-led' gender sensitive human development in this context. The debate revolves around the hypothesis that economic growth per se is necessary, but not sufficient for gender-sensitive human development; government intervention, in particular fiscal policies at various tiers, has a significant role in redressing capability deprivation. The role of government policies at all tiers is to ensure basic capabilities across gender; hence, the significance of gender budgeting.

In terms of Sen's theory of capabilities, there are three crucial layers, which needs interpretation in the context of local-level gender-responsive budgeting. These crucial layers are capabilities, functioning and commodities. The first step is to propose a list of basic capabilities. Basic capabilities can be a set of capabilities that should have only a few elements and this set is common for all individuals. These capabilities can be the capability to stay alive and live long, the capability to lead a healthy life, the capability to have knowledge, the capability to have social interaction, etc. The second step would be to gather relevant information on the functioning, which are observable gender disaggregated data, viz., life expectancy, age-specific mortality rates, literacy rate, nutritional disadvantage, enrolment ratio, participation in the governance process, etc. The third step is to analyse the existing commodity space, especially the fiscal policy stance at the local level. In the third step, ideally, we need to estimate the optimal commodity space first, which is necessary to be at the individual's command to match commodity characteristics and capability requirements and then try to capture the actual commodity space (Table 2).

The first and foremost capability of an individual is to stay alive and in a healthy state. This capability can be achieved by reducing mortality rates (especially preventable deaths) or by increasing life expectancy. Women outlive men, but this is a pure biological advantage. The gender diagnosis exercise across countries revealed that the gap between male and female life expectancy is reduced, especially in South Asia, which reflects that the biological advantage has been neutralised by gender discrimination. Ideally, we should analyse the disaggregated data on capabilities across regions within a country to understand the regional variations of the achieved capabilities to design the gender budgeting. However, the paucity of readily available data at disaggregated levels by

Table 2: Relating Sen's Capability Framework to Gender Budgeting

Capabilities	Functioning[1]	Commodity Space ('Ought' and Actual)		'Ought Budget'	Actual Budget
		Budgetary Policies			
Capability to stay alive and live long	1. Life expectancy 2. IMR 3. CMR 4. Sex ratio	1. Food security 2. Environmental policies			
Capability to ensure (biological) reproduction	1. TFR 2. MMR	1. Policies on reproductive health			
Capability to have knowledge	1. GER 2. Literacy rate 3. Drop-out rate 4. Completion rate	1. Education policy			
Capability for healthy living	1. Morbidity statistics 2. PEM malnutrition 3. Per cent access to water and sanitation	1. Hospitals/medicine availability/ doctors/nurses/services 2. Immunisation programmes 3. Nutrition programmes			
Capability for social interaction	1. Mobility 2. Security and safety	1. Public transport system 2. Better road infrastructure 3. Public safety and security (law and order)			
Capability to earn a livelihood	1. FEAR	1. Employment policies 2. Micro-finance programmes			
Capability to communicate/ decision making/governance	1. Participation in politics	1. Accommodating political cycles in budgets			

Note: [1]Observable data disaggregated by gender. List is preliminary and open-ended.

region 'within a country' may thwart the analysis and analysis therefore needs to be confined to the aggregate level or 'between nations', rather than without analysing both. Gender budgeting has an important role in improving life expectancy, especially when publicly provided goods in lieu of the lack of private income to reduce mortality rates becomes significant.[12]

Ideally, gender budgeting requires gender disaggregated information on the personal characteristics of every individual to arrive at the resource cost estimates to ensure such a basic capability to stay alive and live long. However, we might use the social indicators of age-specific mortality rates or life expectancy to analyse the personal characteristics (Desai, 1990). Financing of health care and access to physical infrastructure like water and sanitation also crucially determine a healthy existence.

An important question at this point is to list capabilities as small as the number of basic needs, which Sen quoted as Pigou's list in his Tanner lecture, as the "minimum which includes some defined quantity and quality of housing accommodation, of medical care, of education, of food, of leisure, of the apparatus of sanitary convenience and safety where work is carried out, and so on".[13]

Apart from the capability to stay alive and live long, the other listed six capabilities are capability to ensure (biological) reproduction, to have knowledge, to earn a livelihood, to interact in the social sphere with safety and security, to participate in decision making/governance. In terms of gender budgeting, there will be some overlap between these capabilities. It is to be noted that the capabilities we have listed is beyond the listing of basic needs to encompass the various facets of empowerment and to map the role of fiscal policy intervention. The capability to (biologically) reproduce is yet another capability which requires budgetary resources to redress deprivation related to malnutrition and other health problems of the reproductive age, which may iterate to malfunctioning of the children born to them, suffering from anaemia or being underweight. The capability to reproduce has dual dimensions – one is the biological dimension and the other is the social one.

Incorporating the care economy in budgetary policies is yet another way of redressing this capability. A major input for the labour force in the market economy comes from the socially determined labour tax ('reproductive tax') paid by women in the hours they spend in the care economy. If the government can design some policies to reduce the burden of social reproduction, the labour force locked up in the care economy in less productive work can be released for income earning work. This labour force in the care economy is in effect a part-free public good largely financed in a regressive way (Palmer, 1991). In the market economy, the public investment in baby care or childcare facilities, sufficient maternity leave and flexible working hours can increase the female economic activity rate and in turn enhance the productivity of the care economy labour force. But it is to be noted that only 4 per cent of women, who work in the organised sector of India, benefit from these policies.

Fiscal policies to ensure basic capabilities to females may cost more than ensuring the same capabilities to males. The unit cost of providing public services cannot be assumed as being the same across gender. For instance, the public provisioning of elementary and secondary education to a girl will cost more than that for a boy as the utilisation of education provisioning by the former is more constrained by demand side and supply side constraints than the latter. Demand constraints include negative parental attitudes towards investing in girls' education and educational costs. Poorer families find it difficult to bear the direct and opportunity costs of investing in female education. Supply constraints include inadequate infrastructure at school such as not enough classrooms, no water and lack of sanitary facilities. Shortage of single-sex schools and female teachers sometimes act as inhibiting factors. School location can be important as it is found that the greater the distance, the less the female participation in education. Child labour and a girl's work burden in the care economy are also principal barriers in achieving universal primary education.

Gender Budgeting: An Empirical Analysis with Expenditure Budgets of India

Theoretically, the methodology for gender budgeting can be dichotomised into: (a) ex-ante gender budgeting, in which, the capability approach framework can be applied to identify the capabilities and functionings and then budgeting it (analysing the gaps in the commodity space between 'ought' and actual budgets) and (b) ex-post gender budgeting, in which the budget is analysed through a gender lens, assuming that the existing budgets are formulated not out of the blue, but with an intrinsic identification of capability deprivation across gender. The attempt of the Ministry of Finance, Government of India, is an ex-post gender budgeting. The ex-ante gender budgeting is more appropriate at the sub-national levels of government, in which the identification of the needs of women at the local level is relatively easy and then budgeting for them, which is also usually referred to in literature as the 'bottom-up approach of gender budgeting'.

NIPFP methodology of ex-post gender budgeting identifies three categories of public expenditure: (i) specifically targeted expenditure for women and girls (100 per cent targeted for women); (ii) pro-women allocations, which are composite expenditure schemes with a women component (at least 30 per cent targeted for women); and (iii) gender-neutral expenditure that has insignificant gender-differential impacts (NIPFP, 2003). This methodology has been accepted by the Ministry of Finance in undertaking gender budgeting across sectors. The Expert Group on Classification of Budgetary Transactions has identified seven matrices to collate gender disaggregated data across sectors.

Methodologically speaking, it is relatively easy to identify the specifically targeted programmes (Category A) for women across ministries from the expenditure budgets. But the information on the pro-women allocations (Category B) is not readily available in the budget documents. It is in the Union Budget 2006–07 that for the first time, Expenditure Budget provided information on pro-women allocations. However, the analysis is partial as the maiden exercise is confined to only 13 demands for grants. In earlier budgets, the information on the female component intrinsic in the composite programmes is not readily available. The NIPFP attempted an illustrative analysis of the pro-women allocation of the expenditure budgets for the period between 1995–96 and 2003–04 (NIPFP, 2003). The NIPFP study depended on the in-house document provided by the Department of Women and Child Welfare to arrive at the pro-women component. The following sections deal with the analysis of specifically targeted programmes for women and the pro-women allocations, respectively.

Specifically Targeted Expenditure on Women

The analysis of expenditure budgets from a gender perspective revealed that only a few ministries/departments have specifically targeted programmes for women in India, other than the gender allocation in the fiscal transfers to UTs. However, this exercise exploded the myth that only the Department of Women and Child Development (DWCD) has budgetary allocations for women. Apart from the departments of DWCD, Health and Family Welfare and Rural Development have relatively higher allocations for women in their respective budgets (Table 3). In 2006–07, the specifically targeted programmes for women constitute around 10 per cent of total budgetary allocations of all the identified demands with specifically targeted programmes for women. However, the share of these demands for grants in total budgetary allocation is only around 15 per cent.

Table 3: Distribution (%) of Gender Budget (Category A) in the Total Budget of Each Ministry/Department

	1995-96	1996-97	1997-98	1998-99	1999-2000	2000-01	2001-02	2002-03	2003-04	2005-06	2006-07
Women and Child Development	99.66	99.61	99.62	99.66	99.58	99.60	99.61	99.80	99.72	99.77	99.79
Agriculture and Cooperation	0.16	0.08	0.04	0.03	0.00	0.00	0.00	0.00	0.00	–	–
Health	2.37	2.04	2.37	2.32	2.90	2.83	2.39	2.61	2.72	*	*
Family Welfare	18.30	25.23	28.68	31.36	26.27	28.46	30.96	12.23	15.89	13.46	12.56
Elementary Education	0.19	0.13	0.10	1.67	1.37	0.66	0.40	0.24	0.64	1.99	0.92
Labour	6.61	7.29	6.64	5.19	4.52	4.17	7.29	9.08	0.00	–	–
Rural Development	8.13	7.42	5.40	5.17	1.90	0.82	0.00	0.00	0.00	12.88	12.14
Textiles	0.00	0.00	0.81	0.88	1.44	2.19	2.49	1.66	1.64	–	–
Tribal Affairs	0.72	0.71	0.79	1.39	1.75	0.93	0.73	0.69	1.10	–	–
Social Justice and Empowerment	0.90	0.89	1.13	2.66	4.87	0.80	1.48	1.56	1.36	1.75	1.76
Secondary Education										0.11	0.09
Police (D52)										0.04	0.03
Home Affairs (D54)										0.18	0.17
Non Conventional Energy Sources (D64)										0.00	0.02
Science and Technology (D81)										0.28	1.72
Small Scale Industries (D86)										0.08	0.19

Contd.

Contd.

	2005–06	2006–07
Assistance for Nutrition for Adolescent Girls: Andaman and Nicobar Islands (D 94)	0.03	0.03
Assistance for Nutrition for Adolescent Girls: Chandigarh (D95)	0.08	0.08
Assistance for Nutrition for Adolescent Girls: Dadra and Nagar Haveli (D96)	0.41	0.43
Assistance for Nutrition for Adolescent Girls: Daman and Diu (D97)	0.25	0.26
Assistance for Nutrition for Adolescent Girls: Lakshadweep (D98)	0.02	0.02
Youth Affairs & Sports (D104)	0.54	0.42
Secondary & Higher Education (D56)	0.11	0.09

Note: Data for 2004–05 is not available. *Allocations for Health and Family Welfare are aggregated for the years, 2005–06 and 2006–07.

Source: NIPFP (2003) for the years, 1995–96 to 2002–04; Chakraborty (2003) for 2003–04 and Expenditure Budget, 2006–07 for 2005–06 and 2006–07.

The point to be noted in this analysis is that the Ministry of Finance computations for 2005–06 and 2006–07 are not strictly comparable with the estimates of NIPFP for the years 1995–06 to 2003–04. The Ministry of Finance computation is based on the increased information of specifically targeted programmes for women under various demands collated from the recently constituted gender budgeting cells of various ministries/departments. NIPFP estimates were based on the expenditure budgets of the respective years, in which the allocation for specifically targeted programmes for women under Demand 52 (Police), Demand 54 (Home Affairs), Demand 54 (Non-conventional Energy) etc., which were reported for recent years by the in-house information from the departmental gender budgeting cells.

Yet another point to be noted here is that prima facie gender-neutral demands like Police (Demand 52), Home Affairs (Demand 54), Science and Technology (Demand 81), etc., reported gender-specific allocations. The details of these schemes/programmes (Category A) for the recent years are given in Appendix A. It is revealed from the analysis that although around 50 programmes were identified as specifically targeted programmes for women, only around 15 programmes have allocations greater than Rs 10 crore. The problem of proliferation of too many programmes with too little money continued over the years.

Despite the proliferation of women-specific programmes, it is surprising to note that the amount allotted to specifically targeted programmes for women in the Union Budget 2006–07 is Rs 9,577 crore, which is only 1.70 per cent of total public expenditure in the Union Budget of the same year (Rs 5,63,991 crore). The corresponding figure of share of specifically targeted programmes for women in total public expenditure was 1.02 per cent, 0.94 per cent, 0.88 per cent, 0.87 per cent and 0.82 per cent in the Budgets of 1998–99, 1999–2000, 2000–01, 2001–02 and 2002–03, respectively, calculated by the NIPFP (Figure 1).

There is a significant spread between the budget allocations and the revised estimates and, in turn, actual spending. Higher budgetary allocation per se does not necessarily translate into higher expenditure on women. The deviation of Revised Estimate (RE) from Budget Estimate (BE), broadly measured through the ratio of RE to BE, is given in Table 4. The ratio of RE to BE nearing one depicts less deviation between the budget estimates and revised estimates. The significant deviation of revised estimates from the budget estimates is noted for the specifically targeted programmes for women in the Departments of Police, Home Affairs and Non-Conventional Energy Resources. The sectors of health and family welfare and social justice and empowerment showed an in-

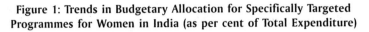

Figure 1: Trends in Budgetary Allocation for Specifically Targeted Programmes for Women in India (as per cent of Total Expenditure)

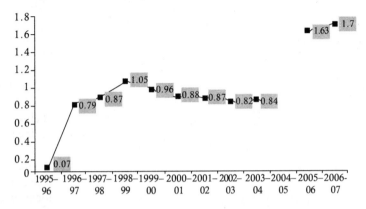

crease in allocation in RE when compared to BE. The allocation of specifically targeted programmes for women in the Departments of Science and Technology, Small Scale Industries, Sports and Youth Affairs and Secondary Education, and the assistance provided in the nutritional programmes for adolescent girls in the Union territories showed no deviation between RE and BE; however, the quantum of these allocations is negligible.

Category B: Expenditure with Pro-Women Allocations

Category B includes those public expenditure schemes with intrinsic gender allocations, though not exclusively targeted at women. Prima facie, it is difficult to identify these pro-women shares from the budget documents. However, in the Union Budget 2006–07, selected ministries/departments have reported the pro-women allocations, with an aggregate allocation of Rs 19,160 crore. In earlier budgets, the information on the woman component intrinsic in the composite programmes is not readily available. As noted above, this paper depends on the estimates of the NIPFP for the previous years. The details of the pro-woman allocation as per the scheme are given in Appendix B. It is noted that the share of the women's component of composite public expenditure in the total expenditure of the Central government showed a decline from 3.89 per cent in 1995–96 to 2.02 per cent in 2001–02, though it rose to 2.65 per cent in 2002–03 and marginally declined to 2.19 per cent thereafter. These figures are not strictly comparable to the recent figures of 3.14 per cent in 2005–06 and 3.40 per cent in 2006–07 (Figure 2).

Table 4: Deviation of Revised Estimates (RE) from Budget Estimates (BE): Category A

(RE/BE) of Depts	1995-96	1996-97	1997-98	1998-99	1999-2000	2000-01	2001-02	2002-03	2005-06
Women and Child Development	1.12	1.00	1.13	0.93	0.95	0.92	1.00	0.95	1.00
Agriculture and Cooperation	1.00	1.00	1.00	1.00	0.00	0.00	0.00	0.00	–
Health	1.16	1.08	1.14	1.05	0.91	0.93	0.83	0.93	*
Family Welfare	1.00	0.96	1.00	0.82	1.02	0.86	0.86	0.57	1.41
Elementary Education	1.00	0.94	0.79	0.95	0.34	0.12	0.59	0.24	0.98
Labour	0.94	0.69	0.51	0.72	0.94	0.99	0.91	0.00	–
Rural Development	2.29	0.64	0.71	0.67	0.82	1.00	0.00	0.00	0.99
Textiles	0.00	0.00	1.00	1.00	1.00	1.00	1.37	1.91	–
Tribal Affairs	1.00	1.00	0.95	1.00	1.00	0.58	0.71	0.58	–
Social Justice and Empowerment	1.00	1.00	0.03	0.11	0.93	0.94	1.01	1.00	#
Police (D52)									0.29
Home Affairs (D54)									0.84
Non Conventional Energy Sources (D64)									0.002
Science and Technology (D81)									1.00
Small Scale Industries (D86)									1.00
Assistance for Nutrition for Adolescent Girls: Andaman and Nicobar Islands (D 94)									1.00
Assistance for Nutrition for Adolescent Girls: Chandigarh (D95)									1.00

Contd.

Contd.

Assistance for Nutrition for Adolescent Girls: Dadra and Nagar Haveli (D96)	1.00
Assistance for Nutrition for Adolescent Girls: Daman and Diu (D97)	1.00
Assistance for Nutrition for Adolescent Girls: Lakshadweep (D98)	1.00
Youth Affairs and Sports (D104)	1.00
Secondary and Higher Education (D56)	1.00

Note: Data for 2003–04 and 2004–05 is not available. * Allocations for Health and Family Welfare are aggregated for the years, 2005–06 and 2006–07. # the BE of Social Justice and Empowerment for the year, 2005–06, was Rs 0.01 crore and RE was Rs 2,800 crore, which gives RE/BE an abnormal estimate of 2,800; therefore not reported.

Source: NIPFP (2003) for years, 1995–96 to 2001–02; Chakraborty (2003) for 2002–03 and 2005–06 figures are computed from Expenditure Budget, 2006–07.

The distribution of pro-women expenditure across sectors for the recent year is given in Figure 3. The sectors of health and family welfare; elementary and secondary education; and social justice and empowerment showed higher allocation of pro-woman allocations.

The deviation between RE and BE of the pro-woman allocations (Category B) presented in Table 7 revealed that there is no deviation between the budget estimates and revised estimates in the case of industry, IT, elementary and secondary education, and biotechnology. Around 10 per cent of budgetary allocations remain as deviation in the sectors of health and family welfare, labour and employment and youth affairs, and 3–4 per cent in Ayush and social justice and empowerment. The

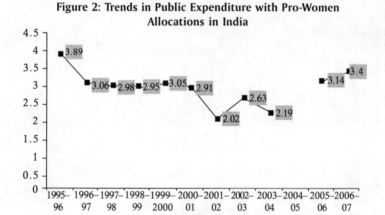

Figure 2: Trends in Public Expenditure with Pro-Women Allocations in India

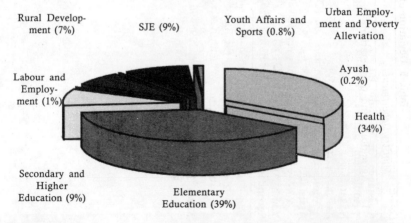

Figure 3: Distribution (%) of Pro-Women Allocations (Category B)

Table 5: Deviation of Revised Estimates (RE) from Budget Estimates (BE): Category B

Ministry/Department	1995-96	1996-97	1997-98	1998-99	1999-00	2000-01	2001-02	2002-03	2005-06
1. Agriculture and Cooperation	0.81	0.77	0.89	0.84	0.79	2.07	0.00	0.00	3.75
2. Health	1.01	1.01	1.03	0.94	0.95	0.95	0.96	0.96	*
3. Family Welfare	1.37	1.02	1.00	0.95	1.09	0.93	0.38	0.74	0.89
4. Indian Systems of Medicine and Homoeopathy (Ayush)	1.01	1.00	1.17	1.04	0.95	0.93	0.81	0.77	0.97
5. Education	1.35	0.83	0.90	0.91	0.94	1.01	0.33	0.88	1.00
6. Youth Affairs and Sports	1.00	1.06	0.99	0.93	0.96	1.00	1.02	1.00	0.93
7. Labour	1.09	0.99	0.95	0.96	0.97	0.99	0.83	0.89	0.93
8. Non-Conventional Energy Sources	1.58	0.95	0.69	0.70	0.98	0.96	0.99	0.95	–
9. Science and Technology	1.01	0.99	1.10	0.89	0.94	0.97	0.96	0.92	–
10. Small Scale Ind. Agro and Rural Industries	1.00	0.83	1.07	1.06	0.92	0.96	0.04	0.87	–
11. Urban Employment and Poverty Alleviation	0	0	0	0	0	0	0.88	0.58	–
12. Rural Development	0.98	0.71	0.99	0.86	0.70	0.57	0.27	1.00	0.00
13. Social Justice and Empowerment and Tribal Affairs	1.08	0.92	0.94	0.97	0.94	0.97	1.14	1.66	1.29
14. Industrial Policy and Promotion	1.01	1.00	0.79	0.79	1.00	0.91	0.79	1.30	0.96
15. Information Technology									1.00
16. Secondary and Higher Education									1.06
17. Biotechnology									1.00

Note: Data for 2003-04 and 2004-05 are not available. *Allocations for Health and Family Welfare are aggregated for the years, 2005-06 and 2006-07.

Source: NIPFP (2003) for years, 1995–96 to 2002–04; Chakraborty (2003) for 2002–03 and Expenditure Budget, 2006–07, for 2005–06.

reasons for these significant deviations in the budget estimates and revised estimates need to be highlighted and analysed through expenditure tracking surveys. However, the lack of gender disaggregated data on the outcome budget restrict the analysis only to the financial inputs on gender.

Conclusion and Policy Suggestions

Prima facie, budgets appear to be gender neutral. But the budgetary policies can have differential impacts across gender due to the systemic differences between men and women in relation to the economy. A gender-sensitive budget aims at examining budgetary allocations through the gender lens and also gives a thrust to the statistically invisible care economy. Sen's capability approach towards gender budgeting might be a better approach in gender sensitising financial inputs at the national and sub-national levels.

The empirical analysis reveals that visible gender allocations in the recent budget – both specifically targeted programmes for women and pro-women allocations – constitutes only 5 per cent of the total budget; however it cannot be dismissed upfront as an unpleasant gender arithmetic because of the partial revealing of gender-sensitive allocations of non-rival and non-excludable public expenditure. A further sectoral analysis revealed that higher budgetary allocations in certain sectors per se do not mean higher spending; there exists significant deviation between budget estimates and actual spending. The policy implications arising from the analysis is that transparency of gender-sensitive budgetary allocations in the budget needs to be ensured for accountability; however earmarking public expenditure for women is only a second best principle of gender budgeting. The specific policy conclusions drawn from the study are:

- Given the institutional mechanism of gender budgeting cells across ministries, the first and foremost step ahead is to *strengthen the gender disaggregated database* within the relevant departments/ministries, which enables an effective monitoring of targets and achievements across gender.
- In order to ensure transparency and accountability of allocations for women, *open a budget (major) head on Gender Development*. This helps in protecting these provisions earmarked for women by placing restrictions on their reappropriation for other purposes.
- *Consolidate the schemes with provision of Rs 10 crore or less*, to avoid

proliferation of programmes with little money, which can hardly make any impact on women.

- *Expenditure tracking survey:* This paper revealed that there is a significant deviation between budget estimates and revised estimates; the provisions earmarked for women are reduced during the course of the year; in many cases, schemes suffer or fail to take off due to procedural delays in their finalisation or getting the appropriate approvals etc.

- *Monitor the output rather than input:* Gender budgeting cells should analyse the budgetary policies through the gender lens at three levels: in terms of budget estimates shortly after the presentation of budgets, in terms of revised estimates as and when they come out and in terms of actual outlays when audited figures become available. The departures of revised estimates from budget estimates and actual outlays from revised estimates need to be highlighted and analysed.

- *Periodic benefit incidence analysis:* It is important to analyse how budgetary allocations have benefited the targeted beneficiaries, viz. women and girls, as the follow-up study of this report. Selective primary surveys need to be conducted to develop the system of *unit cost* and *units utilised.*

- *Ex-post gender sensitive analysis of budgets at all tiers of government:* In the three-tier federal set-up of India, the ideal way of conducting gender-sensitive analysis of budgets is to review the expenditure and revenue policies of all three levels of government at the Centre, states and local levels. Therefore, gender-sensitive budgeting at the sub-national government levels needs to be strengthened.

- *Incorporate care economy in budget making;* Evidence from time-use surveys indicating the statistical invisibility of the unpaid care economy work of women needs to be unveiled; appropriate policies need to be designed to address the issues related to the care economy, viz., adequate infrastructure, employment policies, etc.

- *Sectoral studies of gender budgeting:* As a follow-up of this report, a sectoral analysis of budgetary allocations and their impact on women needs to be undertaken. The important sectors to be covered in the initial phase include education, health, forestry and agriculture.

- *The tax side of gender budgeting needs to be strengthened.* The first step is to create gender disaggregated data for direct taxes and make it public.

Appendix 1: Specifically Targeted Programmes for Women (Category A)

Ministry/ Department	2005-06 (BE)			2005-06 (RE)			2006-07 (BE)		
	Plan	Non-Plan	Total	Plan	Non-Plan	Total	Plan	Non-Plan	Total
Demand No. 46									
Department of Health & Family Welfare									
A. Health wing									
1. RAK College of Nursing	0.85	2.85	3.70	0.57	2.85	3.42	0.76	3.05	3.81
2. Lady Reading Health School	0.60	0.83	1.43	0.60	0.83	1.43	0.43	0.88	1.31
Total	**1.45**	**3.68**	**5.13**	**1.17**	**3.68**	**4.85**	**1.19**	**3.93**	**5.12**
	0.00	0.00	0.00						
			0.00						
B. Family welfare wing									
1. Training for ANM/LHVs	77.73		77.73	60.93		60.93	67.00		67.00
2. Strengthening of basic training schools	2.15		2.15	2.15		2.15	2.15		2.15
3. Free distribution of contraceptives	172.52		172.52	163.00		163.00	100.00		100.00
4. Sterilisation beds	2.02		2.02	3.47		3.47	3.02		3.02
5. RCH-II flexible pool	420.52		420.52	925.18		925.18	1349.43		1349.43
6. Social marketing of contraceptives	241.04		241.04	143.00		143.00	49.50		49.50
Total	**915.98**		**915.98**	**1,297.73**		**1,297.73**	**1,571.10**		**1,571.10**
Total (A+B)	**917.43**	**3.68**	**921.11**	**1298.90**	**3.68**	**1,302.58**	**1,572.29**	**3.93**	**1,576.22**
Demand No. 52									
Police			0.00			0.00			0.00
			0.00			0.00			0.00
1. Day care centre		1.27	1.27		0.16	0.16		0.31	0.31
2. Family Accommodation		0.17	0.17			0.00		1.75	1.75
3. Gender Sensitisation		0.06	0.06		0.02	0.02		0.07	0.07
4. Health care centre		1.19	1.19		0.09	0.09		0.21	0.21

Contd.

Contd.

5. Improvised service	2.17	2.17	0.05	0.05	0.14	0.14
6. Nutritional care centre	0.18	0.18	0.08	0.08	0.21	0.21
7. Women's hostel	1.10	1.10	1.41	1.41	1.29	1.29
Total	**6.14**	**6.14**	**1.81**	**1.81**	**3.98**	**3.98**
BPR&D						
1. 2nd National Conference for Women in Police	4.90	4.90	4.90	4.90	0.00	0.00
2. Common room for women staff	0.00	0.00	0.00	0.00	0.61	0.61
Total	**4.90**	**4.90**	**4.90**	**4.90**	**0.61**	**0.61**
Demand No. 54						
Ministry of Home Affairs						
Transfer to UT Governments						
Assistance for Nutrition Programme for Adolescent Girls (NPAG): Delhi and Pondicherry	2.03	2.03	1.71	1.71	2.03	2.03
Total	**2.03**	**2.03**	**1.71**	**1.71**	**2.03**	**2.03**
Demand No. 55						
Department of Elementary Education and Literacy						
1. Kasturba Gandhi Balika Vidyalaya Scheme (for SC/ST & OBC women)	225.00	225.00	225.00	225.00	128.00	128.00
2. Mahila Samakhya for Women	30.00	30.00	24.00	24.00	30.00	30.00
Total	**255.00**	**255.00**	**249.00**	**249.00**	**158.00**	**158.00**

Contd.

Contd.

Demand No. 57

Department of Women & Child Development

Item							
1. Integrated Child Development Services Scheme	3,315.25	3,315.25	3,325.90	3,325.90	3,325.90	4,087.54	4,087.54
2. National Institute of Public Cooperation and Child Development	0.00	0.00	0.00	0.00	0.00	0.00	0.00
3. Rajiv Gandhi National Creche Scheme for the Chilldren of Working Mothers	4.35 (7.00)	4.35	11.35	11.35 (4.50)	11.35	4.50 (7.30)	11.80
4. Other schemes of child welfare	28.50 (13.00)	28.50 (12.90)	41.50	41.40 (13.00)	81.00	94.00	
5. Condensed courses for women's education	13.55 (3.67)	12.90 (3.75)	17.22	16.65 (4.33)	18.12	22.45	
	5.40	5.40	5.40	5.40	5.40	5.40	
6. Balika Samridhi Yojana	0.03	0.03	0.03	0.03	0.03	0.03	0.03
7. Hostels for working women	6.00	6.00	4.50	4.50	4.50	4.50	4.50
8. Support to training and employment programme	13.50	13.50	13.50	13.50	13.50	13.50	13.50
9. Central Social Welfare Board	31.00 (13.50)	31.00 (13.50)	44.50	44.50 (12.00)	23.45	35.45	
10. Swawlamban	14.00 (7.50)	14.00 (7.50)	7.50	1.80	1.80	1.80	
11. Short-stay homes	13.50 (1.50)	13.50 (1.50)	15.00	14.40 (1.50)	15.00	15.90	
12. Awareness generation programme	4.50	4.50	4.50	4.50	4.50	5.00	5.00
13. National Commission for Women	3.60 (2.17)	3.60 (2.17)	5.77	5.77 (2.45)	3.60	6.05	
14. Swashakti Project	5.00	5.00	3.00	3.00	2.00	2.00	
15. Rashtriya Mahila Kosh	0.01	0.01	0.01	0.01	0.01	10.00	10.00
16. Swayamsidha	18.50	18.50	18.50	18.50	18.50	27.00	27.00

Contd.

Contd.

17. Swadhar	5.50	5.50	5.50	5.50	7.00	7.00
18. Scheme for rescue of victims of trafficking	0.25	0.25	0.25	0.25	0.45	0.45
19. Relief & rehabilitation of rape victims						
20. Other programmes of women's welfare	0.00	0.00	0.15	0.15	0.90	0.90
21. Nutrition	5.07	5.07	11.53	11.53	5.07	12.17
			6.46		7.10	
22. Provision for projects/schemes for the benefit of the Northeastern region & Sikkim	0.00	0.00	0.00	0.00		0.00
Total	**387.53**	**387.53**	**387.53**	**387.53**	**479.59**	**479.59**
	3,875.04	**3,922.49**	**3,875.04**	**3,922.47**	**4,794.85**	**4842.68**
		47.45		47.43	4,7.83	
Demand No. 64						
Ministry of Non-Conventional Energy Sources		0.00	0.00		0.00	0.00
		0.00	0.00		0.00	0.00
1. Women and renewable energy development	5.00	5.00	0.01	0.01	0.10	0.10
Total	**5.00**	**5.00**	**0.01**	**0.01**	**0.10**	**0.10**
Demand No. 78						
Department of Rural Development						
		0.00	0.01		0.01	0.10
		0.00	0.00		0.00	0.00
		0.00	0.00		0.00	0.00
		0.00	0.00		0.00	0.00
1. Rural housing – Indira Awas Yojana (IAY) 2,775.00	2,775.00	2,775.00	2,750.00	2,750.00	2,920.00	2,920.00
Total	**2,775.00**	**2,775.00**	**2,750.00**	**2,750.00**	**2,920.00**	**2,920.00**
		0.00	0.00		0.00	0.00

Contd.

Contd.

Demand No. 81						
Department of Science & Technology	0.00	0.00		0.00		0.00
1. Women component plan	4.00	4.00	4.00	4.00	30.00	30.00
Total	**4.00**	**4.00**	**4.00**	**4.00**	**30.00**	**30.00**
Demand No. 86						
Ministry of Small-Scale Industries	0.00	0.00		0.00		0.00
1. Trade Related Entrepreneurship Assistance and Development for Women (TREAD)	0.40	0.40	0.40	0.40	1.00	1.00
Total	**0.40**	**0.40**	**0.40**	**0.40**	**1.00**	**1.00**
Demand No. 87						
Ministry of Social Justice & Empowerment	0.00	0.00		0.00		0.00
1. Girls hostels for SCs	0.01	28.00	28.00	28.00	32.00	32.00
Total	**0.01**	**28.00**	**28.00**	**28.00**	**32.00**	**32.00**
Demand No. 94						
Andaman and Nicobar Islands						
Assistance for Nutrition Programme for Adolescent Girls	0.45	0.45	0.45	0.45	0.50	0.50
Demand No. 95						
Chandigarh						
Assistance for Nutrition Programme for Adolescent Girls	0.73	0.73	0.73	0.73	0.80	0.80

Contd.

Contd.

Demand No. 96			0.00	0.00			0.00	0.00			0.00	0.00
Dadra and Nagar Haveli			0.00	0.00			0.00	0.00			0.00	0.00
Assistance for Nutrition Programme for Adolescent Girls	0.47		0.47	0.00	0.47		0.47	0.00	0.52		0.52	0.00
Demand No. 97			0.00	0.00			0.00	0.00			0.00	0.00
Daman and Diu			0.00	0.00			0.00	0.00			0.00	0.00
Assistance for Nutrition Programme for Adolescent Girls	0.29		0.29	0.00	0.29		0.29	0.00	0.32		0.32	0.00
Demand No. 98			0.00	0.00			0.00	0.00			0.00	0.00
Lakshadweep			0.00	0.00			0.00	0.00			0.00	0.00
Assistance for Nutrition Programme for Adolescent Girls	0.06		0.06	0.00	0.06		0.06	0.00	0.06		0.06	0.00
Demand No. 104			0.00	0.00			0.00	0.00			0.00	0.00
Ministry of Youth Affairs and Sports			0.00	0.00			0.00	0.00			0.00	0.00
Scheme for National Championship for Women		0.60	0.60	0.00		0.60	0.60	0.00		0.60	0.60	0.00
Total	**2.00**	**0.60**	**2.60**	**0.00**	**2.00**	**0.60**	**2.60**	**0.00**	**2.20**	**0.60**	**2.80**	**0.00**

Contd.

Contd.

Demand No. 56								
Department of Secondary and Higher Education								
1. Access and equity	6.40	6.40	0.00	6.40	0.00	0.00	6.40	6.40
Total	**6.40**	**6.40**	**0.00**	**6.40**	**0.00**	**0.00**	**6.40**	**6.40**
Grand Total: Part A	**7,844.31**	**62.77**	**7,907.08**	**8,217.46**	**58.42**	**8,275.88**	**9,521.07**	**56,959,578.02**

Source: Budget Documents, 2006–07, Govt of India.

Appendix 2: Pro-Women Allocations (Category B)

Ministry/ Department	2005-06 (BE)			2005-06 (RE)			2006-07 (BE)		
	Plan	Non-Plan	Total	Plan	Non-Plan	Total	Plan	Non-Plan	Total
Demand No. 1									
Department of Agriculture & Cooperation									
1. Development and strengthening of infrastructure facilities for production and distribution of quality seeds		0.50	0.50	0.50		0.50		1.00	1.00
2. Extension support to Central institutes/DOE		0.50	0.50	0.25		0.25		0.50	0.50
3. Macro-management: Andhra Pradesh Training of Women in Agriculture (ANTWA)				3.00		3.00			
Total		**1.00**	**1.00**	**3.75**		**3.75**		**1.50**	**1.50**
Demand No. 12									
Department of Industrial Policy & Promotion									
1. Scheme of salt works	5.00		5.00	5.00		5.00	5.50		5.50
Total	**5.00**		**5.00**	**5.00**		**5.00**	**5.50**		**5.50**
Demand No. 15									
Department of Information Technology									
1. DOEACC	1.80		1.80	1.80		1.80	2.40		2.40
2. TDIL	2.10		2.10	2.10		2.10	2.70		2.70
3. IT for masses	1.80		1.80	1.80		1.80	4.20		4.20
Total	**5.70**		**5.70**	**5.70**		**5.70**	**9.30**		**9.30**

Contd.

Contd.

Demand No. 46
Department of Health & Family Welfare
A. Health wing

Item									
1. Safdarjung Hospital & VMC, New Delhi	84.30	72.25	156.55	84.30	72.25	156.55	78.00	74.58	152.58
2. Dr RML Hospital & SPM, PGIMER, New Delhi	47.30	49.30	96.60	37.30	49.30	86.60	40.34	52.38	92.72
3. Kalawati Saran Children's Hospital, New Delhi	8.62	9.45	18.07	8.62	9.45	18.07	10.94	11.00	21.94
4. All India Institute of Medical Sciences, New Delhi	201.26	170.00	371.26	163.36	275.00	438.36	205.86	283.00	488.86
5. Lady Harding Medical College & S.K. Hospital	27.00	42.15	69.15	20.04	42.15	62.19	28.00	49.00	77.00
6. PGIMER, Chandigarh	35.00	96.00	131.00	40.00	121.00	161.00	40.00	122.00	162.00
7. JIPMER, Pondicherry	62.00	42.15	104.15	42.00	42.15	84.15	70.00	25.18	95.18
8. National Cancer Control Programme	69.00	3.50	72.50	70.50	3.50	74.00	87.00	5.00	92.00
9. Grants to Kasturba Health Society,	13.00		13.00	13.00		13.00	13.80		13.80
10. Indian Nursing Council	1.00	0.10	1.10	0.40	0.10	0.50	1.00	0.10	1.10
11. National Vector Borne Disease Control Programme (including filaria and kala azar)	348.45	5.71	354.16	264.22	5.71	269.93	371.58	6.47	378.05
12. National TB Control Programme	186.00		186.00	186.00		186.00	202.17		202.17
13. National Leprosy Eradication Programme	41.75		41.75	28.32		28.32	42.25		42.25
14. National Blindness Control Programme	89.00		89.00	92.28		92.28	90.00		90.00
15. Development of nursing services	20.00		20.00	15.00		15.00	20.00		20.00
Total	1,233.68	490.61	1,724.29	1,065.34	620.61	1,685.95	1,300.94	628.71	1,929.65

Contd.

Contd.

B. Family welfare wing

1. Rural family welfare services	1,964.40		1,964.40	1,279.85		1,279.85	1,556.68		1,556.68
2. Urban family welfare services	135.33		135.33	123.05		123.05	125.00		125.00
3. Routine immunisation programme	507.00		507.00	164.94		164.94	495.00		495.00
4. Pulse polio immunisation	877.00		877.00	822.08		822.08	1049.00		1049.00
5. IEC (RCH)	60.50		60.50	48.98		48.98	60.50		60.50
6. Training (RCH)	30.93		30.93	30.93		30.93	7.38		7.38
7. RCH-II flexible pool	410.97		410.97	910.30		910.30	1318.77		1318.77
Total	**3,986.13**		**3,986.13**	**3,380.13**		**3,380.13**	**4,612.33**		**4,612.33**
Total (A+B)	**5,219.81**	**490.61**	**5,710.42**	**4,445.47**	**620.61**	**5,066.08**	**5,913.27**	**628.71**	**6,541.98**

Demand No. 47
Department of Ayush

1. Central Council for Research in Ayurveda & Siddha, New Delhi	6.00	13.23	19.23	6.00	12.37	18.37	7.97	12.76	20.73
2. Rastriya Ayurveda Vidyapeeth, New Delhi	0.16	0.00	0.16	0.15	0.00	0.15	0.15	0.00	0.15
3. Central Council for Research in Homoeopathy, New Delhi	6.49	2.89	9.38	5.31	2.95	8.26	7.08	3.19	10.27
4. Central Council for Research in Unani Medicine, New Delhi	3.08	4.00	7.08	4.00	4.23	8.23	4.85	5.00	9.85
5. Central Council for Research in Yoga & Naturopathy, New Delhi	0.89	0.00	0.89	0.84	0.00	0.84	0.94	0.00	0.94
6. Morarji Desai National Institute of Yoga, New Delhi	0.00	1.50	1.50	0.00	1.10	1.10	0.00	1.28	1.28
Total	**16.62**	**21.62**	**38.24**	**16.30**	**20.65**	**36.95**	**20.99**	**22.23**	**43.22**

Contd.

Contd.

Demand No. 55
Department of Elementary Education and Literacy

1. Sarva Shiksha Abhiyan		3,588.00	3,588.00		3593.00	3,593.00		5,060.00	5,060.00
2. National Programme of Nutritional Support to		0.00	0.00			0.00		0.00	0.00
primary education		1,572.00	1,572.00		1572.00	1,572.00		2,044.00	2,044.00
3. Teacher education		80.00	80.00		80.00	80.00		72.00	72.00
4. Bal Bhawan Society		3.01	3.01		3.01	3.01		2.40	2.40
5. District primary education programme		282.00	282.00		282.00	282.00		94.00	94.00
6. Shiksha Karmi		2.99	2.99		2.99	2.99		0.00	0.00
7. National Council for Teacher Education		2.00	2.00		0.10	0.10		0.20	0.20
8. Literacy campaigns & operation restoration		15.00	15.00		24.00	24.00		27.00	27.00
9. Continuing education		110.67	110.67		100.59	100.59		128.40	128.40
10. Jan Shikshan Sansthan		23.70	23.70		26.61	26.61		30.00	30.00
11. Support to NGOs		15.00	15.00		13.20	13.20		15.00	15.00
Total		**5,694.37**	**5,694.37**		**5,697.50**	**5,697.50**		**7,473.00**	**7,473.00**

Demand No. 56
Department of Secondary & Higher Education

1. NVS	148.50	43.16	191.66	142.20	45.26	187.46	175.50	46.55	222.05
2. KVS	49.41	179.68	229.09	49.41	191.98	241.39	63.45	193.80	257.25
3. University Grants Commission	314.16	487.34	801.50	314.52	555.84	870.36	507.92	584.28	1,092.20
4. Indira Gandhi National Open University	21.60	0.36	21.96	21.60		21.60	36.00	0.36	36.36
5. Community Polytechnics	12.18		12.18	6.86		6.86	10.50		10.50
6. NITTTR	6.05	6.00	12.05	6.93	5.45	12.38	7.11	6.25	13.36
7. SLIET		3.10	3.10		3.10	3.10		3.50	3.50
Total	**551.90**	**719.64**	**1271.54**	**541.52**	**801.63**	**1343.15**	**800.48**	**834.74**	**1,635.22**

Contd.

Contd.

Demand No. 59				
Ministry of Labour & Employment				
1. Improvement in Working Conditions of Child/Women Labour	125.05	125.05	115.76	127.46
Total	**125.05**	**125.05**	**115.76**	**127.46**
Demand No. 78				
Department of Rural Development				
1. Sampoorna Gramin Rozgar Yojana (SGRY)	1,200.00	1,200.00	1650.00	900.00
2. Swarnajayanti Gram Swarozgar Yojana (SGSY)	384.00	384.00	400.00	480.00
Total	**1,584.00**	**1,584.00**	**2,050.00**	**1,380.00**
Demand No. 83				
Department of Biotechnology				
Biotechnology programmes for women	5.00	5.00	5.00	5.00
Total	**5.00**	**5.00**	**5.00**	**5.00**
Demand No. 87				
Ministry of Social Justice & Empowerment				
1. Special Central assistance for SCP	491.22	491.22	398.28	440.12
2. Post-matric scholarship for SCs	371.89	371.89	371.89	440.00
3. Machinery for implementation of PCR Act 1955 & Prevention of Atrocities Act 1989	0.00	0.00	0.00	0.00
	36.91	36.91	36.91	36.91
4. Pre-Matric scholarship for SCs	0.01	0.01	16.00	16.00

Contd.

Contd.

Scheme							
5. Assistance to voluntary organisations for welfare of SCs	26.00	0.00	26.00	26.00	26.00	30.00	0.00
6. Supporting project of all-India or inter-state nature for SCs	0.50	0.50	0.50	0.50	0.50	0.50	0.50
7. Dr BR Ambedkar Foundation	1.00	1.00	1.00	1.00	1.00	1.00	1.00
8. Coaching and allied schemes	0.01	0.01	3.20	3.20	3.20	3.20	3.20
9. Grants to non-govt institutions for running pre-examination training centres for SCs		0.00	4.80	4.80	4.80	4.80	4.80
10. Upgrading of merit of SC students	0.01	0.01	18.00	18.00	18.00	3.00	3.00
11. Assistance to meritorious students belonging to SCs for pursuing study in residential public school	0.01	0.00	0.00	0.00	0.00	0.00	0.00
12. Setting up of residential schools for SC students	5.00	5.00	5.00	5.00	5.00	0.01	0.01
13. National Commission for SCs	5.58	5.58	5.58	5.58	5.58	6.26	6.26
14. National Commission for Safai Karamcharis	1.59	1.59	1.54	1.54	1.54	1.72	1.72
15. National Commission for De-Notified, Nomadic & Semi-Nomadic Tribes	0.30	0.30	0.82	0.82	0.00	1.45	0.00
16. Scholarships to students of SC & other categories for study abroad	1.00	1.00	1.33	1.33	0.00	1.40	0.00
17. Rajiv Gandhi National Fellowship for SCs	16.03	16.03	16.03	16.03	16.03	35.13	35.13
18. Share Capital to SC Development Corporation	31.50	31.50	31.50	31.50	31.50	33.00	33.00

Contd.

Contd.

No.	Scheme						
19.	National Safai Karmachari Finance & Development Corporation	22.00	0.00	22.00	22.00	0.00	0.00
20.	National SC Finance & Development Corporation	16.60	22.00	16.60	16.60	22.00	80.00
21.	Misc. schemes for SCs		16.60			16.60	37.00
22.	Pre-matric scholarship for BCs	23.99	0.00	27.00	27.00	0.00	6.00
23.	Boys & Girls' hostels for BCs	0.01	23.99	15.24	15.24	27.00	22.50
24.	Post-matric scholarships for BCs	29.95	0.01	32.17	32.17	15.24	18.80
25.	Assistance to voluntary organisation for BCs	5.00	29.95	5.00	5.00	32.17	31.49
			5.00			5.00	5.50
26.	National Commission for Backward Classes	1.45	1.45	1.40	1.40	1.45	1.45
27.	Maulana Azad Education Foundation	30.00	30.00	30.00	30.00		0.00
28.	National BCs Finance & Development Corporation	10.00	10.00	10.00	10.00	27.00	27.00
29.	Grants-in-aid to Wakf Board	1.70	1.70	1.91	1.91	2.06	2.06
30.	National Commission for Minorities	3.38	3.38	3.38	3.38	3.67	3.67
31.	National Minorities Finance & Development Corporation	19.60	19.60	19.60	19.60	16.47	16.47
32.	Special Officer for Linguistic Minorities	0.99	0.99	0.96	0.96	1.04	1.04
33.	National Commission for Economically BCs	0.60	0.99	0.13	0.13	1.12	1.04
34.	National Commission for Economically BCs among religious and linguistic minorities	0.48	0.48	2.16	2.16	0.73	0.73
35.	Pandit Deendayal Disabled Rehabilitation Scheme	80.00	80.00	74.00	74.00	81.00	81.00

Contd.

Contd.

No.	Institution	Plan	Non-Plan	Total	Plan	Non-Plan	Total	Plan	Non-Plan	Total
36.	National Institute of Social Defence	4.80	0.55	5.35	4.80	0.55	5.35	5.50	0.60	6.10
37.	National Institute of Visually Handicapped, Dehradun	5.00	4.57	9.57	5.00	4.57	9.57	5.00	4.77	9.77
38.	National Institute of Orthopaedically Handicapped, Kolkata	4.00	2.99	6.99	4.00	2.99	6.99	4.00	3.14	7.14
39.	National Institute for Hearing Handicapped, Mumbai	9.00	4.85	13.85	7.50	4.85	12.35	6.50	5.06	11.56
40.	National Institute for Rehabilitation Research & Training, Cuttack	6.25	4.05	10.30	6.25	4.05	10.30	7.00	4.24	11.24
41.	Pandit Deendayal Institute for Physically Handicapped, New Delhi	2.00	4.20	6.20	0.75	4.20	4.95	1.00	4.38	5.38
42.	National Institute for Mentally Handicapped, Secunderabad	10.00	2.70	12.70	10.00	2.70	12.70	10.00	2.82	12.82
43.	National Institute for Multiple Handicapped	6.50		6.50	6.50		6.50	6.50		6.50
44.	Aids and appliances for the handicapped	60.00		60.00	60.00		60.00	63.90		63.90
45.	Establishment of rehabilitation centres	4.85		4.85	3.41		3.41	0.01		0.01
46.	Rehabilitation Council of India	3.00	0.90	3.90	3.00	0.85	3.85	3.00	0.93	3.93
47.	Spinal Injury Centre	3.50		3.50	3.50		3.50	3.50		3.50
48.	Implementation of the Persons with Disabilities Act, including scheme for disabilities	20.34	0.00	20.34	8.57	0.00	8.57	11.00	0.00	11.00
49.	Technology development projects in mission mode	2.00	0.00	2.00	2.00	0.00	2.00	1.00	0.00	1.00
50.	Chief Commissioner for Disabilities	1.00		1.00	1.07		1.07	1.26		1.26
51.	Centre for Visually, Hearing & Orthopaedically Disabled Persons	1.00	0.00	1.00	1.00	0.00	1.00	1.00	0.00	1.00

Contd.

Contd.

52. Distribution expenses of commodity	0.00	0.00	0.00	0.00	0.00	0.00	0.00	0.00	0.00
assistance under bilateral agreements	4.00	0.00	4.00	0.00	3.60	3.60	0.00	4.05	4.05
53. Welfare of working children in need of protection and care	7.00	0.00	7.00	2.00	0.00	2.00	3.00	0.00	3.00
54. Central Adoption Resource Agency	1.35	0.00	1.35	1.30	0.00	1.30	0.00	1.50	1.50
55. Scheme for street children	17.20	0.00	17.20	10.80	0.00	10.80	12.00	0.00	12.00
56. Assistance to homes for infant & young children for promoting in-country adoption	5.00	0.00	5.00	2.00	0.00	2.00	2.50	0.00	2.50
57. Assistance to voluntary organisations for old-age homes	24.05	1.25	25.30	18.00	1.00	19.00	26.00	1.00	27.00
58. Assistance to voluntary organisation for providing social defence services	5.50	0.00	5.50	4.50	0.00	4.50	3.50	0.00	3.50
59. Prevention and control of juvenile social maladjustment	0.00	0.00	0.00	0.00	0.00	0.00	23.00	0.00	23.00
60. Grants-in-aid for research studies & publication	0.60	0.00	0.60	0.60	0.00	0.60	0.60	0.00	0.60
61. Information and Mass Education Cell	6.00	0.00	6.00	6.00	0.00	6.00	7.40	0.00	7.40
62. National Handicapped Finance & Development Corporation	11.00	0.00	11.00	11.00	0.00	11.00	11.00	0.00	11.00
63. Artificial Limbs Manufacturing Corporation	0.00	0.00	0.00	0.00	0.00	0.00	1.30	0.00	1.30
64. Lump-sum allocation for NE & Sikkim	64.71	0.00	64.71	64.51	0.00	64.51	67.85	0.00	67.85
Total	**1,495.69**	**54.33**	**1,550.02**	**1,428.00**	**54.35**	**1,482.35**	**1,656.49**	**54.66**	**1,711.15**

Contd.

Contd.

Demand No. 102
Ministry of Urban Employment & Poverty Alleviation

1. Swarnajayanti Shahari Rojgar Yojana				29.00		29.00	75.00		75.00
Total				**29.00**		**29.00**	**75.00**		**75.00**

Demand No. 104
Ministry of Youth Affairs and Sports

1. Nehru Yuva Kendra Sangathan	34.00	18.00	52.00	34.00	18.15	52.15	45.00	18.02	63.02
2. National Service Scheme	20.45	2.40	22.85	22.41	2.40	24.81	25.90	2.51	28.41
3. Promotion of national integration	4.95		4.95	5.50		5.50	9.00		9.00
4. Youth hostels	4.50		4.50	4.50		4.50	4.50		4.50
5. Scouting & guiding	1.35		1.35	1.35		1.35	1.22		1.22
6. National Service Volunteers Scheme	5.40		5.40	5.40		5.40	9.00		9.00
7. Rashtriya Sadbhavana Yojana	8.10		8.10	4.00		4.00	6.30		6.30
8. Rural youth and sports clubs and evaluation	6.75		6.75	4.00		4.00	5.40		5.40
9. Promotion of adventure	2.70	0.50	3.20	2.70	0.50	3.20	2.70	0.15	2.85
10. Promotion of youth activities & training	9.00		9.00	5.00		5.00	6.30		6.30
11. Institute of Youth Development	3.60		3.60	3.60		3.60	3.60		3.60
12. Commonwealth Youth Programme	0.18		0.18	0.18		0.18	0.18		0.18
13. Development and Empowerment of Adolescents	11.70		11.70	12.20		12.20	10.80		10.80
14. Scheme relating to talent search and training	3.00		3.00	0.50		0.50	1.80		1.80
Total	115.68	20.90	136.58	105.34	21.05	126.39	131.70	20.68	152.38
Grand Total – Part B	14,819.82	1,307.10	16,126.92	14,448.34	1,518.29	15,966.63	17,599.69	1,561.02	19,160.71

Source: Budget Documents, 2006–07, Govt of India.

Notes

1. I sincerely acknowledge my gratitude to Dr N.J. Kurien, Director of CSD, for his inspiration to write this paper.
2. Under *quota-based* gender budgeting money was earmarked even for ballroom dancing under the GAD budget in one of the ministries in the Philippines. Also, as there was no penalty for not utilising the GAD budget fully and efficiently, many of the departments ended up with unspent surpluses in the GAD budget. Ideally, differential targeting of expenditure emanating from the identification of appropriate programmes for women in various sectors or reprioritising the expenditure based on a generic list of right programmes and policies for women might be more effective than uniform targeting at 5 per cent across sectors. Refer Rao, Bagchi and Chakraborty (2006).
3. For details on the cross-country analysis of gender budgeting, refer to Diane (1999), Chakraborty (2002 a, b), Chakraborty (2004), NIPFP (2003).
4. The expert group was under the chairmanship of the Chief Economic Advisor of India, Ashok Lahiri, and the report is posted at *www.cgaindia.org/pdf/Classification per cent20Report.pdf*; Section II of the report is on gender budgeting.
5. Refer Expenditure Budget, 2005–06. It was also noted that the Department of Women and Child Development (DWCD) and National Institute of Public Finance and Policy (NIPFP) would be undertaking a *review of the public expenditure profile* of the Departments of Rural Development, Health and Family Welfare, Labour, Elementary Education, Small Scale Industries, Urban Employment and Poverty Alleviation, Social Justice and Empowerment and Tribal Affairs, through a gender lens; conducting a gender disaggregated benefit incidence analysis (BIA) and recommending specific changes in the operational guidelines of various development schemes so as to improve the coverage of women beneficiaries of public expenditure. Subsequently, the NIPFP developed a working paper titled 'Gender Budgeting in Select Ministries: Conceptual and Methodological Issues' and, based on this working paper, the DWCD organised two workshops for the selected ministries for training in gender budgeting.
6. Arndt, 1998.
7. Empirical literature draws attention to the efficiency dimensions of integrating the gender perspective into macroeconomic policies. For example, the striking *good mother thesis* noted that women tend to have a higher marginal propensity to spend than men on goods

that enhance the capabilities of children. Such empirical evidence suggested that the likelihood of children being enrolled in school goes up with their mother's educational level, and the mother's extra income has a more positive impact on household investments in nutrition, health and education of children than extra income accruing to fathers. Also, literature on gender inequality in the labour market shows that eliminating gender discrimination in occupation and wages could increase not only women's income, but also national income.

8. How can fiscal policy address the alarming issue of the declining juvenile ratio across different states in India? If not through direct budgetary policies, it is important to incorporate juvenile sex ratio in the formula-based grants given to states by the Finance Commission, indicating a penalty to states with an adverse sex ratio. The magnitude of female survival disadvantage is far from a minor issue, and macropolicy makers cannot afford to remain indifferent, considering it an intrahousehold issue. Amartya Sen set off this debate when he estimated that there were 100 million 'missing women' in the world, with India having the dubious distinction of having the largest share. Studies noted that it ranks among the worst human catastrophes of the 20th century as it is larger than the combined casualties of all the famines in the century and it also exceeds the combined death toll of both World Wars and the casualties of major epidemics including the currently ongoing HIV/AIDS pandemic.

9. The human development index [HDI] is a gender-neutral measure of the average achievements of a country in three basic dimensions of human development: longevity, knowledge, and a decent standard of living. Longevity is measured by life expectancy at birth, knowledge by adult literacy and the combined gross primary, secondary and tertiary enrolment ratio, and standard of living by gross domestic product (GDP) per capita in US dollars in purchasing power parity (PPP) terms. Let L denote life expectancy at birth in years, A adult literacy as per cent, E combined gross primary, secondary and tertiary enrolment ratio in per cent, and Y per capita GDP in PPP US dollar terms. The value of each variable for a country is transformed into its deviation from the minimum possible value of the variable expressed as a proportion of the maximum deviation possible, i.e., maximum less minimum. Thus, after transformation we have $L^* = (L-25)/(85-25)$, $A^* = A/100$, $E^* = E/100$, and $Y^* = (Y - \min Y)(\max Y - \min Y)$. Given the minimum life expectancy for women and men of 27.5 years and 22.5 years, respectively, the average minimum life expectancy is taken as 25 [= (27.5 + 22.5)/2]. Similarly, maximum life expectancy is taken

as 85. The maximum and minimum of both adult literacy and enrolment are taken as 100 and 0, respectively. The maximum and minimum for Y are exogenously fixed. HDI is computed as $\{L^* + (2/3 \times A^* + 1/3 \times E^*) + Y^*\}/3$. The gender development index (GDI) uses the same variables as the HDI, but adjusts for the degree of disparity in achievement across genders. The average value of each of the component variables is substituted by 'equally distributed equivalent achievements'. The equally distributed equivalent achievement for a variable is taken as that level of achievement which, if attained equally by women and men would be judged to be exactly as valuable socially as the actually observed disparate achievements. Taking an additively separable, symmetric and constant elasticity marginal valuation function with elasticity 2, the equally distributed equivalent achievement X_{ede} for any variable X turns out to be $X_{ede} = [\, n_f(1/X_f) + n_m(1/X_m)]^{-1\cdot}$ where X_f and X_m are the values of the variable for females and males, and n_f and n_m are the population shares of females and males. X_{ede} is a 'gender-equity-sensitive indicator' (GESI). Thus, for this chosen value of 2 for the constant elasticity marginal valuation function, GDI is computed as $\{L_{ede} + (2/3 \times A_{ede} + 1/3 \times E_{ede}) + Y_{ede}\}/3$.

10. The capability approach has been central to the Human Development Reports series (HDRs) launched by the UNDP since the 1990s by Sen's close associate, the late Mahbub ul Haq, and has subsequently influenced policy at the World Bank during the Wolfensohn era (Gasper, 2002).

11. Empirical evidence showed that in a semi-logarithmic framework of regressing proportionate shortfalls of life expectancy against per capita GDP, nearly half of the variations in life expectancy could be attributed to differences in GNP per head (Anand and Ravallion, 1993). In this context, it is important to note that the substantial impact of higher GDP per head on life expectancy and other social outcomes of better literacy levels, low mortality rates among children and better schooling among children seem to work via factors in which the public policy stance plays a significant part. Chakraborty (2005), using a fixed effects model of pooled least squares for the early 1990s, the analysis of link between per capita combined expenditure on health and education and the human development index, revealed that there is a positive functional relationship between the two. The subsequent analysis of the link between per capita expenditure on human capital formation and the gender development index also showed the same result. This result is in confirmation with the trend that public expenditure on human capital formation gets transformed to the end results of

better gender-sensitive indicators, despite the constraints of intra-household disparities in resource allocation.

12. For a detailed discussion, see M. Desai (1990): 'Poverty and Capability: Towards an Empirically Implementable Measure', The Development Economics Research Programme, London School of Economics, London.

13. Pigou (1920/1952) p. 759 quoted by Sen (1987), p.14.

References

Anand, S. and M. Ravallion. 1993. 'Human Development in Poor Countries: On the Role of Private Incomes and Public Services' in *Journal of Economic Perspectives*. 7 (Winter).

Cagatay, N., M. Keklik, R. Lal, and J. Lang, 2000. *Budgets as if People Mattered: Democratizing Macroeconomic Policies*. New York: United Nations Development Programme.

Central Statistical Organization. 2000. *Report of the Time Use Survey*. New Delhi: Ministry of Statistics and Programme Implementation.

Chakraborty, Lekha. 2003a. 'Macroscan of Union Budget 2003 in India: A Glimpse through Gender Lens'. UNIFEM.

———. 2003b. Gender Based Analysis in Canada: Lessons for India. Report prepared under DFAIT Canadian Faculty Fellowship, Carleton University, Canada.

———. 2003c. 'Budgetary Allocations and Gender in Sri Lanka: A Categorization of Financial Inputs'. UNIFEM (Prepared for Government of Sri Lanka/UNIFEM).

———. 2005. 'Public Investment and Unpaid Work: Selective Evidence from Time Use Data'. Paper presented at UNDP-Levy Conference at The Levy Institute of University of Bard, New York.

——— 2005a. 'Public Policy Stance and Human Development: A Panel Investigation' in B.B. Bhattacharyya and Arup Mitra (eds.), *Macroeconomics and Welfare*. Academic Publishers.

Desai, M. 1990. 'Poverty and Capability: Towards an Empirically Implementable Measure'. The Development Economics Research Programme, London School of Economics, London.

Dreze, J. and A. Sen. 1995. *India: Economic Development and Social Opportunity*. Oxford India Paperbacks.

Government of India. 1995–96. 'Budget Documents'. New Delhi: Ministry of Finance.

———. 1996–97. 'Budget Documents'. New Delhi: Ministry of Finance.

———. 1997–98. 'Budget Documents'. New Delhi: Ministry of Finance.

————. 1998–99. 'Budget Documents'. New Delhi: Ministry of Finance.

————. 1999–2000. 'Budget Documents'. New Delhi: Ministry of Finance.

————. 2000–01. 'Budget Documents'. New Delhi: Ministry of Finance.

————. 2001. 'National Human Development Report'. Planning Commission.

————. 2001–02. 'Budget Documents'. New Delhi: Ministry of Finance.

————. 2002–03. 'Budget Documents'. New Delhi: Ministry of Finance.

————. 2003–04. 'Budget Documents'. New Delhi: Ministry of Finance.

————. 2004–05. 'Budget Documents'. New Delhi: Ministry of Finance.

————. 2005. 'Classification of Budgetary Transactions', Ministry of Finance Report, Government of India.

————. 2005–06. 'Budget Documents'. New Delhi: Ministry of Finance.

————. 2006. 'Economic Survey 2002–03, Economic Division, Ministry of Finance.

————. 2006–07. 'Budget Documents'. New Delhi: Ministry of Finance.

Lahiri, Ashok, Lekha Chakraborty and P.N. Bhattacharrya 2000. 'India-Gender Budgeting', Report submitted to UNIFEM, South Asia and Ministry of Human Resource Development, Government of India.

————. 2001. 'Gender Budgeting in India: Post Budget Assessment Report 2001'. Report submitted to UNIFEM, South Asia and Ministry of Human Resource Development, Government of India.

————. 2002a. 'Gender Budgeting in India'. Report submitted to UNIFEM, South Asia and Ministry of Human Resource Development, Government of India.

————. 2002b. 'Gender Diagnosis and Budgeting in India'. Report submitted to UNIFEM, South Asia and Ministry of Human Resource Development, Government of India.

————. 2003. 'Gender Budgeting in India'. UNIFEM, South Asia.

Mahbub ul Haq Human Development Centre. 2000. *Human Development in South Asia 2000: The Gender Question*. Oxford University Press.

Mundle, S. 1998. 'Financing Human Development: Some Lessons from Advanced Asian Countries' in *World Development*. 26(4), 659–672.

NIPFP. 2003. *Gender Budgeting in India*. Follow the Money Series, UNIFEM.

NIPFP. 2005. 'Gender Budgeting in Selected Ministries: Conceptual and Methodologies Issues'. Working Paper for DWCD, Govt of India.

Noorbakhsh, F. 1998. 'A Modified Human Development Index' in *World Development*. 26(3), 517–528.

Palmer. 1995. Public Finance from a Gender Perspective in *World Development*. 23(11), pp. 1981–1986.

Rao, Bagchi, and Chakraborty. 2006. 'Fiscal Decentralisation and Gender Budgeting: An Empirical Analysis of Selected Countries', NIPFP. mimeo.

Rao, Govinda, Amaresh Bagchi and Lekha Chakraborty. 2006. 'Fiscal Decentralisation and Gender Budgeting'. NIPFP.

Rao, M.G. 1998. 'Accommodating Public Expenditure Policies: The Case of Fast Growing Asian Economies' in *World Development*. 26(4), 673–694.

Sarraf, Feridoun. 2003. 'Gender Responsive Government Budgeting'. IMF Working Paper. Fiscal Affairs Department, International Monetary Fund.

Sen, Gita. 1996. 'Gender, Markets and States: A Selective Review and Research Agendas' in *World Development*. Vol. 24, No. 5, pp. 821–829.

———. 1999. *Gender Mainstreaming in Finance: A Reference Manual for Governments and Other Stakeholders*. Gender Management System Series, Commonwealth Secretariat, UK.

———. 2000. 'Gender Mainstreaming in Finance Ministries' in *World Development*. Vol. 28, No. 7, pp. 1379–1390.

Sen, Gita and Caren Grown. 1985. *Development Alternatives: Crises and Alternative Visions*. New Delhi: DAWN Secretariat.

Sen, Gita and Chiranjib Sen. 1984 'Women's Domestic Work and Economic Activity: Results from the National Sample Survey'. *Working Paper No. 197*. Thiruvananthapuram: Centre for Development Studies.

UNDP. 2005. 'Human Development Report'. UNDP

United Nations Development Programme (various issues). 'Human Development Reports'. Various issues.

Van de Walle, D. 1998. 'Assessing the Welfare Impacts of Public Spending'. *World Development*. 26(3): 365–379.

World Bank. 2000. World Development Database, Electronic Version.

13

Crafting Democratic Citizenship
Towards a Continuum Approach to Political Participation

This paper is an attempt to explore the meaning and significance of political participation within (a) the conceptual framework of democratic citizenship and (b) debates surrounding representative democracy. It consists of three parts the first examines the idea of representative democracy and the manner in which democratic politics may be sought to be crafted as a continuum between representation and participation; the second looks at the global experience and experiments in electoral designs and political reservation for women; and the third examines election data in order to identify possible patterns in women's political participation, followed by a discussion of the ways in which civil society organisations have sought to address themselves to reforming the electoral system, in particular by addressing the voter or empowering her through specific rights.

The defining feature of citizenship, distinguishing it from subjecthood, is the sense of belonging, horizontal camaraderie and full and equal membership in the political community. The latter derives not only from equal protection of the autonomous space of the individual, but also through an ethic of participation. The ethic of participation, in turn, makes for *thick* citizenship as distinct from a *thin* or passive notion of citizenship. Active citizenship is embedded in continual creation of public spaces through dialogue, deliberation, expression and demonstration within a mutually agreed framework of democratic norms. A strand within the citizenship theory sees the idea of activity and participation as the crux of citizenship, giving it its historical validity as a momentum concept, and as a countervailing force against domination in all its manifestations, foregrounding its relational and collective aspects.

While the relational aspects of citizenship are expected to unfold within a mutually agreed framework of participation comprising meta-rules like constitutions, institutions like the courts, representative/political bodies like parliaments, schools, universities, hospitals, etc., as a principle of activity, citizenship may be seen as a framework for effecting change, or creating and sustaining an order through which its promise of equality may be made effective. Politics is integral to such a framework, since envisaging and moving towards such an order, in many cases, would involve a radical rupture from existing systems of deliberation, communication, dialogue, participation, methods of representation and power sharing. In other words, democratic citizenship is integrally associated with and embedded in notions of equality and participation. Politics in turn is conceived not merely in terms of institutions through which authoritative allocation of values is made, nor only as understanding the processes through which power permeates and makes itself manifest in society and polity, but primarily as processes through which the constitution of such power and its institutionalisation may continually be opened up for scrutiny and transformative change, in order to make its spread 'democratic', and coincident with principles of popular sovereignty and horizontal equality.

Over the years, questions pertaining to representation of groups and the relative appropriateness of specific electoral designs and electoral systems for their adequate representation have become germane to devising ways of deepening democracy and crafting democratic citizenship. These questions have prompted animated debates around the meaning of representation, what constitutes adequate representation, and what are the ways in which it can be achieved. These debates have generated areas of tension around 'appropriate' and 'effective' electoral systems, compelling a more rigorous examination of the ways in which democracies have addressed issues concerning the edging out of social groups from the electoral process, and the structural and societal constraints that contribute to this.

Debates around women's representation in elected bodies and positions of political decision making, and their visibility and participation in the political process, have been particularly acrimonious. This is not surprising since they threaten to unsettle hegemonic notions of women's 'proper' roles and place in family and society. The contours of the debate have for a long time been framed by contests over what constitutes politics and women's relationship with it. While feminists have differed over the definition of politics, the ways of 'doing' it, and the manner in which women can charter for themselves a more significant political presence, over the last one decade, questions regarding available choices in electoral design and their relative effectiveness in assuring women's representation have begun to be explored with greater assurance and confidence.

Debates around models of representation ultimately have at their core the issue of adequacy of representative democracy, in particular questions around universal and differentiated/proportionality models. Apart from the conceptual framework of citizenship, this paper will, therefore, also examine debates around representative democracy, in particular (a) the 'participatory or political deficit' that representative democracy is seen as entailing, seen especially in comparison with direct or participatory democracy, as exemplified by the classical model of democracy – the elusive ideal for modern political systems; (b) the 'crisis' in mediated or representative democracy, and the different ways in which the crisis is sought to be resolved; and (c) developing a democratic and effective system of representation so that groups are adequately represented. The focus in the examination will not only be on 'appropriate' systems of representation, but also on the ways in which the system is able to translate itself into an 'effective' system, bridging thereby the difference between what Mills calls 'talking' and 'doing' systems. This focus, as the discussion in the following sections will show, will help build a case for what has been called a continuum approach, aimed at linking issues of representation with those of participation.

Representation and Participation in Democratic Citizenship

Redefining Categories

Given that modern political systems work on the principle of indirect or representative, rather than direct or participatory, democracy, there have been considerable debates around how to make representation just, fair and democratic, which is to say, to make it reflective of and commensurate with group-differentiated interests. Alongside concerns around developing appropriate systems of representation, corresponding anxieties around participatory deficit and passive and thin notions of citizenship, which systems of (indirect) representation necessarily entail, have persisted. Some strands have looked for a semblance of directness within civil society, envisaging it as a participatory space embodying 'a ceaseless process of political education in citizenship' (Urbinati, 2000: 758). Considering, however, that definitions of civil society vary, radical democrats exhibit a growing concern over the manner in which the public/

political and, corresponding to it, the idea of democratic citizenship and participatory institutions is being redefined through a preoccupation with building a strong civil society. A strong civil society focussing on participatory networks fraught through non-governmental organisations, they argue, may ultimately edge out 'people', as dominant groups take over, thereby generating greater powerlessness and exclusion (Joseph, 2003). The notion of the public as a democratically negotiated and, therefore, an inclusive collective space may be effaced in such a situation, increasing the vulnerability of disadvantaged groups. In the light of the above, I will examine in the following section feminist engagements with politics, and deriving from these, the ways in which they have attempted to articulate their relationship with representative democracy.

Much of the feminist concern in recent times with 'politics' and the 'political' may be seen as embodying what Anne Phillips has characterised a 'double movement towards both critique and recuperation' (Phillips, 1998: 4). The critique may well be seen as more or less continuing with the issues raised by the women's movement during the 1960s and 1970s of a notion of politics that grounded itself in gendered oppositional dichotomies and dualities of social life, around the private/personal and the public/political.[1] At the crux of the feminist critique has been the analytical worth of categories spelling oppositional duality, which it has for quite some time questioned, or being consonant with the frameworks of domination, viz., patriarchy, or with the ideology and practices of exploitative rule, viz., colonialism. The public and the private, feminists have constantly reminded us, can exist as oppositional and dichotomous categories only in contexts where all persons are not equally free. Taking the public and private as discrete categories, moreover, without analysing the socio-historical contexts within which they get articulated, they argue, is inaccurate and also inadequate for explaining social processes, since it effaces the complexities that actually exist in political and social life. Feminists have not only pointed out the exclusionary nature of these boundaries, but also the ways in which in different historical contexts, women have either negotiated with them to render them permeable, or dismantled them redefining their constitutive elements, and their mutual relationships. As far as recuperation is concerned – the other movement that Anne Phillips alludes to – feminists have chosen different paths, either through equal access or presence in the public-political, or alternatively, seeing the personal and political as a bridged/breached continuum – reconstituting thereby their relationship and content. At the crux of recuperation or reconstruction, however, is not dissolving politics as a distinct category, but rather a 'calling back to politics', bringing in its wake a retheorisation of citizenship. In the history of citizenship, the public and the private have distinctive and interrelated chronosophies, figuring integrally as Gurpreet Mahajan (2003) terms it, 'two modes of enhancing democratic citizenship'. Conceived as two co-eval and co-equal modes of enhancing citizenship, their development is no longer seen as antagonistic, but of mutual imbrication, in an ongoing process of democratisation – imbued in different historical and cultural contexts with different meanings and correlative boundaries.

Immanent in the rethinking of the relationship between the private and the public is the 'relocation' and 'reconstitution' of the abstract citizen. The process of relocation is central to the project of building democratic citizenship since the abstract, unmarked, and masked citizen, integral to liberalism, is constitutive of the dichotomies of social and political life. Following again the method of 'critique and recuperation', the critique of the abstract citizen may be done on the ground that it conceives of the citizen as an unencumbered, un-embedded, disconnected self, who seeks actualisation, not through political activity, but through a range of other commitments and activities that take place in diverse and loosely connected associations. Moreover, feminists, along with multiculturalists, and theorists on the Left, have also criticised the 'uniformity' and 'generality' that liberal citizenship entails since it overlooks the inequalities that exist in real life. The idea of the un-embedded and unencumbered self, the abstract citizen in the liberal framework has been rejected for advocating a context-free and apolitical citizenship – the floating and unconnected individuality of the citizen is not seen as conducive to building relational/democratic citizenship.

In its recuperation mode, feminist politics concerns itself with comprehending the ways in which differential citizenship reproduces itself, so that it no longer silences or marginalises women and, as mentioned earlier, 'calling back to politics' in a way that 'women' like the masked citizen does not become a dangerous 'neutral' abstraction. Guarding against this abstraction, involves not only a reconstruction of the private/public distinction so that its 'recurring power' may be rolled back, but also taking into account the differences that exist among women – of race, class, caste, etc. – that determine their specific experiences of citizenship. It is only by comprehending these differences that the specificity of women's experiences can come together in broad political alliances, alliances that are not fragmented along the lines of differences, nor forged through their occlusion, but rather as struggles that weave them together through action and engagement with specific and shared/common experiences of oppression. The association between feminism and a politics of difference is particularly marked in Iris Young's definition of a 'differentiated citizenship' that would explicitly recognise differences of sex, race, class, sexuality or language in order to guarantee that all groups are fully included and Nancy Fraser's exploration of tensions between those struggles for recognition that are most closely associated with identity politics and those struggles of redistribution that arise in the context of traditional socialist politics. In both cases, feminism provides the tools with which to deconstruct exclusionary notions of common good or the class-defined preoccupations of earlier struggles for social equality. It also generates the insights that clarify the importance of particular identities, while questioning at the same time, the solidity of these identities. The issues that are addressed, therefore, are not simply identifying a notion of 'women's politics' or a politics centering on 'women's issues'. It rather, as Philips points out, holds out the promise of transforming the ways in which we think about any kind of politics at all (Phillips, 1998: 16).

While transformative politics is central to the feminist project, it does not automatically assume a unity of women in a unified feminist politics. Feminists like Judith Butler have pointed out that as a subject of politics, or a subject of feminist politics, 'women' does not – and may never – exist. Arguing that the 'unity' of the category of women is neither pre-supposed nor desired, Butler points out that it would be wrong to assume in advance that there is a category of women that simply need to be filled in with various components of race, class, age, ethnicity, and sexuality in order to become complete. Problematising 'identity' premised in unity and fixidity and its relationship with feminist politics, Butler points out that identity is ambiguous and may not be treated as a normative goal. Feminist politics too may not be seen as emanating necessarily from some 'stable, unified and agreed-upon identity', and without this compulsory expectation of unified identity, feminist actions may 'well get a quicker start and seem more congenial to a number of women' (Butler, 1998: 288). What is important to keep in mind, therefore, following Phillips' framework of a feminist politics of recuperation, is that in the course of engaging in and thinking about transformative politics, the political sub-jectivity of women gets continually constituted.

The difficulties of articulating women as a unified category, cutting across the equality/difference and private/public divide, and 'women's interest', become all the more pronounced where issues of political representation are concerned. But, as Butler herself puts it, the 'political task is not to refuse representational politics – as if we could' (Butler, 1998: 277). Following the track of critique and recuperation, it may be suggested that politics does matter, but what we understand by politics must first be transformed. While feminism provides a much needed counterweight to the resulting cynicism of apathy about politics, enabling us to think more critically about the exclusions still practised under apparent inclusiveness, and enables us to think more imaginatively about the many ways in which politics can still be transformed (Phillips 1998), it is also important to see how, following Butler, feminism is able to weave into the 'historical present' or 'the contemporary field of power' (Butler, 1998: 277) a feminist political practice which bridges the gap between the notional 'woman' with diverse claims to representation.

Towards a Continuum

Since this paper takes up issues of representation, participation and democracy, it would be important to identify first the relationship that it envisages between the three. The delineation of this relationship is important in order to articulate the position that the paper puts forth regarding women's relationship with politics and women's political citizenship within the contours of the existing debate on the relative merits of representative and participatory democracy. As stated at the outset, this paper proposes a continuum framework, which bridges the participatory and representative models of democracy. It also argues for a framework of representative democracy which brings together the agora model consisting of continually evolving multilayered activity with agonistic politics, which subscribes to recognising difference and plurality within a dialogical framework.

While the complexity of modern societies has made the directness of democracy impossible, and the distancing between the processes of ruling and [those] being ruled gets more pronounced as one moves up across the layers/tiers of government, the participatory model of democracy continues to be influential as an ideal form, embodying an elusive state of perfection which one must constantly aspire to emulate, and wherever possible, replicate. The shift in the paradigms of government, with direct participation in ruling giving way to being ruled through representatives, has not eroded the normative value of direct democracy, ironically as something that the 'moderns' can never have, and yet cannot cease to want (Dunn, 1993: 28). This uncritical nostalgia for directness in democracy generates corresponding concerns about the inadequacy or deficiency of modern representative forms of democracy.[2] These debates have become more pronounced with questions around issues of equality in representation, forms of representation of groups, and the appropriate ways of achieving it, having become progressively significant. The above concerns are also attended by anxieties around the thin and passive citizenship which accompanied the shift from participatory and direct democracy to representative democracy. A lament of 'crisis' in representative democracy has emerged in recent years, stemming from the assumptions of democratic deficiency and political passivity in representative democracy. Critics of representative democracy consider it a weak form of democracy, a poor substitute for self-government and active citizenship.

The concerns around indirectness and political deficit may be seen as having been addressed in two ways, each approaching the relationship between representation and participation in divergent ways. The manner in which the question is addressed at each level has a special resonance for women and their engagement/relationship with politics:

(a) *The universality approach* looks at the relationship in terms of cohabitation in an inclusive model. This approach transcends/resolves the anxieties around political deficit by pointing at its moral distinctiveness and value. Focussing on the ways in which an articulated public sphere is created through and in the intervening period between elections, it points in particular to the ways in which the processes of deliberation provide a continuum between the representatives and participation, bridging the spatial and temporal gap, or the absence of simultaneity between the voting and decision making. An articulated public sphere, while filling up the temporal hiatus between 'electoral trials', they argue, adds to the ideological content of elections by going beyond the here and now to connect also with the past and look towards the future. This approach sees both participation and representation as significant elements of democracy and seeks to bridge the distinction between the participatory and representative forms of democracy by locating them in a framework of dialogue, rather than in any kind of contradictory cohabitation, where the existence of representative democracy means a political and participatory deficit. The framework of cohabitation is constituted by the deliberative character of democracy. The focus on deliberation allows the perception of participation and representation, not as two alternative forms of democracy, but as related, and constituting the framework of political action in modern democracies. Seen from this vantage point, the emphasis on the deliberative character of modern democracies is seen as providing the institutional and sociocultural space within which the various components of political action – from opinions and will formation to decision making – take shape (Urbinati: 759).

(b) *The proportionality or group-specific approach* sees representation and participation as distinctive, but rejects the elevation of participatory democracy as the only 'real' form of democracy. The primary purpose of this approach, therefore, is not to devise ways by which representative democracy could as closely as possible replicate participatory democracy. It rather makes the problems and patterns of exclusion central, rather than the participatory deficit that representative democracy might entail. Thus, David Plotke states that in a representative democracy, the 'opposite of representation is not participation', but exclusion (Plotke, 1997: 19). Iris Marion Young considers 'political representation as both necessary and desirable' concerning herself with exclusion and group-differentiated citizenship (Young, 1997: 352; Kymlicka, 1996; Young, 1989).

Significantly, both formulations steer clear of the nostalgia for direct democracy as the only pure form of democracy, enabling participation. Moreover, both look for frameworks of inclusion with the universalist approach locating it in public discourses and deliberations that intervene and connect periodic 'electoral trials', and the group-specific approach concerning itself with the ways in which a differentiated citizenship could make universalism commensurate with proportionality. It would be useful, therefore, to weave into the universalism of the first approach the differentiated universalism of the group-specific approach to address the political and democratic deficit that is seen as informing representative democracy. The concerns around passivity may be addressed by seeking a continuum between representation and participation, by seeing representation as constitutive of democracy and embodying the processes of 'comprehensive filtering, refining and mediating' that is crucial for 'political will formation and expression'. It is this process of mediation that opens up room for deliberation and a public discourse that fosters a relationship between the assembly and the people, a relationship that gets refreshed and renewed with each electoral trial. Moreover, it is through public discourse that intermediating electoral trials, that the 'here and now' aspect of elections, is transcended – to look forward to the future filling in the temporal and spatial gap as distinct from the simultaneity of voting and deciding, which direct democracy assumed. As mentioned earlier, while the deliberative framework works with a notion of universality, bringing in more and more people within its integrative framework, the group-specific framework works on principles of differentiated universalism to make it more compatible with democratic principles of equality and recognition of difference. One may derive from this framework a notion of politics which is founded on principles of agonism, and representation as based on the principle of group-proportionality. Yet, proportionality may not by itself bridge the relationship of verticality or the gap that exists between citizens and their representatives, which requires that the agonism of proportionality must be wedded to the multilayered activity and dialogue that holds together the agora. Thus, both must go together, since proportionality may remain descriptive unless it makes the representative body a talking and deliberating body *and* an acting and governing body with the purpose of making representation effective, imbued with mutual trust and accountability.[3] The spatial and temporal gap opened by representation opens up and requires a speech filled or articulated public sphere, connecting the collective moments of political participation which elections embody. The structures of representation are, moreover, layered, in the sense that public speech and deliberation are also encompassed by mediated participation. The agora paradigm – assumes representation as a complex institution that encompasses several layers of political action that fill the 'interval between one parliamentary election and another and they replace a spatial agora that no longer exists with a temporal one. Representation becomes a 'course of action', rather than a 'simple act' – a practice of political interaction among citizens, which goes well beyond voting.

Reservation for Women: Frameworks for Proportionality

In conformity with the Vienna Declaration and Programme of Action, the United Nations emphasised measures 'to assist in the strengthening and building of institutions relating to human rights, strengthening of a pluralistic civil society, and the protection of groups which have been rendered vulnerable'.[4] In this context it identified as 'of particular importance', 'assistance [to be] provided upon the request of governments for the conduct of fair and free elections, including assistance in the human rights aspects of elections and public information about elections' (Vienna Declaration Part II, Para 67). The provision of conditions ensuring fair and free elections was envisaged within the broad framework of basic human rights, and democracy as a condition in which these rights could be realised, while assisting in the election process was seen as helping the process of democratisation. Democratisation, in turn, was seen not only as ushering in political democracy, but also broadening and deepening it through the inclusion of vulnerable groups. The United Nations booklet, *Human Rights and Elections*, part of its professional training series, lays down the legal, technical and human rights aspects of elections, emphasising non-discrimination and inclusion. While emphasising equal, universal and non-discriminatory suffrage as a basic element of fair elections, the booklet also highlights the instruments providing for non-discriminatory and positive measures, e.g., the Declaration on the Elimination of Discrimination against Women (Article 4 (a) and (c)), the Convention on the Elimination of All Forms of Discrimination Against Women (Article 7 (a) and (b)) and the Convention on the Political Rights of Women (Articles II and III) (United Nations 1994).

The effective representation of specific groups, women in particular, and the terms of their inclusion – as voters and representatives – has been a matter critical to both the theory and practice of democracy. The question of 'fair representation' in particular has been contentious, when seen in terms of parity or proportionate representation in terms of specific numbers or quota. While the demand for parity of women and men in politics was grounded in biological differences between them, the rationale behind a quota system is women's historical marginality in politics and the effects it has on the political system (Siim, 2000: 69; Hust, 2004: 35). In a manifestation of the replacement of the politics of ideas with the politics of presence, certain influential strands in feminist theory have stressed the importance of women's presence in public/political/decision making bodies in a 'critical mass'. While the notion of critical mass subscribes to the view that the presence of women as a 'critical mass' would somehow set in motion a process that would engender politics, the difference between presence as a 'critical mass' and 'critical action' has been emphasised by others foregrounding the necessity of moving beyond numbers into the realm of transformative actions (Dahlerup, 2001: 108).

Concerns around enabling women's equal access to the political process, and with offering technical assistance for the reform of the electoral system and management of the election process, have focussed attention on gender equality relating to (a) design of the electoral systems: analysis of the implications for women's representation of different options in electoral systems (including the number of seats, the size of electoral districts, whether proportional representation is adopted, etc.); (b) voter registration: supporting approaches to registration and training of officials to ensure that women get on the list on an equal basis with men; (c) voter education: ensuring that education reaches women as well as men, and promotes respect in the community for women's equal rights to participate; and (d) access to the polls: promoting approaches that reduce risks to voting that could reduce women's participation, e.g., separate queues in polling booths for women (Schalkwyk and Woroniuk, 1998).

While questions of women's representation in elected bodies and positions of political decision making, and their visibility in the political process have been raised for a long time now, questions regarding the available choices in electoral design and their relative effectiveness in assuring adequate representation for women have begun to be asked relatively recently. Different kinds of electoral designs and political and electoral procedures have been subsequently examined so as to craft a system which gives adequate representation to women, facilitating their emergence as a critical mass. Among these, the 'quota' system or reservation of seats in elected bodies, aiming at 'guaranteed outcome' rather than providing an equal or level playing field as in the gender parity list system for parties, has become the most contentious. While there have been divergent positions on the quota system and its implications for feminist politics, a comparative study of electoral systems has shown that in electoral systems based on the principle of first past the post, quota is perhaps the best way of assuring the presence of women in substantial numbers in representative bodies. The Platform for Action arrived at in the 4th UN World Conference on Women in Beijing in 1995, has become an important reference point for the demand for quotas by the women's movement worldwide. In many ways, the Beijing programme of action reflects the general shift in the way in which participation was being envisaged in different UN instruments. Like the Vienna Declaration, which stressed the importance of rolling back discrimination and structures that generate group vulnerability by strengthening institutions, the Beijing Platform of Action suggested a discursive shift from women to structures and institutions. The justification of reservation is mostly made with reference to some kind of historically experienced or inherent group disadvantage, vulnerability, inadequacy or weakness. In the case of women's representation, while previously the focus was on women's lack of resources or lack of will to participate, the Beijing platform talks about structures of exclusion – 'discriminatory attitudes and practices' and 'unequal power relations', which have led to the under-representation of women in arenas of political decision making. Importantly in the new discourse the responsibility for promoting change has shifted from the individual woman to those institutions that are expected to take action to identify and correct the causes of women's under-representation. While suggesting affirmative action as a possible means of attaining the goal of women's equal participation in political decision making, the Beijing Platform recommended that governments use 'specific targets and implementing measures... if necessary through positive action'. Moreover, the platform attempts to expand the discourse on critical mass by focusing on equal representation rather than insisting on any minimum representation. It demands a commitment from governments to 'take measures, wherever appropriate, in electoral systems that encourage political parties to integrate women in elective and non-elective public positions in the same level and at the same levels as men', and directs political parties to 'consider examining party structures and procedures to remove all barriers that directly or indirectly discriminate against the participation of women'.[5]

Theoretically and historically, two kinds of tracks have been considered for increasing women's representation in elected bodies, viz., the incremental track and the fast track. The two tracks are identified with two distinct discourses. The incremental track recognises the existence of social prejudices and the fact that women do not have the same political resources as men. Following a linear view of progress, it assumes that as society progresses, with the increase in its resources and people's access to it, *gradually*, women's representation in decision making and other public bodies will increase. The fast track rejects gradualism and even the assumption that an increase in resources might lead to equal representation. It sees exclusion and discrimination as the core of the problem and believes that equality will not come by itself and will have to be pushed.[6] The fast track and the fast track policy constitute an important part of the new direction set out in the Beijing platform.

Reservations or electoral quotas are fast tracks to equal representation of women. In the debates on gender quotas, the high representation of women in Scandinavian parliaments is commonly used as an argument in support of the introduction of gender quotas. Drude Dahlerup, however, considers these examples as misleading since the trajectory of women's representation in these countries may be seen as having followed the incremental track. The representation of women in Denmark, Norway and Sweden occurred in the 1970s and in Iceland in the 1980s, all before the introduction of quotas. Moreover, gender quotas in these countries was voluntary, never a legal requirement, and used only by some political parties at the centre and the Left. It took approximately 60 years from women's enfranchisement for Denmark, Sweden and Norway to cross the 20 per cent threshold and 70 years to reach 30 per cent. This means that the Nordic countries, in spite of the high level of women's representation, can no longer be considered the model, or at any rate the only model for increasing women's representation.

At present, only 16 per cent of the world's parliamentarians are women, and according to the feminist movement as well as feminist theory, this shortage of women in political institutions may have serious consequences for the articulation of women's interest and for the legitimacy of democratic institutions (Phillip, 1995; Norris, 2004). Today, around 40 countries have introduced gender quotas in elections to national parliaments, either by means of constitutional amendment or by changing the electoral laws (legal quotas). In more than 50 other countries, major political parties have voluntarily set out quota provisions in their own statutes (party quotas). Even if quota provisions are often controversial, the use of the quota tool to make historical leaps or jump starts in women's representation is becoming a global trend. In 2003, Rwanda surpassed Sweden as the number one country in the world in terms of women's parliamentary representation – women received 48.8 per cent of the seats as opposed to 45.3 per cent in Sweden. Rwanda came to signify a new trend in world politics, which the study conceptualises as the fast track to gender balance in politics using which countries as disparate as Argentina, Uganda, South Africa, Bosnia and Herzegovina, France and Costa Rica have, through the use of gender quotas, attempted to rapidly change women's historical under-representation in political institutions (Dahlerup, 2006).

A question that may well be asked here is to what extent do electoral quotas fit or accommodate into, rather than challenge, dominant conceptions of citizenship? Electoral quotas or reservations for women clearly involve a demand for women's increased participation in public-sphere activities. An influential strand within feminist theory challenges the norms of 'public' citizenship and questions the 'passivity' ascribed to non-political and non-economic/productive activity. While the active or participatory model which associates rights and entitlements to performance or practice of citizenship, drawing from the civic republican model, is dominant among American feminist theorists, prioritising women's public-ness or their public roles to their domestic activities, other forms of citizenship have focussed attention on social and cultural rights, the associated welfare regime and responsibilities of the state and claims for recognition of women's contribution in the domestic sphere (Bacchi, 2006).[7] There is, therefore, a degree of ambivalence among feminists, particularly from the Eastern European countries, to the strategy of electoral quotas. Feminists have sought to overcome the dichotomies structuring the contours of the debate by arguing that specific forms of citizenship may take precedence depending on the context. While the notion of context-based or context-sensitive citizenship may facilitate the alleviation of the debate to a level of co-existence of contrasting arguments, on the issue of quotas, feminists have insisted that it actually cuts across the entrenched dichotomies that have inhibited women's claims to citizenship, irrespective of their form. First, they straddle the public/private divide by insisting that women, because they are women, deserve representation; second, they draw attention to the importance of having a voice in defining the nature of citizenship rights and responsibilities (Bacchi, 2006: 42). The suggestion that quotas cut across the public/private divide challenges the dichotomy of the mind/body implicit in the 'politics of ideas', which was challenged by the counter-argument of a 'politics of presence'. The insistence on presence in critical numbers or a 'critical mass' to set in motion significant change, has led on to yet another measure of transformative change – 'critical act' – put forth by feminists in the context of Scandinavian politics, where women have a substantial presence.[8] While the critical mass theory may be inhibited by reference to minimum and relative numbers, weakened in turn by expectations of a turning point, the theory of 'critical act' put forward by Dahlerup, hopes to diminish weakness by shifting attention to actions rather than numbers, actions which involve men as well as women, for transformative change.[9]

Frameworks of Women's Political Participation in India

The Missing Women? Exploring the Gender Gap in Politics in India

The presence of women in parliament in India, as Table 1 shows, has remained remarkably low and stable, ranging from an average of 5 per cent till the 1990s, when it increased to an average of 8 per cent. In 1999 with 8.8 per cent women, the highest so far, India was 82nd of the 180 countries for which data on women in the Lower House was reported by the Inter-Parliamentary Union. In 2004, of the 498 elected representatives in the Lok Sabha, only 8.26 per cent or 45 were women. While women from all communities are under-represented, Muslim women's representation has remained especially low.[10] The caste-class composition of women members of Parliament, moreover, shows that class forms an important factor in the successful inclusion of women into the political system in decision making positions.[11]

The smaller proportion of women in the Lok Sabha is replicated in the state legislative assemblies as well. The number of women legislators remains low in single digits for almost every state. Moreover, the proportion of women candidates in all major political parties remained around 10 per cent of the total candidates nominated by the party. While political parties have evidently doubted their winning ability, election data shows that the success rates of men and women candidates do not differ in a major way. By implication, this means that voters are not apprehensive of women candidates (Deshpande, 2004: 5433).

Following the continuum approach to politics, it may be proposed that democratic citizenship entails not merely frameworks of representation, which necessitates that we talk about a critical mass of numbers. It involves, as discussed earlier in the paper, that people's representatives,

Representation of Women and Muslim Women MPs in Parliament

Year of Election	No. of Women MPs	No. of Muslim Women MPs
1952	23	0
1957	24	2
1962	37	2
1967	32	0
1971	26	0
1977	18	3
1980	32	2
1984	45	3
1989	28	0
1991	40	0
1996	40	1
1998	44	0
1999	47	1
2004	45	2

See Sanjay Kumar, 'Muslim Women in India: Opinions, Attitudes and Participation in Politics' (Unpublished Paper).

the voters, electoral processes and actors through each electoral trial are tied in a multilayered relationship, which creates a democratic agora or dialogical spaces, marked by critical action and recognition of difference or agonism. Thus, when one talks about representation and the invisibility of women in political bodies, it is important that we also look at another aspect of participation – women voters – and thereafter at the manner in which an articulated public sphere bridges the temporal and spatial distance between representation and participation.

Both the Election Commission and the National Election Survey data show that women have consistently turned out in less numbers to vote than men, although the gender gap or the turnout differential between men and women has decreased over the years, steadying at 8 per cent through the elections of 1998, 1999 and 2004 (Tables 1, 2, 3 and 4; Figures 1 to 3). In an interesting analogy, Sudhir Varma, the Chief Election Officer in the Government of Rajasthan at the time of doing this study, extended the category of 'missing women', normally used in the context of the declining sex ratio, to women absent from the electoral rolls (Verma, 1997: 79-124). Varma correctly points out that whereas the trend of decline in the sex ratio in India has been primarily in the 0–18 age group which is the non-voting population, and the sex ratio of the voting population is better than the general sex ratio, under ideal conditions, the electoral sex ratio should have reflected this. Yet, the electoral sex ratio (ESR) is actually adverse. In the 1991 Lok Sabha elections, for example, out of a total of 49.8 crore voters, only 23.6 crore were women, which meant that nearly a crore women voters were left out of the voters' list. While the pattern of ESR is complex, a pattern of absences may be identified in terms of differences across states, between rural and urban constituencies, between general and reserved constituencies, as well as among reserved constituencies across states.[12]

Election data shows that there is no correlation between women's turnout and the number of women elected as representatives. As evident from Table 3, which shows male and female voter percentages, 1998 showed the highest female poll percentage in the 1990s at 57.69 per cent, coming close to the two highs in the 1980s (58,59 per cent in 1984 and 57.31 per cent in 1989). In the corresponding years the percentage of women representatives in the Lok Sabha was 7.9 per cent in 1984, which was an increase from 5.1 per cent in 1980. In 1980, however, the percentage drops to 5.3 per cent, to rise again to 7.9 per cent in 1991. For the 1990s high, the corresponding percentage of women representatives was 7.9 per cent, almost one percentage point lower than the highest achieved in the subsequent year at 8.8. per cent. In the same year, however, the female poll percentage dropped from the 57.69 per cent of 1998 to 55.63 per cent.

As evident from Table 2 and Figures 1 and 3, there is an overall increase in the size of the electorate and in the numbers of women and men voters over the years, alongside a consistent gender gap. Despite the gender gap, one can identify 'a definite participatory upsurge' among Indian women in the 1990s (Yadav, 2000; Deshpande, 2004), seen both in terms of increase in the proportion of women voters among total voters, and their turnout (Tables 2, 3 and 4; Figures 1, 2 and 3). While as mentioned earlier, 1984 remained the peak for women voter percentage, in 1998, the female poll percentage reached close to the landmarks of 1984 and 1989. Unlike the peak in the 1980s, when the increase was associated with the fortunes of the Indian National Congress in a phase of transition after the demise of Indira Gandhi, the increase in the 1990s has been explained on two counts, both of which demand empirical evidence, however.

The increase may possibly be associated with the 'second democratic upsurge', as Yogendra Yadav termed the phenomenon, referring to the process of democratisation in the decade of the 1990s, especially the dynamism which the electoral process witnessed in the period, characterised by a hitherto unprecedented upsurge in political participation by the lower classes of the Indian electorate.[13] It is significant that

the second democratic upsurge is also put forward by Yadav as a coun-
terpoint to proceduralism and 'design fallacy', focussing attention on the
processes whereby the democratic will of the people *is able* to make itself
effectively manifest, irrespective of electoral design. Apart from the
upsurge among the backward classes, the increase in women voters may
as well be attributed to the panchayati raj reforms, which boosted participation among women. While the increase may in all probability have
been associated with the democratic upsurge and churning which the
panchayat elections brought in their wake, the relationship cannot be
conclusively established unless the caste gender data for the period are
examined. Moreover, the two may not be seen as exclusive and the
political upsurge among the backward classes may be seen as simulta-
neous and intertwined. The turnout of women voters as a proportion of
total voters by states in the Lok Sabha elections for 1991, 1996, 1998,
1999 and 2004 shows that in certain states like Bihar, Gujarat, Madhya
Pradesh, Rajasthan and Uttar Pradesh, there was a jump in the proportion
of women among total voters from previous election years. In the case
of Bihar, the numbers leapt from 39.8 per cent in 1996 to 47 per cent in
1998. In Gujarat, the increase was incremental, increasing from 40.1 per
cent in 1996 to 45.2 per cent in 1998, climbing yet again to 48.4 per cent
in 1999. In Madhya Pradesh the proportion of women voters increased
from 42 per cent in 1996 to 48.1 per cent in 1998 and stabilised thereon.
Like Gujarat, in Rajasthan, the number increased incrementally, from 40
per cent in 1996 to 43.4 per cent in 1998, to 47.3 per cent in 1999 and
47.7 per cent in 2004.

Seen in terms of gender gap or differential voter turnout in men and
women, the picture is more complex, however. In her study based on
National Election Study (NES) data, Rajeshwari Deshpande points out
that after the 1998 elections which witnessed a significant rupture in
women's political participation, there occurred a plateau, which when
unravelled would show that whereas for most states, the gender gap in
turnout remained at 5 percentage points, it widened in states like Bihar,
Uttar Pradesh, Madhya Pradesh, Rajasthan, Jharkhand and Gujarat. The
latter were the same states which had witnessed a significant rise in the
number of women voters in the 1998 elections. If the gender gap in
turnout in these states in the recent elections is explained vis-à-vis their
social backwardness, the rise of women voters earlier may then be linked
to the overall increase in the participation of marginalised groups in the
1990s.

The NES Lok Sabha post-poll data for 1999 and 2004 for Uttar
Pradesh and Bihar (Tables 5 to 8) shows an interesting pattern.[14] What
is interesting about these figures is that they afford a comparison among

communities on the basis of the proportion of women who voted in each community. The comparison is interesting despite the fact that a lesser percentage of upper caste women voting may work out more in absolute numbers. In 1999, more men irrespective of caste and community consistently claimed to have voted, e.g., 86 per cent of Muslim men said they voted as did 67.8 per cent of upper caste men, and 80 per cent of others. On the other hand while more Muslim and SC women voted (both at 57.7 per cent) and 52.5 per cent of upper caste women and 69 per cent of other women voted, in all categories, the number of women who voted was significantly less than the men in the same category (Table 5). In 2004, however (Table 6), the picture changes somewhat as the percentage of upper caste (Brahmin and Rajput) and Muslim men who said they voted showed a decline from 1999. The decline is also seen in all categories among women, including upper caste women and Muslims. The picture in Bihar, too, for the 1999 elections shows a consistently high voting percentage for men in all caste/tribe categories averaging in the eighties, except the scheduled tribes. The percentage of women voting remained considerably less, with the proportion of Muslim women (56.7 per cent) who claimed to have voted again surpassing women from all other categories (Table 7). Remarkably, in the 2004 polls, the percentage of upper caste women who voted declines, as the percentage of Yadav women claiming that they voted increases dramatically from 46.2 per cent to 61.8 per cent, and the percentage of Muslim women declines from 56.7 per cent to 50.6 per cent (Table 8). The stabilisation of turnout of women voters from 1996 and 1998 to 1999 and 2004 thus shows internal and regional differentiation.

Discussion

Contemporary frameworks of gendering electoral governance – comprising initiatives by the United Nations, NGOs, the women's movement, and feminist theorists – may broadly be described as frameworks of *differentiated universalism*. In other words, these frameworks adhere to a principle of inclusion that starts from the premise that the universal principles of electoral governance may not reflect the special needs that emerge from women's societal contexts and, the specific structural constraints that women suffer. The right to vote and to be represented may then exist in law, but can be denied in practice to women. Women, moreover, may feel overwhelmingly about women's issues, especially on reservation of seats for women in the Lok Sabha and the legislative assemblies, and issues of right to higher education, to work, and political participation, cultural constraints on public contact between women and men, and the manner in which the public space remains debilitating for women, may place limits on their mobility Rajeshwari Deshpande's study based on NES data shows that while there appears to be a consensus among women on women's issues, including reservations in elected bodies and women's right to work, cutting across social groups and communities, there is little to indicate that this consensus translates itself into concerted political action. On another set of questions relating to economic issues, women across social sections, along with men, share common ground. On a set of social issues relating to inter-caste and inter-community relationships, however, women seem to cling to community ties more than men, favouring closed inter-community relationships (Deshpande, 2004). Often, however, the electoral system and the management of the system may also be such that it may inhibit women's participation. Sudhir Varma's study shows that the exclusion of women from the electoral list and their lack of access to the ballot box produce a low electoral sex ratio and gender gap in voting, respectively. Often, moreover, the increase in the number of women voters on the electoral rolls, as in 1996, is deceptive since the electoral sex ratio may continue to be worse than the sex ratio at 896. In 1991 in particular, the electoral sex ratio fell to 886 from 938 in 1981. The fall could have been due to the fact that between 1981 and 1991, the voting age was lowered to 18, and a number of 18 year old girls may have been left out of the voters' list. Moreover, different groups seem to be showing different patterns of ESR. Thus in 1991, in certain states such as Haryana, Himachal Pradesh, Karnataka, Madhya Pradesh, Orissa and Rajasthan, constituencies reserved for SCs have a substantially lower ESR than the ESR of the state. For general constituencies also in some states, the ESR was worse than the ESR for the state (Verma, 1997: 84-86).

The continuum model, as discussed earlier, seeks to bring together differentiation with universalism through creating a talking and doing space that bridges the hiatus between voting and decision-making, which is performed by different sets of people at different moments. It is, therefore, this space that needs to be strengthened for all differentially included groups. In the case of women in particular, bringing up women's issues as significant issues in the electoral agenda of political parties and in the public space is important. Again, continuous dissemination of information on poll issues and candidates as well as programmes is important, since women too need to know in order to perform the act of voting well. While groups like Lok Satta,[15] Association for Democratic Reform,[16] Lok Raj Sangathan,[17] and Lok Samvad of Bihar which is a network of organisations working on electoral reforms and the right to information, have taken the lead in suggesting reforms for the electoral system, women's groups like Sakhi[18] in Kerala and Vimochna[19] in Karnataka have, over the years, campaigned to inform women about their candidates.

Several women's groups have prepared women's manifestos and undertaken 'know thy candidate' campaigns and issued leaflets highlighting women's issues. They have also, over the years, campaigned against candidates with a criminal background or a past record of violence against women. Vimochana, for example, campaigned against such candidates by distributing leaflets,[20] organising street corner meetings, and writing in newspapers. Feminist organisations demanded 'a code of conduct' for party cadres in the context of complaints of sexual violence against CPI(M) party cadres in Kerala and Bengal. In Maharashtra, the Stree Mukti Sampark Samiti (Women's Liberation Coordination Committee), a state-level united front of the progressive and Left women's organisations, issued a leaflet before the Lok Sabha elections in February 1990, putting forth the perspective of the women's organisations on the elections and suggesting to voters the principles and programmes which should determine their choice of candidates. The issues that were highlighted in the leaflet as significant for women pertained to fundamentalism, family laws and issues of development and ecology, identifying women's concerns that needed to be addressed, viz., fuel-fodder-water issues, electrification, dams, education, health, employment, violence against women, media's depiction of women, and rural and tribal women's struggles for survival. The leaflet also suggested that candidates should be accountable to their constituencies on these issues (Patel, 2005: 43–44).

Kerala Streevedi, an autonomous network of women's groups in Kerala, including Sakhi, carried out campaigns against candidates accused or convicted in sexual violence cases in the assembly election of 2006. The network campaigned against Neela Lohita Dasan Nadar, contesting from the Kovalam constituency, who originally belonged to the Janata Dal (U) and was part of the LDF. Nadar was convicted in two cases of sexual harassment at the workplace and, as a result of the campaign, the LDF withdrew his candidature, with the result that he stood as an independent candidate. A similar campaign was waged against Kunjalikutty, a former minister who was commonly believed to have been involved in a case of sexual harassment, though his name was not among the accused, in Kuttipuram from where he contested.

The need to strengthen and continually recreate a vibrant political space, and bridge thereby the gender gap both in voting and decision making remains, however. While specific states have had experience of women participating in the political process at the local level even before the 73rd and 74th Amendments,[21] since the 1990s concerted effort by women's organisations to appeal to women voters at the national level has also emerged. Women's groups, as seen above, have put up manifestos, conducted educational campaigns, and put up codes of conduct for party candidates and cadres. In the 1990s, the Forum of National Women's Organisations, based in Delhi, had appealed to women to vote judiciously and articulated their intention to directly intervene in the electoral processes.[22] A perspective that has gained some clarity within a wide range of organisations is the relevance of influencing decisions of those in power and placing gender issues on the political agenda. Women's groups in different states in India have also experimented with networks to promote ideas and consolidate issues on a common platform.[23] An interesting development has been the setting up of the Womanist Party of India (WPI), or the Bhartiya Streevadi Paksha, in 2003, which claims to have a constructive approach in politics to bring equal representation for women in Parliament through 50 per cent reservation and pursuing a development agenda that recognises and affirms women's rights over natural resources – land, water, fuel-wood, etc.[24]

To understand these efforts by non-party associations and women's organisations to consolidate a common platform for electoral reforms one may go back once again to the point where the paper began, i.e., the imperative to bridge the temporal, spatial and ideological hiatus – between 'electoral trials', representatives and the people, and the act of voting and decision making. Such a notion of active citizenship differs from frameworks that explain this activity within the framework of the 'crisis of representation' thesis, which proposes that when citizens perceive the traditional forms of representation such as 'political parties and trade unions' to be inadequate, or face recalcitrant and unresponsive political institutions, as in the case of the countries of Eastern and Central Europe in the 1980s, they 'turn their back on the political domain and form self-help organisations in civil society to solve their problems'.[25] The shift to organisations in civil society has taken place, the thesis argues, since traditional modes of representation such as political parties have exhausted their capacity to represent the aspirations of their constituencies, have become hierarchical, bureaucratic, and rigid, have followed the political logic and impulse of power seeking more assiduously than pursuing the task of representing the needs and the interests of their constituents, and have, unlike civil society organisations, been out of touch with the exigencies of everyday life, in particular at the local levels. Examining the crisis of representation thesis in the Indian context through a survey conducted in Delhi in 2003, however, Neera Chandhoke argues that the findings showed that there existed among respondents, excessive reliance on personalised contacts to resolve problems. While the latter pointed to the fact that neither political parties nor civil society organisations inspire confidence in the minds of the citizens, it also showed the ways in which the 'profoundly undemocratic' consolidation of patron-client relationships takes place isolating people and 'pre-empting the forging of solidarity on crucial issues that are common to all, in civil society'.[26] The lessons that one can draw from the study while building a case for a continuum approach, whereby a continual and concerted multi-layered activity creates an agora of democratic politics, is looking at ways which block the consolidation of such trends. We must at this point, emphasise yet again, the importance of revitalising/ democratising the public sphere through communication, speech and action, which are empowering and conducive to building alliances for a shared common perspective, and work towards democratising participatory institutions by focusing our energies both for information about them and for purging them on them. The ultimate aim of strengthening political and representative institutions would also help preclude the emphasis that participatory networks created through non-governmental organisations have come to assume as being of value by themselves. As mentioned at the outset, such an approach may ultimately edge out the people, as dominant groups take over the mediating and negotiating spaces, thereby generating greater powerlessness and exclusion. The notion of the public as a democratically negotiated and, therefore, an inclusive collective interest may be effaced in such a situation, increasing the vulnerability of groups that already have a differential access to the public. It is significant that the efforts at reforms attempted by some of the groups mentioned above, have addressed themselves to the voters, creating thereby the space where the 'talking and doing' will translate into critical action, with significant bearing on the nature of representation.

Notes

1. Feminists, in particular Carole Pateman, point out that the public-private divide is generally seen as referring only to the distinction between state and economy, or state and civil society. Feminists emphasise that the sole allusion to this distinction occludes the further distinction that differentiates between state and civil society from the domestic sphere. See Carole Pateman, 'Feminist Cri-

tiques of the Public/Private Dichotomy' in S.I. Benn and G.F. Gaus (eds), *Public and Private in Political Theory*, Oxford, Polity Press, 1991.

2. Nadia Urbinati (2000) points out that nostalgia may foster resignation, but it may also encourage a realistic disenchantment toward what is actual.

3. Criticising mirror or descriptive representation, Hannah Pitkin suggests that the metaphors of descriptive representation were most commonly found among those who regarded representative democracy as a poor substitute and who therefore looked to more 'accurate' or pictorial representation of the electorate as a way of approximating the older citizen assemblies, instead of recognising the qualitatively new elements that entered into democracy with the development of representative institutions (Phillips, 1995: 34). Pitkin argues that proportional representation while professing equality of representation, may actually be insincere because it can eventually become a way of using minorities' representation to legitimise the majority's decisions. It meticulously reflects the social topography, but at the same time, makes the assembly into a 'talking rather than acting, deliberating rather than governing body' (Pitkin, 1967: 86).

4. The Vienna Declaration and Programme of Action was adopted by the World Conference on Human Rights on June 25, 1993. The Conference was convened by the United Nations General Assembly during June 14-25 to reaffirm the promotion and protection of human rights as a matter of priority for the international community.

5. For details, see Drude Dahlerup (2006).

6. Ibid.

7. Western European feminists contrast welfare regimes, using as their chief point of differentiation whether or not a male breadwinner model of social organisation is in place (Orloff, 1993). Some Scandinavian feminists (Hermes, 1987; Sim, 1990) insist that 'an adequate account of contemporary citizenship' must grasp the interplay between material rights, multi-level participation, and political identities' (Lister, 200: 40). In Eastern Europe, where the dismantling of communism has meant the reduction of social rights and increasing reliance on family, women are trying to establish a claim for recognition in the domestic sphere (Havelkova, 200). In Latin America, Virginia Vargas (2002: 215), a prominent feminist activist, argues that '[t]hose who campaign for political rights while neglecting or ignoring social or cultural rights... sustain and legitimise the exclusionary character of existing democracies and formations of citizenship'. See for a discussion on these issues,

Carol Bacchi. 'Arguing For and Against Quotas' in Drude Dahlerup (ed.), *Women, Quotas and Politics* (2006).

8. In nuclear physics, a 'critical mass' refers to the quantity needed to start a chain reaction, an irreversible take-off into a situation or process. By analogy, the presence of women in substantial numbers is required for the possibility of change.

9. Drude Dahlerup defines a 'critical act' as one which would change the position of the minority considerably and lead to further changes in policies. Critical acts would involve increasing the representation of women through quotas, while simultaneously developing gender-sensitive platforms for change (Dahlerup, 2001).

10. Of the 14 Lok Sabha elections so far, a total of only 16 women from the Muslim community have been elected to the Lok Sabha, and in six elections, not even one Muslim woman was elected. On the other hand, the maximum number of Muslim women who could get elected has been three, in the 1977 and 1984 elections.

11. Shirin Rai's study on class, caste and gender in the Indian Parliament makes some interesting observations. Caste has been an important factor in so far as most of the women MPs in the 10th Parliament were members of the higher castes. There were six women who were Brahmins, constituting thereby 17.14 per cent of the women MPs, while the Brahmins comprise only 5.52 per cent of the population. Of the six, two women MPs were from the CPI, were privileged in terms of class, and had a history of participation in political movements, the nationalist struggles and the anti-emergency movement. The number of women who are able to avail of the caste-based reservation system in the Parliament is small. While 22 per cent of the parliamentary seats are reserved for the scheduled castes, women occupy only 4.1 per cent of the reserved seats. Two women MPs were from the scheduled tribes. Out of the 39 women MPs in the 10th Lok Sabha (representing 7 per cent of the total strength), however, 14 per cent were from the Scheduled Castes. Two women MPs belonged to the backward castes, and represented open constituencies. Class and social position was, however, equally significant. Out of the 39 women MPs in the 1991-1996 Lok Sabha, 32 had postgraduate qualifications. In the Rajya Sabha, 14 out of 17 women MPs were graduates. The class position of these women, points out Rai, was obviously more important to their educational levels than caste. Only one out of the seven lower caste women MPs was not a graduate and the one scheduled caste woman MP in the Rajya Sabha had postgraduate education. The levels of education (and therefore, the class position) is also reflected in the professional profiles of these women. Thirty per cent of women MPs in the Rajya Sabha were lawyers,

and 25 per cent in the Lok Sabha were either teachers or lecturers. See Shirin Rai (2002).

12. Sudhir Varma's study (1997) makes interesting comparisons and also goes into the reasons for women's absence from the electoral rolls and their lack of access to the ballot box even when their names figure in the list.

13. The *second* democratic upsurge, the first being the phase of the 1960s, is the term given by Yogendra Yadav to refer to the 'new phase of democratic politics' in India in the 1990s, particularly in the state assembly elections during the period 1993–95, characterised by a hitherto unprecedented upsurge in political participation, particularly by the lower classes of the Indian electorate. An average of more than 64 per cent in these elections indicated a decisive break in this period with the previous period of Assembly elections, and a sizeable 9 per cent increase over the Lok Sabha elections (Yadav, 1999 and 2004).

14. The National Election Study is a nationwide study conducted across more than 2,000 locations in India. NES 2004, for example, was conducted at 2,380 locations spread across all the 29 states of India. The study is based on a three-stage stratified random sample where the Parliamentary constituencies and Assembly segments are randomly drawn using the probability proportionate to size (PPS) method, and the polling stations (locations) are randomly sampled using the simple random method. In the 2004 study, 35,360 respondents were randomly selected from the electoral rolls of the selected polling booths. The respondents were contacted for interview at their home, using a structured questionnaire. Of the total respondents selected, 27,189 could be successfully contacted and interviewed. With minor variations, the sample was truly representative, with 79.8 per cent Hindus, 11.3 per cent Muslims, 17.9 per cent Dalits and 9 per cent Adivasis. The sample had 46.5 per cent women respondents and 53.5 per cent male respondents. The sample over represented people from rural areas. Compared to India being 72.2 per cent rural, the sample had 78.6 per cent respondents from rural areas. Naturally, the sample underrepresented the urban respondents by nearly 6 per cent. The study was conducted after the 2004 Lok Sabha elections. The field-work for the survey was done with the help of nearly 1,200 field investigators after the polling was over, but was completed before the counting of votes. The description of the survey is taken from Sanjay Kumar, who is the national coordinator of the NES.

15. A Hyderabad-based organisation which describes itself as a 'people's movement for better governance'. While its organisational activities are confined to Andhra Pradesh, its goals are, it argues, na-

tional. Dedicated to good governance and fighting against corruption, it is dedicated, among other things, to fighting against the illegal use of money power in elections.

16. The Association for Democratic Reforms is an Ahmedabad-based non-political, non-partisan group of professors of the Indian Institute of Management, Ahmedabad (IIM-A) and the National Institute of Design (NID), and the alumni of IIM-A, working on 'improving governance' and 'strengthening democracy in India'. A public interest litigation (PIL) filed by the ADR in December 1999 culminated in a landmark Supreme Court judgement on May 2, 2002, emphasising the right to know of the citizen voter, and an ordinance on electoral reforms was promulgated in August 2002. The ordinance was subsequently passed as a Bill in December 2002. It partially overturned the May 2, 2002, Supreme Court judgement, requiring disclosure of criminal background, but not of financial and educational background. The ADR and two other petitioners challenged this Act. In a second landmark judgement on March 13, 2003, the Supreme Court struck down the Bill as unconstitutional and restored its earlier order. Subsequently, the Election Commission issued orders implementing the judgement, requiring candidates to fill in an affidavit giving personal details including financial details.

17. The Lok Raj Sangathan is an all-India organisation set up in May 1998. It describes itself as a 'political organisation of a new type whose mission is to vest sovereignty in the hands of the people'. It argues that the political process is being dominated by a handful of so-called recognised political parties, which are trained for the status quo and aims, among other things, to expand the people's role in the political process.

18. Started in 1996, Sakhi, which literally means a woman friend, is a feminist documentation, training and resource centre. It describes itself as 'a space for women to come together, share their pains, anxieties, pleasures and fun'. In the recent state election in Kerala (April-May 2006), Sakhi campaigned against a candidate who was charged of molestation.

19. Vimochna is a Bangalore-based women's organisation which has led a concerted campaign against torture and violence against women, in particular domestic violence and crimes against women.

20. The following is the text of a leaflet which was published by Vimochana for the 1989 elections, urging women voters to vote against candidates charged with crimes against women:

To All Women Voters, Vimochana is not a political party. Why then do we reach out to you at the time of general elections? In

1979, when we first intervened in the political process, we did so to raise women's issues and put them on the political agenda. We had asked you then to vote for candidates who would recognise and talk about violence against women – dowry, rape, sexual harassment, exploitation in the media, shelter, fuel, water... questions on which politicians are totally silent.

We have come some way since then. Women's issues have become more 'visible'. We are now an essential part of political rhetoric – no speech or manifesto is complete without a formula to draw women into the political and national mainstream. Why then do we need to reach out to you once again?

Perhaps because we all know that in an age of false promises and hollow utopias, this rhetoric too hides the everyday reality of a majority of the women in India. We write to you this time to ask you to expose the hypocrisy behind political promises. All parties speak glibly about giving full representation of women in politics – some have gone so far as to promise 30 per cent reservation in these elections. How many parties have fulfilled this promise? In fact this year the number of women candidates has drastically decreased.

We ask you [to] expose this hypocrisy because we all know that most of our 'representatives' rarely practise at home what they preach on the streets – they cleverly separate private ethics from public morality. Today, wife beaters and rapists can talk of equality of women; mafia dons can talk of justice; fundamentalists can preach secularism.... As women and 50 per cent of the electorate we have to exercise our vote to transform this degenerate political culture. Let us all take a strong stand against 'leaders' like:

- Z.R. Ansari, the Union Minister of State for Forestation, who despite being directly implicated in an attempt to rape charge by Mukti Datta, a woman activist working in Himachal Pradesh, has been given a Lok Sabha ticket.
- Kalvi, a Janata Dal leader from Rajasthan, who openly came out in support of the murder of Roop Kanwar, a young widow burnt alive on her husband's pyre in 1988.
- The 19 CPI(M) activists arrested in connection with the gang-rape of a young woman activist of the Kashtakari Sangathan, an organisation working with the tribals in Dahanu District, Maharashtra.
- Suraj Singh Deo, Bihar's mafia king, who is the trusted lieutenant of Chandrashekhar, senior leader of the Janata Dal.
- H.K.L. Bhagat, who has been directly named by a number of the post-Indira Gandhi murder riot victims in Delhi in 1984 as the

man behind the mass killings of Sikhs and yet continues to be a Union minister and a senior Congress (I) leader.

- R.L. Jalappa, a Janata Dal candidate from Doddaballapur, who has been implicated in the murder of a lawyer.
- Dr Venkatesh, a former Janata Party MP, at present contesting on a Congress (I) ticket from Bethmangala to the Karnataka Assembly, who has not only deserted his wife and child without paying any maintenance despite a court order, but also has a criminal case of assault on his wife pending against him.

The list is endless....

The irony is that none of the political parties involved i.e., the CPI(M), Janata or the Congress (I) have thought fit to initiate any enquiry against these individuals who have all been implicated in serious crimes. The greater irony is that some of these are not even seen as crimes – deserting a wife is seen as a 'personal' domestic issue. Society, too, sanctions such acts with its silence and cynicism about the 'criminalisation of politics'.

Boycott these candidates in your constituency who get up on a public platform and speak of equality for women while denigrating and violating them in their personal lives.

Support those candidates who you are assured will respond positively to issues of violence against women.

Support those candidates who genuinely attempt to put into practice what they speak, both in their public and in their private lives.

It is a small step, but the first one.

Let us vote with our conscience and bring conscience back into politics. November 1989, Vimochana Forum for Women's Rights P.O. Box 4605

21. Maharashtra for example, has several experiences of women participating in the mainstream political processes. There were cases of two villages putting up an all-women panel for panchayat elections and losing. There have also been cases of all-women panchayats getting elected and functioning in Pune district in the early 1980s. The experiences of the Samgara Mahila Agadhi (All Women's Front), a broad platform created by the Shetkari Sangathan Mahila Agadhi in Maharashtra, in putting up nine all-women panels for the *gram panchayat* elections in 1989 have received great visibility in the women's movement. The facilitation of women to contest local self-government elections by the Samagra Mahila Agadhi comes in the midst of the struggles of peasant women in parts of Maharashtra.

22. Newsletter, Vol. 12, No. 2, Research Centre for Women's Studies, 1991, Mumbai.

23. While some of these networks have grown organically from within the women's movement, reacting to certain issues and events, the growth of others have been facilitated by funding agencies and kept alive with a certain agenda. Paradoxically, most networks have not synergised to keep networking efforts alive on a sustainable basis. By and large, several networks seem to come alive to react to specific issues and relapse into inaction till another issue, sufficiently proactive, propels them into action. Classification of networks reveals certain trends. Large organisations such as the AIDWA, Mahila Dakshta Samithi, All India Coordination Committee for Working Women, and the Joint Women's Programme (JWP) have branches in different parts of the country with networking arrangements. The emergence of the two informal national fora – Forum for Women and Politics (FWP) and the Forum of National Women's Organisation (FNWO) in the 1990s is noteworthy in that they reflect a trend to come together for joint action despite differences in ideology and organisational perspectives. The FNWO comprises the AIDWA, CWDS, AIWC, JWF, MDS, NFIW and YWCA. Each of these organisations has promoted lateral networks making efforts to bring their members together through regular visits, workshops, conventions and campaigns. The Forum for Women and Politics, comprising autonomous women's groups such as Jagori, Saheli, JWP, Ankur, Action India, Sabla Sangh, Shaktishalini, Kali for Women and Purogami Mahila Sangathan, have a common past in that they have been coming together for several joint campaigns (Ramaswamy, 1997: 191–2).

24. The details of the document laying out the position of the WPI – 'Let Us Make a History' – in Marathi, is available in Patel (2005: 49).

25. The thesis is discussed and found wanting by Neera Chadhoke (forthcoming) in her article, 'Revisiting the Crisis of Representation Thesis: The Indian Context', *Democratisation* (forthcoming).

26. ibid.

27. Data available at the Election Commission of India website, *http://www.ec.gov.in/*

28. Tables 3 and 4 and Figures 1 to 4 are available at the Election Commission's website, eci.gov.in

29. Table based on National Election Survey from Deshpande, 2004.

References

Agnew, Vijay. 1979. *Elite Women in Politics*. New Delhi: Vikas Publications.

Bacchi, Carol. 'Arguing For and Against Quotas' in Drude Dahlerup (ed.), *Women, Quotas and Politics.* (2006).

Butler, Judith. 2003. 'Subjects of Sex/Gender/Desire' in Anne Phillips (ed.), *Feminism and Politics.* New York: Oxford University Press.

Chadhoke, Neera. (Forthcoming). 'Revisiting the Crisis of Representation Thesis: The Indian Context'. *Democratisation.*

CWDS. 2000. Background Note of the Workshop on Gender and Governance in India. June 22.

CWDS. 1998. *Gender and Democracy at the Grassroots: A Bibliographical Compilation on Women and Panchyati Raj.* New Delhi.

Dahlerup, Drude (ed.), 2006. *Women, Quotas and Politics.* London: Routledge.

Dahlerup, Drude. 2001. 'Women in Political Decision-making: From Critical Mass to Critical Acts in Scandinavia' in Inger Skjelsbaek and Dan Smith (eds.), *Gender, Peace and Conflict.* London: Sage.

Deshpande, Rajeshwari. 2004. 'How Gendered was Women's Participation in Election 2004'. *Economic and Political Weekly.* December 18.

Dunn, John. 1993. *Western Political Theory in the Face of the Future.* Cambridge: Cambridge University Press.

Elshtain, Jean Bethke. 1981. *Public Man Private Women: Women in Social and Political Thought.* Princeton: Princeton University Press.

Faulks, Keith. 2000. *Citizenship.* London: Routledge.

Ghosh, Archana and Stephanie Tawa Lama-Rewal (eds.), 2005. *Democratisation in Progress: Women and Local Politics in Urban India.* Delhi: Tulika Books.

Hust, Evelin. 2004. *Women's Political Representation and Empowerment in India: A Million Indiras Now?* Delhi: Manohar.

John, Mary. 2000. 'Alternate Modernities? Reservation and the Women's Movement in the 20th Century'. *Economic and Political Weekly.* October 28.

Joseph, Sarah. 2003. 'Creating a Public: Reinventing Democratic Citizenship' in Gurpreet Mahajan and Helmut Reifeld (eds.), *The Public and the Private: Issues of Democratic Citizenship.* New Delhi: Sage Publications.

Kumar, Sanjay. 'Muslim Women in India: Opinions, Attitudes and Participation in Politics' (Unpublished Paper).

Lister, Ruth. 2003. 'Feminist Theory and Practice of Citizenship'. Paper presented at the annual conference of the German Political Science Association, September.

Mahajan, Gurpreet. 2003. *The Public and the Private: Issues of Democratic Citizenship.* New Delhi: Sage Publications.

Menon, Nivedita. 2000. 'Elusive Woman: Feminism and the Women's Reservation Bill'. *Economic and Political Weekly.* October 28.

Mohanty, Bidyut. 2005. 'Women and Panchayati Raj and Seventy Third Amendment Act'. *Economic and Political Weekly.* Vol. 52.

Mouffe, Chantal. 1992. 'Democratic Citizenship and the Political Community' in Mouffe (ed.), *Dimensions of Radical Democracy.* London: Verso.

Mozaffar, Shaheen and Andreas Schedler. 2002. 'The Comparative Study of Electoral Governance – Introduction'. *International Political Science Review* 23: 1, pp. 5–27.

Omvedt, Gail. 2005. 'Women in Governance in South Asia'. *Economic and Political Weekly.* October 29, 2005.

Pateman, Carole. 1991. 'Feminist Critiques of the Public/Private Dichotomy' in S.I. Benn and G.F. Gaus (eds.), *Public and Private in Political Theory.* Oxford: Polity Press.

Patel, Vibhuti. 2005. 'Getting a Foothold in Politics: Women in Political Decision-Making Process'. *Social Action.* Vol. 55, January-March 37–54.

Phillips, Anne. 1998. *Feminism and Politics.* Oxford: Oxford University Press.

———. 1995. *The Politics of Presence.* Oxford: Clarendon Press.

Pitkin, Hanna Fenichel. 1967. *The Concept of Representation.* Berkeley: University of California Press.

Plotke, David. 1997. 'Representation is Democracy', *Constellations* 4.

Prokhovnik, Raisa. 1998. 'Public and Private Citizenship'. *Feminist Review.* No. 60, Autumn.

Rai, Shirin. 2002. 'Class, Caste and Gender: Women in Parliament in India'. International IDEA, Women in Parliament, Stockholm (http://www.idea.int).

Rai, Shirin, Farzana Bari, Nazmunnessa Mahtab and Bidyut Mohanty. 2006. 'South Asia: Gender Quotas and the Politics of Empowerment: A Comparative Study' in Drude Dahlerup (ed.), *Women, Quotas and Politics.* Abingdon: Routledge.

Ramaswamy, Uma. 1997. 'Organising with a Gender Perspective' in Ruddar Datt (ed.), *Organising the Unorganised Workers.* New Delhi: Vikas.

Report of the Committee on the Status of Women in India. 1974. Department of Social Welfare, Ministry of Education and Social Welfare, Government of India.

Siim, B. 2000. *Gender and Citizenship: Politics and Agency in France, Britain and Denmark.* Cambridge: Cambridge University Press.

Singh, Ujjwal Kumar. 2004. *Institutions and Democratic Governance: A Study of the Election Commission and Electoral Governance in India.* NMML Monograph No. 9, Nehru Memorial Museum and Library: New Delhi.

The United Nations. 1994. *Human Rights and Elections: A Handbook on the Legal, Technical and Human Rights Aspects of Elections.* Geneva: Centre for Human Rights.

Urbinati, Nadia. 2000. 'Representation as Advocacy: A Study of Democratic Deliberation'. *Political Theory.* Vol. 28, No. 6, December, 758–786.

Varma, Sudhir. 1997. *Women's Struggle for Political Space.* Jaipur: Rawat Publications.

Yadav, Yogendra. 1999. 'Electoral Politics in the Time of Change: India's Third Electoral System, 1989–99'. *Economic and Political Weekly.* August 21–28, 2393–9.

———. 2004. 'Reconfiguration in Indian Politics: State Assembly Elections 1993–1995' in Partha Chatterjee (ed.), *State and Politics in India.* Delhi: Oxford University Press.

Young, Iris Marion. 1997. 'Deferring Group Representation' in Ian Shapiro and Will Kymlicka (eds.), *Ethnicity and Group Rights.* New York: New York University Press.

Appendix

Table 1: Turnout Differential and Percentage of Women in the Lok Sabha

Year	Turnout Differential between Men and Women	% of Women in the Lok Sabha
1952		4.4
1957		5.4
1962	17	6.7
1967	11	5.9
1971	21	4.2
1977	11	3.4
1980	9.5	5.1
1984	10	7.9
1989	9	5.3
1991	10	7.9
1996	9	7.3
1998	8	7.9
1999	8	8.8
2004	8	8.26

Source: Election Commission of India.

Table 2: Male and Female Voters[1]

Total No. of Electors	Year	Male-Female Voters		
		Males	Females	Year
17,32,12,343	1951			
19,36,52,179	1957			
12,77,19,470	1962	6,73,88,166	60,331,304	1962
24,89,04,300	1967	12,95,68,604	11,93,35,696	1967
27,41,89,132	1971	14,35,64,829	13,06,24,303	1971
32,11,74,327	1977	16,70,19,151	15,41,55,176	1977
35,62,05,329	1980	18,55,39,439	17,06,65,890	1980
37,95,40,608	1984	19,67,30,499	18,28,10,109	1984
49,89,06,129	1989	26,20,45,142	23,68,60,987	1989
49,83,63,801	1991	26,18,32,499	23,65,31,302	1991
59,25,72,288	1996	30,98,15,776	28,27,56,512	1996
60,58,80,192	1998	31,66,92,789	28,91,87,403	1998
61,95,36,847	1999	32,38,13,667	29,57,23,180	1999
67,14,87,930	2004	34,94,90,864	32,19,97,066	2004

Source: Election Commission website.

Table 3: Male and Female Voter Percentages

Poll Percentage	Year	Total	Males	Females	Year
44.87	1951			Male-Female Poll Percentage	
45.44	1957	Total	Males	Females	Year
55.42	1962	55.27	60.8	49.11	1971
61.04	1967	60.49	65.62	54.91	1977
55.27	1971	56.92	62.17	51.2	1980
60.49	1977	63.56	68.17	58.59	1984
56.92	1980	61.95	66.13	57.31	1989
63.56	1984	56.73	61.58	51.34	1991
61.95	1989	57.94	62.06	53.41	1996
56.73	1991	61.97	65.86	57.69	1998
57.94	1996	59.94	63.96	55.63	1999
61.97	1998	58.07	61.98	53.63	2004
59.94	1999				
58.07	2004				

Source: Election Commission website.

Table 4: Women Voters as a Proportion of Total Voters by States, Lok Sabha Elections (%)[1]

State	1991	1996	1998	1999	2004
Andhra Pradesh	46.1	47.3	50.7	50.1	50.4
Arunachal Pradesh	43.1	44.8	46.2	47.5	48.6
Assam	44.3	45.8	46.4	47.8	47.9
Bihar	38.2	39.8	47.0	46.9	46.4
Goa	45.4	46.3	47.8	49.1	49.4
Gujarat	40.9	40.1	45.2	48.4	48.5
Haryana	43.6	45.0	43.4	45.5	45.9
Himachal Pradesh	46.1	48.4	49.9	49.4	49.0
Jammu and Kashmir	–	37.2	38.4	45.8	45.5
Karnataka	43.8	45.4	46.3	49.1	49.1
Kerala	50.5	50.9	51.4	51.0	51.8
Madhya Pradesh	38.6	42.0	48.1	48.0	47.8
Maharashtra	42.1	43.7	44.9	47.8	47.9
Manipur	50.3	49.5	49.6	50.9	51.4
Meghalaya	46.1	49.2	50.0	49.6	49.6
Mizoram	48.1	50.4	49.9	49.8	50.2
Nagaland	45.5	46.1	44.9	47.1	47.4
Orissa	40.4	43.8	43.7	48.2	48.2
Punjab	40.2	46.5	45.5	47.2	47.9
Rajasthan	39.1	40.0	43.4	47.3	47.7
Sikkim	39.1	45.5	44.6	48.8	48.3
Tamil Nadu	47.6	48.1	47.0	49.6	50.7
Tripura	44.7	47.8	48.0	48.2	48.2
Uttar Pradesh	40.6	39.9	40.7	45.2	45.2
West Bengal	44.9	46.3	46.2	47.8	47.7
Chhattisgarh					46.5
Jharkhand					48.1
Uttaranchal					43.9
Andaman and Nicobar	41.7	42.3	43.3	41.9	45.5
Chandigarh	42.7	43.5	42.1	42.5	44.5
Dadra and Nagar Haveli	48.1	48.8	48.8	47.4	46.9
Daman and Diu	50.8	51.3	49.7	49.0	50.0
Delhi	40.5	41.8	40.3	42.3	43.4
Lakshadweep	50.3	49.4	49.7	48.2	49.0
Pondicherry	48.6	49.9	49.6	49.2	51.2
All India	42.9	44.0	46.9	47.7	48.0

Source: Rajeshwari Deshpande (2004).

Table 5: Uttar Pradesh Lok Sabha 1999 Post-Poll Caste/Community/Gender

Gender	Did You Vote?		Total
Men	No	Yes	
Upper Castes	55	116	171
	32.2%	67.8%	100.0%
	23.8%	26.4%	25.5%
Yadavs	33	33	66
	50.0%	50.0%	100.0%
	14.3%	7.5%	9.9%
OBCs	88	132	220
	40.0%	60.0%	100.0%
	38.1%	30.1%	32.8%
SCs	44	98	142
	31.0%	69.0%	100.0%
	19.0%	22.3%	21.2%
Muslims	7	44	51
	13.7%	86.3%	100.0%
	3.0%	10.0%	7.6%
Others	4	16	20
	20.0%	80.0%	100.0%
	1.7%	3.6%	3.0%
Total	231	439	670
	34.5%	65.5%	100.0%
	100.0%	100.0%	100.0%
Women	No	Yes	Total
Upper Castes	77	85	162
	47.5%	52.5%	100.0%
	23.9%	26.4%	25.2%
Yadavs	26	23	49
	53.1%	46.9%	100.0%
	8.1%	7.1%	7.6%
OBCs	146	111	257
	56.8%	43.2%	100.0%
	45.3%	34.5%	39.9%
SCs	47	64	111
	42.3%	57.7%	100.0%
	14.6%	19.9%	17.2%
Muslims	22	30	52
	42.3%	57.7%	100.0%
	6.8%	9.3%	8.1%
Others	4	9	13
	30.8%	69.2%	100.0%
	1.2%	2.8%	2.0%
Total	322	322	644
	50.0%	50.0%	100.0%
	100.0%	100.0%	100.0%

Source: CSDS Data Unit.

Table 6: Uttar Pradesh Post-Poll 2004 Caste/Community/Gender

Gender	Were You Able to Vote?		Total
Men	Unable to Vote	Able to Vote	
Brahmins	60	41	101
	59.4%	40.6%	100.0%
	14.9%	8.6%	11.5%
Rajputs	17	32	49
	34.7%	65.3%	100.0%
	4.2%	6.7%	5.6%
Vaishyas	17	16	33
	51.5%	48.5%	100.0%
	4.2%	3.3%	3.7%
Other Upper Castes		9	9
		100.0%	100.0%
		1.9%	1.0%
Jats	9	11	20
	45%	55.0%	100.0%
	2.2%	2.3%	2.3%
Yadavs	46	36	82
	56.1%	43.9%	100.0%
	11.4%	7.5%	9.3%
Other Peasant OBCs	46	79	125
	36.8%	63.2%	100.0%
	11.4%	16.5%	14.2%
Lower OBCs	78	61	139
	56.1%	43.9%	100.0%
	19.4%	12.7%	15.8%
Jatavs	40	60	100
	40.0%	60.0%	100.0%
	10.0%	12.5%	11.4%
Other SCs	17	35	52
	32.7%	67.3%	100.0%
	4.2%	7.3%	5.9%
STs	14	2	16
	87.5%	12.5%	100.0%
	3.5%	0.4%	1.8%
Muslims	49	83	132
	37.1%	62.9%	100.0%
	12.2%	17.3%	15.0%
Others	9	14	23
	39.1%	60.9%	100.0%
	2.2%	2.9%	2.6%
Total	402	479	881
	45.6%	54.4%	100.0%
	100.0%	100.0%	100.0%

Contd.

Contd.

Women	No	Yes	Total
Brahmins	58	32	90
	64.4%	35.6%	100.0%
	11.4%	8.7%	10.3%
Rajputs	23	22	45
	51.1%	48.9%	100.0%
	4.5%	6.0%	5.1%
Vaishyas	14	18	32
	43.8%	56.3%	100.0%
	2.8%	4.9%	3.7%
Other Upper Castes	6	4	10
	60.0%	40.0%	100.0%
	1.2%	1.1%	1.1%
Jats	12	12	24
	50.0%	50.0%	100.0%
	2.4%	3.3%	2.7%
Yadavs	63	36	99
	63.6%	36.4%	100.0%
	12.4%	9.8%	11.3%
Others Peasant OBCs	197	42	149
	71.8%	28.2%	100.0%
	21.1%	11.4%	17.0%
Lower OBCs	84	50	134
	62.7%	37.3%	100.0%
	16.5%	13.6%	15.3%
Jatavs	29	63	92
	31.5%	68.5%	100.0%
	5.7%	17.1%	10.5%
Other SCs	29	25	54
	53.7%	46.3%	100.0%
	5.7%	6.8%	6.2%
STs	6	4	10
	60.0%	40.0%	100.0%
	1.2%	1.1%	1.1%
Muslims	63	52	115
	54.8%	45.2%	100.0%
	12.4%	14.1%	13.1%
Others	14	8	22
	63.6%	36.4%	100.0%
	2.8%	2.2%	2.5%
Total	508	368	876
	58.0%	42.0%	100.0%
	100.0%	100.0%	100.0%

Source: CSDS Data Unit.

Table 7: Bihar Lok Sabha Post-Poll 1999 Caste/Community/Gender

Gender	Did You Vote?		
Men	No	Yes	Total
Upper Castes	8	65	73
	11.0%	89.0%	100.0%
	11.3%	19.9%	18.3%
Yadav	10	50	60
	16.7%	83.3%	100.0%
	14.1%	15.3%	15.1%
Kurmi Koeris	4	19	23
	17.4%	82.6%	100.0%
	5.6%	5.8%	5.8%
Other OBCs	21	82	103
	20.4%	79.6%	100.0%
	29.6%	25.1%	25.9%
SCs	6	36	42
	14.3%	85.7%	100.0%
	8.5%	11.0%	10.6%
STs	14	23	37
	37.8%	62.2%	100.0%
	19.7%	7.0%	9.3%
Muslims	8	50	58
	13.8%	86.2%	100.0%
	11.3%	15.3%	14.6%
Others		2	2
		100.0%	100.0%
		0.6%	0.5%
Total	71	327	398
	17.8%	82.2%	100.0%
	100.0%	100.0%	100.0%
Women	No	Yes	Total
Upper Castes	33	39	72
	45.8%	54.2%	100.0%
	13.8%	16.0%	14.9%
Yadavs	35	30	65
	53.8%	46.2%	100.0%
	14.6%	12.3%	13.5%
Kurmi Koeris	19	19	38
	50.0%	50.0%	100.0%
	7.9%	7.8%	7.9%
Other OBCs	58	63	121
	47.9%	52.1%	100.0%
	24.2%	25.9%	25.1%

Contd.

Contd.

SCs	45	45	90
	50.0%	50.0%	100.0%
	18.8%	18.5%	18.6%
STs	21	7	28
	75.0%	25.0%	100.0%
	8.8%	2.9%	5.8%
Muslims	29	38	67
	43.3%	56.7%	100.0%
	12.1%	15.6%	13.9%
Others		2	2
		100.0%	100.0%
		0.8%	0.4%
Total	240	243	483
	49.7%	50.3%	100.0%
	100.0%	100.0%	100.0%

Source: CSDS Data Unit

Table 8: Bihar Lok Sabha Post-Poll 2004 Caste/Community/Gender

Gender	Were You Able to Vote?		
Men	Unable to Vote	Able to Vote	Total
Upper Castes	44	101	145
	30.3%	69.7%	100.0%
	23.4%	23.9%	23.8%
Yadavs	11	52	63
	17.5%	82.5%	100.0%
	5.9%	12.3%	10.3%
Kurmi Koeris	16	45	61
	26.2%	73.8%	10.0%
	8.5%	10.7%	10.0%
Other OBCs	55	98	153
	35.9%	64.1%	100.0%
	29.3%	23.2%	25.1%
SCs	46	55	101
	45.5%	54.5%	100.0%
	24.5%	13.0%	16.6%
Muslims	16	55	71
	22.5%	77.5%	100.0%
	8.5%	13.0%	11.6%
Others		16	16
		100.0%	100.0%
		3.8%	2.6%
Total	188	422	610
	30.8%	69.2%	100.0%
	100.0%	100.0%	100.0%
Women	Unable to Vote	Able to vote	
Upper Castes	60	58	118
	50.8%	49.2%	100.0%
	19.3%	21.8%	20.5%
Yadavs	21	34	55
	38.2%	61.8%	100.0%
	6.8%	12.8%	9.5%
Kurmi Koeris	39	27	66
	59.1%	40.9%	100.0%
	12.5%	10.2%	11.4%
Other OBCs	87	61	148
	58.8%	41.2%	100.0%
	28.0%	22.9%	25.6%
SCs	53	31	84
	63.1%	36.9%	100.0%
	17.0%	11.7%	14.6%

Contd.

Contd.

Muslims	44	45	89
	49.4%	50.6%	100.0%
	14.1%	16.9%	15.4%
Others	7	10	17
	41.2%	58.8%	100.0%
	2.3%	3.8%	2.9%
Total	311	266	577
	53.9%	46.1%	100.0%
	100.0%	100.0%	100.0%

Source: CSDS Data Unit.

Figure 1: Number of Male and Female Electors

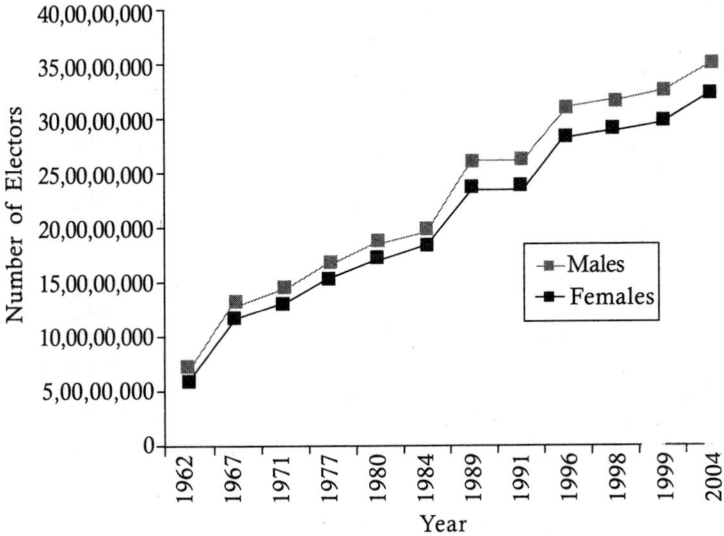

Figure 2: Male-Female and Total Voter Percentage in General Elections

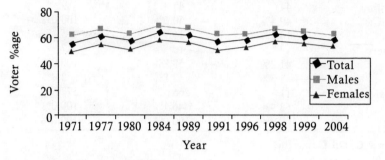

Source: Election Commission website

Figure 3: Size of Electorate

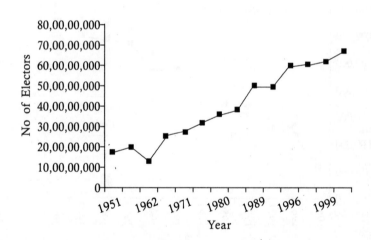

Source: Election Commission website

Contributors

Abhijit Guha is Reader at the Department of Anthropology, Vidyasagar University, West Bengal. He has been teaching for 20 years and has participated and presented papers in several seminars, conferences and workshops in India and abroad. He has published about 60 research papers in refereed national and international journals. His areas of interest include development-caused displacement, ecology, gender issues, and policy studies.

Anita Nuna is Lecturer in the Department of Women's Studies, NCERT, New Delhi. She has been working on gender issues for the past ten years. Her recent research interests include gender issues in education and women's equality and empowerment.

Anupama Datta has been associated with HelpAge India for the last five years in Research and Strategic Development Department and deals with research and advocacy of rights of older persons in the country. The major research projects undertaken by her have been on topics such as elder abuse, non-contributory pensions, need assessment in disaster situations and developing community-based disaster preparedness plans, and an enabling environment for older persons.

Anupama Roy is Senior Fellow at the Centre for Women's Development Studies (CWDS), New Delhi. Her research focuses on debates on citizenship, particularly the issues of gender and citizenship. She is the author of the book, *Gendered Citizenship: Historical and Conceptual Explorations* (Orient Longman, Delhi, 2005), and editor of *Poverty, Gender and Migration* (Sage, 2006). Her research articles have appeared in reputed journals.

Bhaswati Das is a Faculty Member at the Centre for the Study of Regional Development, School of Social Sciences, Jawaharlal Nehru University, New Delhi. She did her graduation from Presidency College,

Kolkata. She continued her higher education in Jawaharlal Nehru University, New Delhi where she completed her M.A. in Geography and M.Phil in Population Studies. She was awarded Ph.D on 'Study of Fertility Behaviour in a Transitional Socio-Economic Condition'. With more than ten years of research experience, she has diversified her areas of interest towards gender issues and rural development.

Dipendra Nath Das is a faculty at the Centre for the Study of Regional Development, JNU, New Delhi. He has been teaching for last 10 years. During his academic career he has presented several papers at national and international seminars.

Lekha S. Chakraborty is Senior Economist at the National Institute of Public Finance and Policy, New Delhi. She has worked extensively on gender budgeting and has presented and published papers in the area.

Murali Dhar Vemuri is Professor of Demography at the Centre for the Study of Regional Development, JNU, New Delhi. During his long career, he undertook researches on different demographic aspects including ageing issues. He has several publications to his credit.

Neetha N. is Senior Fellow at the Centre for Women's Development Studies, New Delhi. She has been consistently working on labour, gender and development issues and has completed detailed research studies on gender and labour issues. She has also been pursuing disaggregate level analysis of NSSO data to understand the changing patterns of women's employment in India. She has published articles on these subjects in various journals and books.

Pradeep Panda is Economics Fellow at the Population Council, and currently spearheads the Financial Sustainability and Capacity Building Initiative in South Asia. He has published papers in peer-reviewed journals and has undertaken policy-relevant research on the issues of poverty and the gender dimensions of poverty, women's employment, women's autonomy and reproductive behaviour and male involvement in reproductive health.

Preet Rustagi is Senior Fellow at the Institute for Human Development, New Delhi. She has been working on labour, gender and development issues for the last ten years. Her recent research interests include gender development indicators; work, employment and institutions; crimes against women; and women's equality and empowerment. She has published several articles on these subjects in various journals and books.

Purnamita Dasgupta is Senior Fellow at the Indian Council for Research on International Economic Relations (ICRIER). Her academic interest and expertise include health economics, natural resource and environmental economics, applied economics, development economics, and interdisciplinary studies related to social sector analysis.

Saraswati Raju is Professor of Social Geography at the Centre for the Study of Regional Development, JNU, New Delhi. She has been researching and teaching on social development issues for the last three decades.

Shobhita Rajagopal is Associate Professor at the Institute of Development Studies, Jaipur. For the past 19 years she has been involved in research and training in the area of women's development and gender issues. Her current areas of research include gender and education, childhood poverty, violence against women, gender, poverty and livelihoods. She has published extensively in national and international journals and books.

Vimal Khawas is Associate Fellow Sikkim University, Gangtok. He was previously associated with the Council for Social Development, New Delhi for more than two years. He has been trained in geography at Jawaharlal Nehru University, New Delhi and in Urban and Regional Development Planning at Centre for Environmental Planning and Technology, Ahmedabad. He has worked extensively in the area of agriculture development; human development/security, environmental security and regional development issues.

Index